# Ivanni Delgado

I0152256

# How We Got Here

*An Enlightened Look at the Past
that Will Change Your Future*

Carmen & Son

How We Got Here
Author: Ivanni Delgado
www.carmen-usa.com

Copyright © 2017 by Ivanni Delgado

Library of Congress Control Number: 2018936735

ISBN: 978-0-9910720-3-3

$21.00
ISBN 978-0-9910720-3-3
52100>

9 780991 072033

Published in USA by Carmen & Son, Houston, TX

www.carmen-usa.com

Follow us on:

First Edition

# To Homo Sapiens
*For his great feat in bringing us here.*

I want to dedicate this book to Homo Sapiens for his great feat to bring us to where we are today. To achieve such a great feat, this wise man had to go through all kinds of adversity, for the world was not yet made—he had to do it. Thanks to this great man, we can live a much more comfortable life today.

We humans evolved from Homo Sapiens, who evolved from Homo Erectus, who evolved from Homo Habilis, who evolved from hominids, who evolved from primates, which in turn evolved from the first mammals. To achieve a better life, Homo Sapiens perfected the things he inherited from his ancestors, such as the making of tools, the mastery of fire, and language. With his cognitive ability, he managed to develop a great intellect capable of designing the strategy and planning necessary to conquer the planet. This wise man managed to tirelessly transmitt his wisdom from generation to generation for about 200,000 years, including to our generation of modern humans less than 7,000 years ago.

Of the Homo Sapiens family, we alone remain. It is our responsibility to continue the work of Homo Sapiens to preserve humanity and to carry forward our civilization, which we inherited from the wise man who preceded us. Throughout these 7,000 years of our civilization, we have seen great progress for the benefit of all. However, it seems we are now going through one of those downturns inherent perhaps to our civilization. We realize that we live in a world full of calamities, with much uncertainty about our society, its economy, and security in general. We see with some concern the future, not only of us, the people, but also of our own humanity. Of course, so much uncertainty can distract people from the desire to move forward, as some people think there is not much that can be done to improve our situation. However, finding out how we got here can dramatically change our perception of life. That's especially true when we meet Homo Sapiens, our ancestor responsible for bringing us here.

Today, despite the gloomy outlook of human civilization, it would not be at all fair for modern man, by doing nothing, to jeopardize the sustained effort of more than seven million years by our ancestors to build the world in which we live today. We must once again become Homo Sapiens—wise men. Wisdom consists in accumulating the necessary knowledge and then using it to improve our lives and that of those around us. That was exactly what our great ancestor Homo Sapiens did. We must know our past and learn from it. In addition, we must learn to live life under a new perspective to guide our thoughts toward what we want to achieve. Finally, we must remember that the great secret to the success of humans has been to remain united and to work together as a team throughout our existence, a value we inherited from the species that preceded us.

# TABLE OF CONTENTS

ACKNOWLEDGMENTS 7

INTRODUCTION 9

1. THE UNIVERSE 15
1.1 Origin and Evolution 17
1.2 The Big Bang 25
1.3 Thought Evolution on the Universe Origin 31
1.4 The Solar System 45
1.5 Destiny of the Universe 74

2. THE EARTH 85
2.1 Origin and Evolution 86
2.2 Today's Blue Planet 98
2.3 Formation of Natural Resources 107
2.4 Formation of the Current Landscape 114
2.5 Destiny of the Earth 133

3. LIFE 135
3.1 Origin of Life 136
3.2 First Organisms and Events Impacting Life 146
3.3 The First Animals 156
3.4 The Cambrian Explosion 160
3.5 Evolution for Survival 166

**4. LIFE CONQERS EARTH'S SURFACE**     177

4.1 Events Toward the Conquest of Suface     178

4.2 Reptiles and Their Evolution     185

4.3 Mammals     194

4.4 Primates     199

4.5 Evolution for Survival at the Surface     201


**5. THE HUMAN BEINGS**     217

5.1 First Hominids: The Australopithecus     218

5.2 The Homos     223

5.3 Great Human Migrations     233

5.4 Human Evolution     239

5.5 Modern Humans     264


**ABOUT THE AUTHOR**     285


**NOTES**     287

# ACKNOWLEDGMENTS

I want to thank each of the people who have served in some way to inspire me in writing this book. I dedicate this work to all those authors who have written about how we got here and to all institutions—such as NASA the Discovery Science Channel™, the History Channel™, and the National Geographic Channel™—that have served as a means to bring a message of knowledge to all people everywhere. I also thank my entire family for their great support in the creation of the book.

# INTRODUCTION

Ever since he appeared, the human being was intrigued about everything that existed in the world around him. He even felt the need to establish his place and purpose in that world. His curiosity was so intense that he became a great observer, not only of his world, but of the whole universe. He always wanted to know how we got here. Today, however, we see a great general apathy about our ancestors' curiosity to discover the origin and formation of everything that exists, all that affects the development of life. We also see a great lack of interest in knowledge in general, especially regarding our past. Many people seem to have decided to take the things they hear for granted without thinking of any consequence or effect that some of these things may have on their daily lives. There may be several causes of so much indifference, but we have noticed that one of them has been the discontinuation of some projects that were designed to teach us how we got here. Another cause could be the amount of so many political, economic, and social problems, as well as so much uncertainty in the world today, which have made people lose interest in knowing what happened before we got here. Rather, people tend to focus only on solving their own problems in an effort to survive.

Perhaps all those problems and the great uncertainty about the future of much of today's people have created a great reluctance to move on. Some of them live their lives as those early beings who lived confined to the great ocean of Earth billions of years ago: drifting by eating something to survive and then dying. During that time, life may seem to us to have had little meaning or purpose, but that life changed through a long and extraordinary process of evolution to make ours much more interesting.

Our life today consists of much more than simple birth and death. It involves thinking, creating, and doing good things to achieve and enjoy a better life. Our immediate ancestors, the Homo Sapiens, managed to live a better life than their ancestors, thanks to their immense talent. We have evolved from them to be what we are today.

Why, then, do so many human beings today act with so much disillusionment and indifference to life? Part of the problem is that people do not know our history, our incredible and fascinating history. That's why I decided to write *How We Got Here*—to teach people today about their origin. I am convinced that by knowing the history of how we got here, we can take up the banner of Homo Sapiens and can all progress and lead our civilization on the right path, one that will continue preserving humanity.

This book will give continuity to the knowledge of how we got here, beginning with the knowledge of everything concerning the existence of the human being. First, we will focus on knowing where we came from. Clearly, this leads us straight to the origin of our universe and how everything formed from the "Big Bang." Thanks to science, we can find answers about the origin of our entire world and where and how we fit into it. We can also find answers about our own appearance as human beings, for, in addition to everything that composes the universe—the stars, galaxies, sun, planets, moons, asteroids, and comets—we are also part of the universe.

Then, we will focus on knowing our own evolution. For this we will start from the fact that life has evolved during a very long process. We must understand that the process that led to the biological material of which we are made is evolution. For centuries men of science have sought the truth about the human being. But that truth can only be found through the knowledge of facts that lie in the process called evolution, for the human being is what evolution has made of him. Evolution is a process of change over time.

Throughout the history of the Earth are numerous evidences indicating that all live organisms originated from earlier, more primitive life forms. That is, all species descend from other species. In other words, all living beings share common ancestors in the distant past.

Throughout the evolutionary process, species are diversifying. For example, when a male and a female of any species mate, the offspring inherits in its DNA the combined genetic information of its progenitors. However, the DNA of the offspring is not exactly like that of the parents, as it contains some variations called mutations that produce the diversity of the species. Mutations can also be generated due to the living environment. Passing genes from generation to generation of this species include those mutations, which can sometimes be problematic; in other cases, they can be beneficial, as they create new opportunities for the adaptation of life to the environment. This preservation of favorable mutations is what Charles Darwin called *natural selection* or survival of the fittest. Species that do not adapt to their environment simply disappear. Throughout the entire evolutionary process of life, 99 percent of the species that have existed have become extinct. Survivors are equipped with mutations that have given them the unique characteristics essential to survival.

To tell the story of how we got here, we have organized the book into five chapters, each consisting of five subchapters.

In the first chapter, "The Universe," we present the origin and evolution of the universe according to the Big Bang theory. We will also present the solar system and its formation, including that of the sun and the planets. We will see that on one of these planets, Earth, there is intelligent life, something that makes us as human beings part of the universe. Finally, we will explore the intriguing theory of the destiny of the universe.

In the second chapter, "The Earth," we will focus on how our planet originated and evolved. We will see how it was formed and how it was transformed during a long evolutionary period to the blue planet of today, a unique planet known to harbor life. We will also talk about how the major natural resources were formed that were essential in order for life and civilization to progress. We will also talk about the formation of the current landscape of the planet for the support of life and civilization. Finally, we will explore the theory of what the future of the planet might be like.

In the third chapter, "Life," we will talk about the origin and evolution of life. We will present the formation of the first forms of life on Earth; the first organisms and events that impacted its development; and the emergence of the first animals, from which all other animals evolved. We will also talk about the Cambrian Explosion, which changed life forever. Finally, we will talk about the evolution of the creatures in the great ocean of the Earth.

In the fourth chapter, "Life Conquers Surface," we will present how life continued its evolution out of water. That includes an exploration of events toward the conquest of the surface, which includes the changes and adaptations required to leave the great ocean and live on the surface of the Earth. We will see how the life that came out of the water evolved into reptiles and how they continued to evolve into mammals and primates. Finally, we will talk about the mechanisms that developed or improved beings, so they could survive on the surface and eventually conquer the planet.

In the fifth chapter, "The Human Beings," we will present the origin and evolution of human beings. We will talk about the first hominids, the Australopithecines, and their evolution into each of the members of the genus *homos*: Habilis, Erectus, and Sapiens. In addition, we will cover the great human migrations from Africa all over the globe as well as all aspects of human evolution. Finally, we will talk about modern humans, who with the development of their extraordinary talent, conquered the world and established the civilization we still have today.

The following pages will tell the story of how we got here. It is our story. Like all history, it has been a chronological narration of events that took place from the formation of the universe, the origin of life, to the evolution of the species that we are today. To better understand this story, we recommend that you read the book from beginning to end, following the established sequence.

# 1

# THE UNIVERSE

To understand how we got here, we must know how the universe was formed and how it evolved to the time we appeared as human beings. We are part of everything that composes the universe—and that's why in this first chapter we will present perhaps the most fascinating and intriguing part of our world: the universe and everything that comprises it. We will see how our universe originated and how everything that exists in it—stars, galaxies, suns, planets, moons, asteroids, and comets—evolved. All this explanation is made possible thanks to our scientists and the the various media that have served as a means of communication to bring all this immense knowledge to all of us. Thanks to them, we have answers about the origin of almost our entire world and where and how we fit into it. So much progress has been made in the study of the universe that we can decipher its origin. In the following pages, we will capture the history of our entire world and how it all began. Please be aware that this continues to be a work in progress as further explorations and new discoveries emerge.

We will begin to decipher the origin of the universe from the things we know and those that are accepted today. We will also see that the origin of everything begins with the famous explosion of the Big Bang. That sounds like something tremendous . . . but it was not. On the contrary, it was something very small—so small that it's difficult to imagine. If we think it's difficult to understand the concept of an atom because it is so small, how can we hope to understand its components, such as protons, neutrons, and electrons?

To get an idea of how small a world we are talking about, a proton is so small that about 500 billion of them can be contained in the space that occupies a dot of ink on a piece of paper. An atom by itself is an entire universe whose components must remain orchestrated to maintain its equilibrium. Each component of an atom in turn forms a smaller universe, and so on. Protons, like neutrons, are constituted by more elementary particles called *quarks*; under normal conditions, quarks do not exist in an isolated state but are always associated in small groups called *hadrons*. In addition to the quarks, there is a second category of elementary particles called *leptons*; unlike quarks, leptons experience only a weak nuclear force. Leptons include the *electron* and the *neutrino*. The electron is a negatively charged particle that helps protons and neutrons form atoms. The neutrino is a particle that, although it interacts very little with ordinary matter, appears in very energetic processes as in the accelerators of particles.

The process of how the universe formed has not been an easy one to understand, as human nature finds it difficult to understand things that cannot be seen with the naked eye. However, thanks to the challenging work of millions of human brains for thousands of years through our evolution, we have finally begun to understand the origin of the universe and how expanded and evolved through the Big Bang theory.

# 1.1 ORIGIN AND EVOLUTION

What we now know as the universe started out as an immense emptiness. Out of nowhere and with the passing of billions of years, however, the universe expanded to what it is today. At first the universe was dominated by radiation in the form of photons and small traces of matter in the form of electrons, protons, and neutrons. As the universe cooled a little during its evolutionary process, protons and neutrons combined to form atomic nuclei, which, when joined with electrons, formed atoms. In this process the free electrons decreased, and atoms formed. These were free to expand to fill the universe completely. Those photons or light particles are referred to as the "Cosmic Microwave Background."

In its initial stage, the universe was only a cluster of matter formed mainly of hydrogen and cosmic dust. Over time, these clusters grew denser and grew into vast regions of clouds called *nebulae*. Within the nebulae, gravity fragmented the immense clouds of hydrogen and dust into clusters from which the first cosmic structures like stars and galaxies began to form.

# Origin

At first there was nothing. Absolutely nothing. Everything was empty, in darkness and without space or time. With the passing of billions of years and out of nowhere, somewhere in that infinite void, something extremely small was formed that is commonly referred to as a singularity or starting point in the formation of the universe. This initial point became very dense and hot until it reached an extremely high energy and "exploded" about 13.7 billion years ago. That explosion, which has come to be known as the "Big Bang," began to form our universe.

In less than a thousand-millionth of a second after the Big Bang, a kind of bubble formed. Much smaller than a fraction of an atom, that bubble was the initial universe. Extremely small and hot, it was comprised of ultra-infinitesimal particles at elevated temperatures. It is believed that within this bubble formed the four known forces of nature that formed the universe at that time: gravity, electromagnetism, the strong nuclear force (or force that holds together the particles of the atomic nucleus), and the weak nuclear force (or force responsible for radioactive decay). These four forces combined into a single super-force. However, as the universe expanded, gravity separated itself from super-force. As the universe expanded, movement was created over space in time and it cooled to produce the energy that drove a hyperinflation. This inflation enclosed the uniformity of the universe. All the happened within less than a second of when the universe was initially formed.

The universe was dominated by radiation with small traces of matter. The radiation was in the form of photons, and the matter was in the form of electrons and a small concentration of protons and neutrons. The universe continued to expand more slowly, becoming less dense and colder. Thus, began the evolution of the universe, where the conversion of energy into matter was very frequent due to elevated temperatures. At such extremely elevated temperatures, the universe was plasma-shaped, and all particles had extremely high energy, which caused them to collide with each other and led to the expansion of the universe. This expansion produced a decrease in the energy of the particles to move from side to side, thus decreasing the temperature of the universe.

Just three minutes after the Big Bang, the universe's temperature had dropped to about 570 million degrees Celsius, cold enough for the lowering of the energy of protons and neutrons to combine to form atomic nuclei. When the nuclei united with the electrons, the atoms were formed mainly of hydrogen, and some atoms of hydrogen were fused to form helium. In this process of formation of the first atoms the Cosmic Microwave Background originated.

## Cosmic Microwave Background

The capture of the electrons to form the atoms diminished the free electrons. As a result, the electromagnetic radiation, or the photons emitted in the formation of the atoms, were free to expand along with the universe until they filled it completely. Those photons or particles of light are referred to as the *Cosmic Microwave Background*. This burst of radiation happened about 380,000 years after the Big Bang, and it was at that moment that light began to shine through the darkness—except, of course, there were still no eyes to see it.

The Cosmic Microwave Background was discovered by New Jersey scientists Arno Penzias and Robert Wilson in 1965 when they were trying to install a large radio antenna that would improve the communications of the company for which they worked. The discovery came when they began to detect a background noise in any direction in which they pointed the antenna. When analyzing the causes of noise, they realized that it came from space. The scientific community then concluded that Wilson and Penzias had discovered the cosmic background radiation; ever since, the Cosmic Microwave Background has been considered as a major remnant and proof of the Big Bang.

# Formation of Cosmic Structures

In its initial stage, the universe was only a cluster of matter formed mainly of hydrogen and cosmic dust. About 200 million years after their formation, these clusters became denser and grew into vast dense regions in the form of clouds called *nebulae*. Within the nebulae, gravity fragmented the immense clouds of hydrogen and cosmic dust into smaller groups that began to form the first cosmic structures like the stars. These cosmic structures, like stars, are celestial bodies composed of hot gases that emit heat, electromagnetic radiation, and light because of nuclear reactions inside. In addition to the nebulae and stars, other cosmic structures include everything we can see in the universe: the planets that revolve around the stars, the moons that revolve around the planets, and the asteroids and comets that revolve around the stars.

When a group of the first stars united about 700,000 years ago, they formed the first galaxies. The process by which that happened continues today when the galaxies in turn come together to form the so-called cumulus and superclusters. Thousands of galaxies form cosmic superstructures called *galactic aggregates*. Thousands of galaxy aggregates in turn form other colossal structures called *macrostructures*. All these cosmic structures are held together by the force of gravity and can cover a total mass equivalent to ten-million-millions of suns.

Galaxies such as our Milky Way and Andromeda form the so-called *Local Group of Galaxies*, which is a set of stars, gas clouds, planets, cosmic dust, matter, and perhaps dark energy that are linked by gravity and that are closer to us. Depending on their form, galaxies can be of three basic types: elliptical, spiral, and irregular. As their name implies, *elliptical galaxies* have the shape of an ellipse. *Spiral galaxies* are comprised of rotating discs of stars and interstellar matter, with a central protuberance composed mainly of older stars. From this protuberance, spiral arms extend. Unlike the other two types, *irregular galaxies* have no defined shape.

Supernova formations and black holes can also be observed within the cosmic structures. *Supernovae* are giant stars toward the end of their lives that explode with a sudden increase in luminosity and a huge release of energy. *Black holes* are regions of space within which there is a concentration of mass high enough to generate a gravitational field that does not let anything escape into it, not even light. Both supernovae and black holes form with the death of stars. If a star is the size of the Sun, before it dies it will become a red giant and will then become a white dwarf. If the star is large, while dying it will form a supernova. As nuclear reactions stop, the gravity-driven core collapses inward and explodes, releasing massive amounts of matter and energy into space. If the star is fifteen to twenty times the mass of the Sun, its core can become a black hole when it collapses.

## The Stars

The first stars began to form about 600 million years after the Big Bang; they have continued to form since that moment. Within the nebulae, regions are formed denser than others and with high concentrations of hydrogen, from which the stars are formed. A nucleus begins to form in the center of the star in a very hot contraction called a proto-star. When the temperature and pressure inside the proto-star become large enough, nuclear fusion takes place and the star begins to glow. Proto-stars take millions of years to evolve from the molecular cloud to become a star. The process of nuclear fusion through which the star begins to glow is called the *main sequence*.

Other elements are formed within the stars. For example, hydrogen fuses to form helium, which in turn fuses into carbon and oxygen, and so on. The stars usually form in groups called *cumulus*, where several develop simultaneously when the cloud that contains them contracts and is fragmented into smaller clouds.

The stars are the most recognized astronomical bodies and represent the fundamental blocks in the formation of other cosmic structures such as galaxies. The size of the stars depends on the mass of the cloud from which they form. Many of these stars attracted to each other by their mutual gravity form clusters of stars with discs of gas and cosmic dust around them, from which later planets, asteroids, and comets may arise.

The life and destiny of the star depends on its size: though it seems paradoxical, the bigger the star, the shorter time it lives. The small stars, called *red dwarfs*—the most abundant in the universe, with masses of 10 percent of that of the Sun—can live for tens of billions of years as they burn their fuel slowly. Medium stars, such as the Sun, live for billions of years. Large stars with masses of a hundred times that of the Sun live for only a few million years.

Most stars spend most of their lives in the main sequence, where they gradually consume their nuclear fuel. A star the size of the Sun requires about fifty million years to mature before the onset of the collapse of its adult age; they stay in that mature phase in the main sequence for about ten billion years. In other words, our sun star still has half of its life left. Small stars end in expanded, cold bodies called *red giants*; average stars like the Sun end up reduced approximately to the size of the Earth in bodies called *white dwarfs*. The biggest stars are more spectacular, ending their lives in supernovae, neutron stars, and black holes.

# The Galaxies

The immense cosmic structures like galaxies are formed when large volumes of matter in the universe collapse. Within the galaxies are formed the stars, which can be attracted to each other by their mutual gravity to form groups of stars or stellar clusters. Some of these stars have planets and form planetary systems with one or more central stars and several celestial bodies orbiting around them. Among these celestial bodies are the planets and their moons, asteroids, and comets. The *planets* are opaque bodies that rotate around the star because of the force of gravity with which it attracts them. The planets do not have their own light, so we only see them as they reflect sunlight. *Asteroids* are rocky bodies smaller than the planets. *Comets* are celestial bodies made up of ice, dust, and rocks.

A cluster of stars forms a *galaxy*, which is a massive system of stars, clouds of gas, and cosmic dust and dark matter gravitationally attached. Galaxies can also include dark energy. Since about 600 million years after the Big Bang when galaxies began to form, billions of galaxies have formed in the universe.

Among the most important galaxies for us are the Milky Way (the galaxy to which we belong) and the Andromeda (our nearest neighbor galaxy). As can be seen in the illustration on the next page, the Milky Way is a galaxy in the form of a spiral with several arms that arise from its center or nucleus. The galaxy has a diameter of about 100,000 light years and has more than 200 billion stars, our Sun being one of them. Our galaxy is so large that it has enough gas and cosmic dust to double the number of stars it now holds in its bosom; as additionally, it has at least ten times more dark matter than all stars and gas combined. The Milky Way revolves around its center at an average speed of about 514,000 miles per hour. At that speed, it would take our solar system about 230 million years to complete an entire circle around the galactic center. The whole galaxy is held together by its immense gravity.

Several galaxies together form a cluster of galaxies, and a cluster of galaxies form a supercluster of galaxies surrounded by vast void areas called dark matter, believed to constitute 90 percent of the mass in most galaxies. There is evidence to suggest the existence of black holes in the nucleus of some galaxies; the Milky Way appears to have one of these large-sized holes in its nucleus. This is a super massive black hole about 4 million times larger than the mass of our Sun and about 28,000 light years from Earth.

The Milky Way is part of a galactic cluster about 10 million light years in diameter made up of more than thirty galaxies that are gravitationally connected to each other. Apart from our galaxy, the most massive in this group is the Andromeda, which scientists predict will hit the Milky Way in about 4 million years.

The galactic cluster to which we belong is just one of many that exist in the universe. These clusters are moving away from each other as more and more space comes to exist between them. This means that the universe itself is expanding. That discovery is what led to the Big Bang theory about the origin of the universe.

# 1.2 THE BIG BANG

The Big Bang is the theory that explains how the universe originated and how it changed in a fraction of a second after the "explosion" to form our universe. After having evolved over the years, the Big Bang is a theory well accepted by current science. The conclusive proof of the Big Bang was the capture in 1965 of the Cosmic Microwave Background. However, the problem that still existed regarding the uniform temperature of the universe was solved with the development of the theory of cosmic inflation, which explains how the universe expanded evenly and very quickly after its birth with the Big Bang about 13.7 billion years ago.

## The Big Bang Theory

This cosmic theory explains how the universe originated and how it changed in a fraction of a second after the "explosion" to form our universe today. About 13.7 billion years ago, the

Big Bang gave rise to the creation of every atom, every star, and every galaxy in our universe. For thousands of years, people all the way from the shamans of the past to the scientists of today have gathered observations of the cosmos. Thanks to our scientists, we now know how it all started: the Big Bang.

As we observe the universe and its galaxies today, we can see that these are moving away from us. They are expanding at great speeds, continuing the expansion that happened after the birth of the universe when it was nothing more than a very dense little spot.

At first, mankind didn't even think about the origin of the universe, perhaps because we assumed it was fixed and eternal. As a result, some scientists were reluctant to accept the Big Bang theory. The term *Big Bang* seems to imply an explosion, but that's a contradiction: it wasn't big (having a tiny starting point), nor was there an explosion (no air transmitted the vibrations). But the name *Big Bang* was eventually accepted, and so was the theory, which is a solid part of current science.

Even though the theory is well accepted, it is not very well understood, because it still does not provide all the answers about the origin of the universe. The Big Bang theory explains only what happened after the explosion but gives no answers about the formation of what exploded. After the Big Bang, all the elements that make up everything we see around us were created. After being born from the Big Bang, the universe began to expand and to evolve, and it continues to expand and evolve today.

## Evolution of the Theory

The knowledge we have about the origin of the universe is the product of a talented team of people who captured the ideas of those who went before and who improved on those ideas. Everything began when our ancestors looked at the sky during the day and saw that it was dominated by the Sun, which provided light, heat, and life. At night, they watched the Moon and stars. What they saw was the universe, with a sun that wandered and changed through the sky as the seasons went from warm to cold.

Primitive peoples needed to understand their world to survive in it. And because they could not understand much about their nature, they turned part of nature into gods to establish some relationship with it. The primitive peoples, without telescopes or sophisticated observatories, relied on observatories of simple structures to help them understand the sky. In places like Goseck in Germany and Stonehenge in England, they tried to connect with the sky, which they believed was the abode of their gods. These first structures were simple instruments of observation and tools of analysis that helped give sense to the universe that danced before their eyes.

Thus, about seven thousand years ago they built in Germany the Solar Observatory of Goseck, one of the oldest instruments related to the Sun, Moon, and stars. It was built by farmers about two thousand years before Stonehenge to determine the seasons of the year and is the oldest known calendar in Europe. During the Winter and Summer Solstices, the shortest and longest days of the year respectively, the setting sun aligned with the gates on the palisades. Knowing these dates helped these people calculate when to sow and when to harvest. Clearly, their life depended on their understanding of the Sun and the sky. Over time, the investigation of the skies by man continued until men formulated the Big Bang theory, whose conclusive proof appeared when least expected.

# The Conclusive Proof

For about five hundred years, science not only searched for evidence of where we came from but sought answers about the origin of everything. The answer was right there in space in the form of noise, but we had not been able to hear it. Then in 1965, scientists Bob Wilson and Arno Penzias were installing a communications satellite when they managed to capture a static noise. These radiations came from every direction of every point in space. Wilson and Penzias had found what the scientist George Gamow had predicted in his theory about the remnant of the Big Bang. They had found the decisive proof that the universe had been formed and that it was not eternal. This source of radiation came from the creation of the universe through the Big Bang. Wilson and Penzias published their findings in 1965 and won the Nobel Prize in 1978. Their finding consolidated the Big Bang theory.

Now we can better understand the origin of the universe and all its elements. We also know what the universe was after only a fraction of a second of its formation, when it was immensely dense at very high temperatures, and we can understand in general how it began expanding and cooling. We now know how the first atoms were formed, and how the first cosmic structures, the first stars, the first galaxies, and eventually the planets and much later life were formed.

Most scientists agree that most of the hydrogen and helium were created in the initial stages of the Big Bang. The other heavier elements, such as nitrogen and carbon, were created later in the hot nuclei of the stars and in explosions of supernovae until the rest of the elements of the periodic table were generated. In all, a number of scientists contributed to the consolidation of the Big Bang theory, which is unanimously accepted in the scientific world.

However, even the theory was not perfect, as there were some problems with the details, especially as it relates to the expansion of the universe.

## Final Details

During the last days of the twentieth century, scientists examined the problems that existed with the Big Bang theory. Although the theory was generally accepted, one of the biggest problems scientists still had was that the temperature in outer space was very uniform. Physicists did not expect the universe to have approximately the same temperature in all places they observed. The universe is simply too large for one end to have the same temperature as the other.

However, this was explained at the beginning of the 1980s with the idea that the universe was very small when it began—so small that within that volume there was enough time for these different points in the universe to communicate and normalize their temperatures. After this idea, it was theorized that the universe expanded faster than light, faster than the cosmic speed limit, which Einstein theorized was the maximum speed. This gives rise to the emergence of cosmic inflation theory.

## Cosmic Inflation Theory

In the first moments of the existence of the universe, the four forces of nature were combined into one super-force. During the Big Bang, this super-force was divided into the four known forces: the weak nuclear force, electromagnetism, gravity, and the strong nuclear force. When the universe was too small to divide, the laws of

Einstein's physics were not yet applied, including the law that says that nothing moves faster than light. Perhaps at that moment something happened that caused the universe to expand even faster than light, at such a speed that it enclosed the uniformity it had when the universe was still very small. It is possible that inflation began when gravity separated from the other three forces, but at a time when the other three forces were probably still unified. If this hyperinflation happened, it had a certain uniformity in temperature.

NASA has launched two missions to study the background of cosmic radiation originated in the formation of the universe and to determine the truth about the theory of inflation. The first of the missions was the Cosmic Background Explorer (COBE) in 1992; and the second was the Wilkinson Microwave Anisotropy Probe (WMAP) in 2001. The WMAP was a much better resolution satellite than the COBE.

Photos were taken with the WMAP of the remaining fossilized heat that Penzias and Wilson had found. In other words, NASA photographed the primary universe to compare it with the universe as it looks today. In 2003, scientists gave their first look at the photo of the primary universe when it was only 380,000 years old with clearly astonishing data. In the photo, you can see patterns representing the seeds of what would later become the vast expanses of stars and galaxies as we known them today.

In this NASA photograph on the Cosmic Microwave Background the data from NASA, apart from proving strongly the theory of inflation, also gave concrete clues about the composition, form, and evolution of the universe. As for the shape of the universe, the WMAP results confirmed that the universe is flat. Also, with the help of NASA it was possible to obtain numerical results on the size of the universe, its age, its rate of expansion, and its contents. Before this NASA strategy, we had no more than a bunch of theories. Now we have a model of events that occurred just after the Big Bang.

# 1.3 THOUGHT EVOLUTION ON THE UNIVERSE ORIGIN

When astrologists first looked at the sky to divine fate, they also observed and learned how the sky moved. But sometimes these observations led to erroneous thoughts, such as the idea that the Earth was the center of the universe. Aristotle proposed the concept of the finite universe with the Earth as the center of everythingThis concept was later modified by Ptolemy, who suggested a different idea regarding the path of the planets. Copernicus proposed that the center of the solar system was the Sun, not the Earth. Then Johannes Kepler continued with the work of Copernicus and stated that the planets did not orbit in perfect circles but in an elliptical path around the Sun.

The great Galileo Galilei would later prove the theories of Copernicus and Kepler with an innovative technology that would change the course of history: The telescope. Galileo also noted that the universe was larger than previously thought. Isaac Newton then appears to explain with his mathematics how the celestial bodies moved and postulated their laws and expressed in equation form the force of gravity that attracted the bodies of the universe.

Later came the thought of Albert Einstein, who reinvented the concept of the universe. Einstein in his theory of relativity formulated that space and time were not separate elements, but the same thing as a kind of tissue interconnecting both elements. He then included gravity and its effects on this tissue and explained that gravity worked because the space-time tissue curved in the presence of matter. Einstein believed that the universe was static and eternal, but this was not compatible with his theory of relativity.

Finally appear the thoughts oriented toward the Big Bang, a term coined by Fred Hoyle. Georges Lemaitre understood that the universe was not static but was expanding, so at first it should have been smaller. Edwin Hubble proved that the universe was really expanding, which would fit the concept of the Big Bang. George Gamow argued that the radiation left by the Big Bang at its inception had to be measured even today.

Obviously, thoughts about the origin of the universe has been in constant evolution since the beginning of astronomy and astrology.

# Beginning of Astronomy and Astrology

During the infancy of astronomy and astrology, *astronomy* attempted to predict the behavior of natural events based on the "movement of the sky," while *astrology* claimed that sky movement predetermined our destiny. For example, people believed that a meteor determined a military victory and that a new star announced the birth of a king.

At that time, astronomy predicted the movement of stars and astrology predicted how those stars affected our behavior. In the ancient mind, it was very difficult to separate these two notions. Astrologers of 2,700 years ago divided the sky into regions and gave them names according to the shapes they stared at in the stars. That's how we got the names of what we know today as the constellations: Aries, Taurus, and Gemini, among others.

But as astrologers watched the starry sky to guess destiny, they also watched and learned how the sky moved.

The first steps in scientific observation arose out of superstitious motives. Sometimes these simple observations led to fundamentally erroneous conclusions, such as the idea that the Earth was the center of the universe and that the sky, the stars, and everything else revolved around us. While that conclusion existed for a long time, we know that the Earth has never been the center of anything.

Knowledge gradually moved forward until we could decipher the origin of the universe. The first significant advances on the evolution of thought about the origin of the universe took place in ancient Greece. Using mathematics, the ancient Greeks provided more detailed information about the Sun and the Moon, which are the most dominant celestial bodies seen from Earth. By that time, more than two thousand years ago, the Greeks already knew that the Earth was round. By observing the shadows that the bodies projected on Earth, they could calculate the size of the Earth with a precision of 10 percent. They also calculated the distance from the Earth to the Moon and from the Earth to the Sun.

In addition to recognizing the small stars that moved together and formed the constellations, the ancient Greeks also recognized other larger stars that moved at random. The latter were the planets, it was centuries before scientists could predict their movements. They still believed the Earth to be the center of the universe. With the naked eye, the Greeks managed to recognize five planets, which they named in honor of their gods. However, today we are more familiar with the designations of the Romans: Mercury, Venus, Saturn, and Jupiter.

When thinking about the concept of how the universe began to evolve, scientists began to change their belief about the Earth being its center.

# The First Thoughts on the Concept of the Universe

Ancient astronomy assumed the concept of the universe proposed by the Greek philosopher Aristotle of the fourth century before Christ (BC). However, this concept was somewhat modified later by Ptolemy, another Greek astronomer.

## Aristotle

Aristotle, born in 384 BC and one of the greatest ancient philosophers, imagined the Earth motionless as the center of the universe, with a sun and a moon, stars and planets spinning in elegant harmony around the Earth in perfect crystalline spheres. The concept of Aristotle's universe was finite and lasted for several centuries until Copernicus in the sixteenth century AD After studying the idea of Ptolemy on the path of the planets, scientists changed the concept and conceived the Sun as the center of the universe.

## Claudius Ptolemy

The Greek astronomer of the first century of our age, Ptolemy brought a different idea to the model of Aristotle in tracing the path of the planets—which do not move at random but follow certain patterns. He showed that the position of the planets could be calculated. Ptolemy's system was a great feat of mathematics in its beginnings, although somewhat complex for his time.

After this great contribution, astronomy remained stagnant for centuries after the fall of the Roman Empire in 476 AD. Then Europe fragmented into smaller powers, and much of Greek wisdom was lost. However, thinking about the universe would resume its evolutionary course after more than a millennium.

# Thoughts that Changed the Concept of the Universe

Among the thoughts that would change the concept of the universe are those of Nicholas Copernicus, Johannes Kepler, Galileo Galilei, and Isaac Newton. Copernicus proposed that the center of the solar system was the Sun and not the Earth. Kepler continued with the work of Copernicus and stated that the planets did not orbit in perfect circles, but in an elliptical path around the Sun. Galileo proved the theories of Copernicus and Kepler with his revolutionary telescope; he also noted that the universe was larger than previously thought. Newton then explained with mathematics how the celestial bodies moved. He also expressed in equation form the force of gravity that attracted the bodies of the universe and postulated the laws of motion.

## Nicholas Copernicus

A thousand years after the fall of the Roman Empire, a new theory confronted accepted beliefs about the functioning of the firmament and took humanity a step closer to the Big Bang theory. During the fifteenth century AD, a new idea called *heliocentrism* proclaimed that the Sun and not the Earth was the center of the universe. Of course, this idea horrified the Catholic Church, which believed such a concept contradicted the word of God. If God had created the Earth and man in His image and likeness, then Earth and its inhabitants should be the center of everything. Ironically the defender of the theory of a universe whose center was the Sun, Copernicus was a very religious man and a great devotee of the Catholic Church.

Nicholas Copernicus was born in Poland in 1473. Apart from his religious work, he also devoted time to astronomy. Copernicus was intrigued by Ptolemy's celestial mechanics and found clarification when he replaced the

Earth with the Sun as the center of the solar system. With that move, Copernicus positioned the planets where they could orbit the Sun in perfect harmony. Copernicus also insisted that the Earth rotated about its axis every twenty-four hours and that Earth, not the skies, moved. Copernicus rightly claimed that the stars created the illusion of scouring the sky every night because of the rotation of the Earth.

To avoid reprisals from the church, Copernicus refrained from publishing his magnificent work until he was on his deathbed in 1543. His book *The Revolutions of the Celestial Spheres*, opened the way for Johannes Kepler.

## Johannes Kepler

Born in Germany in 1571, Kepler, the defender of observational science, continued the work of Copernicus and proclaimed to the world the idea of Copernicus that the Sun was the center of the solar system. Kepler had at his disposal all the observations of Copernicus on the skies. When Kepler analyzed all these observations, he not only realized that the Sun is the center of the solar system, but also that the perfect circles that described the path of the planets was a product of the imagination. He therefore improved the theory of Copernicus in formulating the hypothesis that the planets revolved not in perfect circles, but in ellipses around the Sun.

Kepler also observed something he maintained but could not understand: Kepler observed that the Sun affected the speed of the planets as they traveled through space. As the planets approached the Sun, they turned faster, and as they moved away from the Sun, they slowed down.

## Galileo Galilei

At the beginning of the seventeenth century, the Italian astronomer Galileo Galilei, born in 1564, proved without any doubt the theories of Copernicus and Kepler that the Sun was the center of the solar system. Galileo achieved that proof with an innovative technology that would change the course of history: the telescope, which became the most revolutionary instrument of science as its application spread throughout the world. Galileo improved the design of the telescope in 1609 by fitting his own lenses and creating a lens that could increase the size of an object an unprecedented thirty times Galileo had the most detailed view of skies that any person before him had ever had, and his subsequent observation of the skies changed the scope of astronomy.

Through his telescope Galileo saw thousands of stars, a moon full of craters, satellites surrounding Jupiter, and a Saturn with giant ears. Most significant of all, he saw that Venus was going through phases like our Moon— unmistakable evidence that Venus orbited the Sun and proof that the solar system centered around the Sun, proving for the first time that Copernicus was right.   Galileo also observed that there was a larger universe than the one known until then.

Galileo's telescope marked the meeting point between the old and the modern. Galileo could demonstrate that the dogmas of the Catholic Church that had been in place for centuries were now wrong. With the church still reeling from the episode of the protestant reformation, Galileo's discovery seemed to weaken it even more— dangerous for a church that felt in a state of siege and much more dangerous for the scientist who was proposing the evidence.

Galileo, a devout Catholic, published his observations in a book titled *The Messenger of the Stars* in 1610. The church welcomed Galileo's work in clever ways at first. But, feeling threatened, the church did not accept, the interpretation of Galileo for biblical reasons. After Galileo published his new book about the solar system revolving around the Sun in 1633, the pope called him to face trial for heresy. Galileo was forced to give up his ideas and spend the rest of his days under house arrest in his home on the outskirts of Florence. Galileo was the first modern scientist to make observations with his telescope and actively proposed consistent theories, but perhaps his bravest act was to to challenge the power of the Catholic Church.

Galileo has been considered as the father of modern astronomy. He died in 1642, but shortly before that, he found a key to explaining Kepler's conundrum in relation to the effect of the Sun on the planets of the solar system. It was a key that helped future generations point to the Big Bang theory. His last work was about bodies in free fall, which he noticed fell at the same rate regardless of mass. It is here that another genius emerged to combine these two pieces of the puzzle into a theory of gravity.

## Isaac Newton

Isaac Newton, born in England in 1643, explained the mechanism by which not only the planets moved but how everything in the sky and all things on the Earth moved. With Newton, mathematics gained power and through its use man achieved understanding of the cosmos.

Mathematics is really the language of the cosmos and gravity is the force that holds all things together. Newton not only observed gravity, but also expressed it in the form of an equation demonstrating that it was the force of gravity that bound the planets to the Sunand that bound the objects on Earth to it.

Gravity is the force of attraction that affects all the bodies of the universe, gives order to it, and is described by the science of physics. Newton created the laws of physics, and it was he who first noted the fundamental laws of physics. Newton's laws explained almost everything. He postulated the laws of motion and the universal laws of gravity. Newton began a new era of science using observations and mathematics to describe the laws of nature.

His brilliant book, *The Principles*, revealed that the tides, the speed of the orbiting planets, and even the shape of the Earth could be explained by the attraction of gravity, because everything that has mass exerts a force of attraction.

The Moon attracts the oceans, the Earth attracts the Moon, the Sun attracts the Earth, and the closer these objects are to each other, the greater the force of gravity. Although Newton wrote the laws of gravity, he never understood why gravity worked. That would take another two hundred years until Albert Einstein appeared to explain what Newton could not about gravity, thereby reinventing the universe.

## Albert Einstein: The Thought that Reinvented the Concept of the Universe

Albert Einstein not only formulated new laws, but also reinvented the concept of the universe. Born in Germany in 1879, Albert Einstein is the most famous scientist of all time. He started his work in Bern, Switzerland, in 1905 when he began to wonder how the universe worked (though his intention was not to discover the origin of the universe). At first, the universe was considered dynamic and finite, but Einstein preferred to think of a static and infinite one. That is, he saw an eternal universe, one without a beginning or an end. But this idea was somewhat contradictory, for his understanding of forces such as gravity suggested that the universe was not eternal. Of course, those ideas were very extravagant for his time (and perhaps for ours as well). The truth is that our world is the world of Einstein.

In 1905, Einstein published his theory of special relativity that explored the link between space and time. According to his view, space and time were not separate elements, but were one thing. He thought of this new space-time as an invisible tissue that interconnected space and time.

In 1915, Einstein developed his theory of general relativity that modified special relativity to include gravity and its effects in this space-time fabric. The new theory of relativity told us that gravity worked because the fabric of space and time curved before the presence of matter and could respond dynamically. Space itself could expand and contract in the presence of matter.

On the other hand, *mass* is the term used to describe the energy and matter contained by bodies. The greater the mass of a body, the larger the distortion of the space-time tissue and the stronger the effects of gravity. Gravity was no longer seen as a straight line. Einstein said that even light could not escape the effects of gravity.

Einstein was proved right in 1919 in the form of a great astronomical experiment based on a solar eclipse. General relativity said that if a star were observed from Earth in a path of light passing in front of the Sun, that path of light would be curved a little by the gravity of the Sun but would still reach the observer on Earth. Einstein's theory could be demonstrated during the 1919 solar eclipse by photographing the star when the Sun was being blocked by the Moon; even then, it was possible to see the star behind the Sun. The ability to see bodies behind the Sun showed that bodies can bend space-time.

Einstein received the Nobel Prize for Physics in 1921. But the theory of relativity opened a Pandora's box for Einstein. One of the consequences of this theory was that the universe should be expanding or contracting, but never be static and eternal. This was a big problem, because if you introduce mass into a static universe, all that mass will be attracted by gravity. As a result, you have an unstable universe. To prevent gravity from collapsing the universe, Einstein postulated a force that equated gravity but that acted in the opposite direction. This constant and opposing force of gravity maintained the balance of the universe in a static universe. Einstein believed that this constant could be hidden among his equations, but it was not so.

The static universe Einstein assumed was not compatible with his formulated theory. On the contrary, his theory pointed out that the universe was not static but was expanding. Einstein might not have predicted what would happen in the expanding universe, so as not to cause more commotion than he had already caused, and he did not risk making that prediction. Einstein's theory inevitably leads to the idea of a moment of formation, a moment where the universe was much smaller.

Although Einstein could not make the leap, others would later. A dynamic and expanding universe would then fit perfectly into a Big Bang theory. At the beginning of the twentieth century, Albert Einstein might have led us to consider the scientific possibility that our universe had begun at some point. But the idea of a beginning for everything had serious religious consequences. But any culture has the right to wonder where they came from, for if we do not know where we came from then we will never know who we are and where we are going.

For thousands of years the origin of the universe was the subject of scholars of religion, not scientists. Religion and science by their own definitions have very different and even opposing points of view. Religion is a matter of faith, whereas everything in science is based on facts. Science has always sought truth. When religious men embark on a project to seek the truth, they become scientists, as in the case of the priest Georges Lemaitre, whose thoughts would lead the way to the Big Bang theory.

# Thoughts Leading the Way to the Big Bang Theory

The thoughts of Georges Lemaitre, Edwin Hubble, Fred Hoyle, and George Gamow are among those geared toward the Big Bang theory, a term coined by Fred Hoyle. Lemaitre understood that the universe was not static but was expanding, so at first it should have been smaller. Edwin Hubble proved that the universe was really expanding. Gamow argued that the radiation left by the Big Bang at its inception had to be measured even today.

## Georges Lemaitre

It is ironic that one of the first proponents of an objective scientific theory for the origin of the universe was this Catholic priest, and that his solution, based on science, maintained that the universe had not always existed but that there had been a beginning. Belgian Father Georges Lemaitre, born in 1894, argued that the universe had had a birth, like all things. Lemaitre was the one who best understood an expanding universe and presented many of the ideas that are still being explored.

Lemaitre thoroughly studied Einstein's theories during the 1920s and proposed a radical idea, one that even the great Einstein would reject. Lemaitre said that the universe was not static but was expanding. And if the universe is expanding, then it was smaller yesterday than it is today. Consequently, the universe at first must have been much smaller. Lemaitre believed that the universe had begun with what he called the original atom: an infinitely hot and dense cosmic egg that at some point had exploded, putting the universe in motion and leading to the formation of everything we know today.

Lemaitre's theory of universe expansion was validated in 1925 in the United States, when American astronomer

Edwin Hubble saw something in his telescope that destroyed Einstein's cosmological constant and altered our image of the universe. Until then, we believed the universe was just the huge wave of milk that was seen in the night sky consisting of a hundred billion stars. That was the Milky Way some 100,000 light years away. But Hubble would go much further.

## Edwin Hubble

Edwin Hubble, born in the United States in 1889, was one of the most important American astronomers of the twentieth century, famous for demonstrating the expansion of the universe by measuring the redshift of distant galaxies. Hubble is considered the father of observational cosmology. He looked at the universe more deeply than Galileo could have imagined. Using the most sophisticated telescope of his time, he saw that the Sun was just one more star among millions of others within the Milky Way galaxy.

Hubble could locate a known or standard bright star within the Andromeda nebula, which had been believed to be just a cloud of star dust within the Milky Way. According to the brightness of the standard star (brighter when it is closer and fainter as it moves away), Hubble was able to calculate the distance to a star. He then realized that the galaxy was a million light years away and discovered that Andromeda was another another galaxy like the Milky Way. At that moment, the universe changed from a single galaxy of 100,000 light years to a universe of billions of light years consisting of about one billion galaxies like ours.

This discovery immortalized Hubble, who went even further in 1929 to conclude that galaxies were moving away from the Milky Way. In other words, the universe is constantly expanding, enlarging every second, which proves that if we go back in time the universe must have been smaller.

Based on the velocity of expansion he measured, Hubble could calculate the age of the universe, but the results were very low. Although it was on the right track because its formula to determine the age of the universe was correct, the measurements were not. This discrepancy gave some scientists the space to disagree with Lemaitre's theory, which certainly could be measured, but that was not so easy to do. By the middle of the twentieth century it was said that this theory would never have wide acceptance, but Hubble's incorrect estimate of the age of the universe allowed another theory to move on. This theory was that of a steady state— that is, a universe that has always existed with its same appearance and average density and the same temperature. This was the theory of Fred Hoyle of Cambridge College.

## Fred Hoyle

Fred Hoyle was born in England in 1915 and is known mainly for his model of Stationary Universe. The theory proposed by Hoyle said that all elements of the periodic table were formed by fusion of hydrogen and helium in the stars, which is known as *nucleosynthesis*. Hoyle's theory also said that hydrogen, which constitutes more than 70 percent of the detectable universe, had always been there. But there was a problem: people already knew that the universe was expanding, so the task of going back to a theory of a steady state was very difficult.

## George Gamow

Amid the debate between the steady state and the dynamic state of the universe, Russian scientist George Gamow, born in 1904, admired the original atom of Lemaitre. Gamow suggested that hydrogen and helium were created early in the formation of the universe in a big explosion when temperatures were thousands of degrees warmer than they are at the core of any star. Gamow drew on the help of mathematical students, and together they refined Lemaitre's prediction of the traceable heat of the formation of the universe. This was a strong element in support of the Big Bang theory.

Gamow argued that if the Big Bang had been so hot, the echoing of the glow or the radiation after the Big Bang should not have cooled so much, and the residue should be measurable today. The problem then was how to measure these radiations. No one had special telescopes in 1949 that could measure the radiation or residual heat at the moment of creation.

At that time, there were also other problems with the Big Bang theory, because it offered no explanation as to the origin of elements beyond hydrogen and helium. At the same time, steady-state theory was hoarding coverage.

Ironically the term *Big Bang* was coined by Fred Hoyle in 1949 as a satire. By 1960, Hubble's calculations on the age of the universe had been corrected to produce more accurate results. Stationary state theories and the Big Bang theory were kept abreast. Then decisive proof arrived, as old as the universe itself: the radiation of the Cosmic Microwave Background was detected by Arno Penzias and Robert Wilson in 1965.

# 1.4 THE SOLAR SYSTEM

Today, the formation of the solar system has been predicted quite accurately, thanks to observations of the formation of other stars and their planets as seen through the Hubble telescope positioned about 380 miles above Earth and with an excellent view of 20/20. Our solar system was formed about 4.5 million years ago in a nebula formed in turn by an explosion of a supernova. The first to form was the Sun; the gas and cosmic dust subsequently led to formation of the planets, moons, asteroids, and comets.

There are eight planets and a group of comets and asteroids spinning around the Sun, forming orbits in the form of an ellipse. Those eight planets include Mercury, Venus, Earth, Mars, Jupiter, Saturn, Uranus, and Neptune. Mercury is the closest planet to the Sun; Neptune is the farthest. The four planets nearest the Sun—Mercury, Venus, Earth, and Mars—are called terrestrial planets because they have solid, rocky surfaces. The two outer planets beyond the orbit of Mars, Jupiter and Saturn, are known as gaseous giants. And the most distant planets, Uranus and Neptune, are called ice giants.

An intriguing feature of some planets are the rings that are spinning around them. In addition to Saturn, rings have been discovered around Jupiter, Uranus, and Neptune. Astronomers have also seen rings around an asteroid and around a moon.

Also known to date are 173 moons, 3,319 comets, and about 670,452 asteroids. Moons, also called satellites, are usually solid bodies that rotate around the planets and sometimes around the asteroids. Moons that revolve around the planets are called planetary moons. Most of the moons were formed from gas and dust disks and other small space bodies that circled the planets in the primitive solar system; some have atmospheres.

The solar system also includes the asteroid belt between the planets Mars and Jupiter. Beyond the solar system is the Kuiper Belt, made up of thousands of icy bodies, and the Oort Cloud, home to ice comets. The solar system covers a length of about 9 billion miles from the Sun outward.

# Formation of the Solar System

More than six billion years ago, a huge supernova explosion blasted into a gigantic cloud of dust and gas. Ironically, the last breath of that dying star would be the beginning of life for a new star. After the great explosion of the supernova, gas and cosmic dust were ejected and formed huge clouds called *nebulae*, such as the Veil Nebula and the Eagle Nebula, with its large columns carved by time and wind on the cosmic dust as seen in the illustration. Our solar system was formed in a nebula like this.

The dust was concentrated by waves of galactic vibrations, and gravity attracted and accumulated more material around the cloud. The heat and pressure in the nucleus became very intense, enough to turn the molecular cloud into a nuclear reactor by firing gas jets. This surprising mixture formed our solar system. The first to form was the central star within the molecular cloud formed by the remains of dust and gas resulting from explosions from hundreds of previous stars. The molecular cloud was composed mainly of the most common element in the universe: hydrogen, whose atoms are held together by gravity. With the help of the Hubble telescope, it has been observed that in stars that end in supernovae, a gigantic detonation occurs, where small atoms are combined to form larger and more exotic ones. During this intense atomic activity and with a unique cosmic alchemy, precious metals like gold and platinum are created.

Over the course of a million years, the cloud was compressed and then collapsed. More and more material gradually accumulated near the center. In the molecular cloud, molecules, as they usually do, rotated faster in the center of the cloud, making it progressively denser until the atoms in the center become so compact and so compressed that they overheat.

The temperature of the cloud rose to millions of degrees, so hot that the hydrogen atoms collided with each other and fused. Huge explosions of energy were released. The force of these explosions pushed the center of the cloud outward against the force of gravity. Throughout its life, the Sun will be in a constant struggle between these two forces.

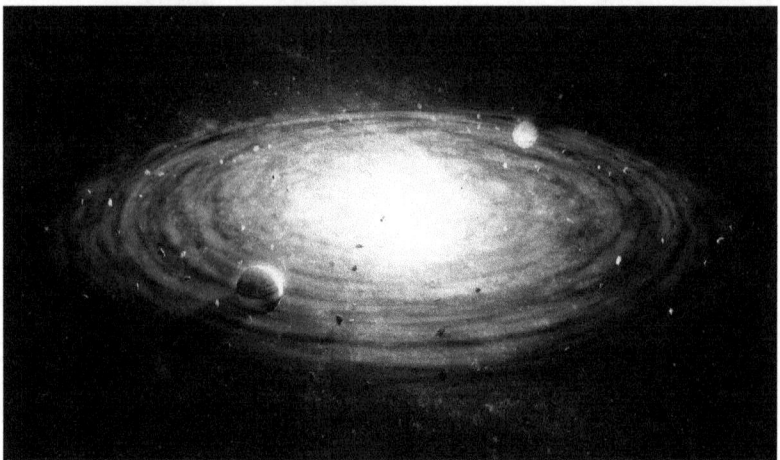

When the cloud finally stabilized, the pressures were balanced, and the Sun was born, as seen in the illustration on the previous page.

The birth of the Sun occurred about 4.5 billion years ago in a dark, shapeless molecular cloud that floated inside one of the arms called Orion of a galaxy in the form of a spiral called the Milky Way. This cloud was just one of the thousands that populated the galaxy. While other of these clouds dispersed, this one stayed more united and went through spectacular transformations. As the cloud contracted, its center became hotter and denser. From this center came the Sun, which at this stage was only a very agitated hot gas ball compressed by the crushing pressure of gravity. When the temperature and pressure reached the point of ignition, nuclear reactions took place and the Sun started its activity.

Meanwhile, the material of the cloud around the Sun swirled to form a sort of disk in the form of a miniature spiral galaxy called the *solar nebula*. Particles in the cloud combined for millions of years later to form many larger bodies called *planetesimal bodies* that were grouped into planets, moons, asteroids, and comets around the central star. The Sun agglomerated 99.8 percent of the original molecular cloud. The planets formed out of the remaining 0.2 percent and began revolving around the central star, or Sun.

Near the Sun, radiation swept light gases, leaving only heavy elements like rocks and metals. Thusthe rocky planets like Mercury, Venus, Earth, and Mars formed closest to the Sun. Farther away from the Sun, planets composed mainly of hydrogen, helium, and ice formed as Jupiter and Saturn, also called the "gas giants." In the most remote area, planets called "ice giants" were formed: Uranus and Neptune are composed of ammonium, methane, and carbon monoxide. For millions of years, the gravity of the planets and their moons swept away the remains of the rocks and dust, leaving only the planets, the asteroid belt, and large, seemingly empty spaces, as shown in this illustration of our solar system.

    The solar system in its first moments was much more compact than it is now. Where the four planets of the inner space of the system are now orbiting, a chain of smaller planets orbited the Sun 4.5 billion years ago. Some of these small planets drew near each other when the force of gravity caused them to merge. The forces and heat of those collisions melted the parent rock of the planets involved, but gravity kept the two rocky bodies together and solidified them into one. With each collision, the planets combined to get bigger. Of the four planets inside the Sun, it is believed that Mercury was formed by only one or two collisions, while Venus, almost the size of Earth today, was formed by eight collisions. Earth, however, got the most hits: it was formed by about ten collisions, which caused it to be bigger. The last impact on Earth, some 4.5 million years ago, had a profound effect on our world. A gigantic rocky body hit the center of the planet, giving Earth its iron core and forming the Moon that orbits around the Earth.

Now that we've established how our solar system was formed, let's take a closer look at its components, starting with the Sun.

# The Sun

The Sun—or *Helios*, as it was called by the ancient Greeks— is the most powerful force in the solar system. With its gravity, the Sun holds together the entire solar system, including its planets, moons, asteroids, comets, and everything that exists in it.

The Sun is a medium-size star that is about 4.5 billion years old, with a diameter of 864,337.2 miles and a mass of $4,385 \times 10^{30}$ pounds. In other words, its mass is 333,000 times greater than that of the earth. The Sun is so large that more than a million planets like Earth would fit in it.

The Sun, which generates the heat and light that give us life, is a huge orange ball formed by 92.1 percent hydrogen, the element that constitutes most of the universe. In addition to hydrogen, the Sun also contains 7.8 percent helium. The Sun converts hydrogen into helium to produce its energy, which reaches us on Earth in the form of light. That energy is the fuel of life on Earth. Without it nothing could live, neither animals nor plants, which are so essential to the food chain on which we all depend.

The energy of the Sun is generated at its core at temperatures of more than 27 million degrees Fahrenheit. At that point, the Sun compares to an immense nuclear plant; every four hydrogen nuclei that fuse produce a helium nucleus, which is even lighter than the four hydrogen nuclei. That difference in material becomes pure energy using Albert Einstein's famous formula: $E = mc^2$ where $E$ represents energy, $m$ represents mass, and $c^2$ represents the speed of light squared. This energy is what produces the tiny particles of light called photons, which are the components of each beam of light.

Every second, almost 600 million tons of hydrogen are converted into helium, which represents more energy in a second than could be produced by six million nuclear plants in a year, according to the *National Geographic* Channel. That energy comes to us thanks to the incredible journey that photons make to Earth. The photons that finally reach the Earth were created more than a million years ago, and the reason for that lengthy time is that it is extremely difficult for them to leave the Sun. The biggest obstacle in their journey is just to leave the dense nucleus of the great star. When the photons enter the radioactive zone, they are bombarded by particles of hot hydrogen gas or plasma, where they begin to change directions at random, zigzagging for many years. Some of the photons that were formed when the Sun originated have not yet been able to leave the Sun. But those that do leave the Sun release their energy and travel at the speed of light, making the journey of 93 million miles to Earth in only eight minutes. These photons have been providing us with heat and light since the Sun began to shine.

The Sun consists of six zones: three zones in its interior and the other three outside. The nucleus, the radioactive zone, and the convection zone are in the interior. The outside consists of the surface (or visible part, also called the *photosphere*), which is about 300 miles thick; the chromosphere; and the crown.

The surface is where the radiation of the Sun comes out; on Earth, we see it as sunlight. The temperature on the surface of the Sun is about 10,000 degrees F, which is the coldest part of the Sun. The temperature increases by about 2 million degrees F in the crown, which is a kind of white halo or aura.

The Sun is not only heat and light; it is also an immense and complex magnetic field generated by its electric currents. Thanks to the work of the solar winds, this magnetic field extends in all directions toward outer space to form the interplanetary magnetic field.

Magnetism is the invisible force that influences every aspect of the behavior of the Sun. It does not always behave in the same way, because it changes according to its own solar cycle of approximately eleven years. At the end of each cycle, geographic poles change their magnetic polarity. When that happens, changes in the crown can range from calm situations to busy situations. In busy situations, solar storms occur, and we can see some solar activities like the black spots of the Sun and the solar prominences.

The black spots of the Sun are the darkest and coldest points, where a very strong local magnetic field prevents heat from increasing at that point. The prominences or solar flares are gigantic arcs of gas columns above the black spots of the Sun. Solar flares can be dangerous because they throw vast amounts of particles and radiation into space. This material is swept away by the normally constant breeze of the electrically charged gas coming out of the Sun, and it can suddenly turn into a solar windstorm that can be directed to Earth. At a speed of about two million miles per hour, this breeze hits the Earth's magnetic field, forming the light of auroras. Solar storms are caused when the lines of the Sun's magnetic field are twisted so that they seem to break like rubber bands, causing the Sun's flares to burst into space. When the particles of these solar storms collide with the Earth's magnetic field, these particles are diverted to the Earth's poles, creating bundles of lights of assorted colors. This phenomenon is known as *polar auroras*. If the phenomenon is seen on the North Pole, they are called *boreal auroras*; those seen on the South Pole are called *austral auroras*.

The only form of the Sun's radiation that we have felt so far has been its light, which is composed of ultraviolet light. Much of this light can cause skin burns or cancer. But the ozone layer of the Earth protects us from the damaging effects of ultraviolet radiation. However, solar activity can have a dark side, as it can affect the Earth's technology system, satellites, power plants, and the planet's climate.

# The Planets

When our solar system was born more than 4.5 billion years ago, both heavy and light elements swirled and revolved around the Sun. The gravity of the central star kept the whirlpool in balance; the heavier elements, such as rocks and metals, remained near the center, while the lighter elements, such as hydrogen and helium, escaped to the more distant regions. This separation gave the planets that were being formed their distinctive characteristics.

The spiral of rocks and dust around the Sun rotated in the same direction, dancing to the same rhythm, but this dance was not always serene. The fragments collided and clustered. From this mixture of dust and particles, the planets slowly formed, with so much material flying around that it was not always easy for these bodies to survive in peace. Some young planets were impacted, some others were annihilated, and some were reformed. As the planets grew, their gravity increased, drawing even more material.

A few large planets formed; some were large enough to have their own environment of dust and particles. This complex dance of activity eventually stabilized, and a few new planets paraded around the central star. It was finally possible to have only a handful of planets spinning around the star. Terrestrial planets—planets like Earth that are formed from rocks and silicates—are found near the Sun. Giant gas planets—made primarily of hydrogen, with some water and helium—are farther away. Even farther from the Sun are dwarf bodies like Pluto that are formed by frozen balls. Let's look at each of them starting with Mercury, the one closest to the Sun.

## Mercury

Mercury got its name from the Roman messenger of the gods, which were as fast as the planet Mercury in their orbit around the Sun. At about 36 million miles or 0.39 Astronomical Units (AU), Mercury is the closest planet to the Sun. An AU is the distance between the Sun and Earth and is the unit of measurement used as a standard for measuring distances in the universe.

Given the proximity of Mercury to the Sun, the Sun appears gigantic from Mercury's surface: three times larger than seen from Earth. It is possible that Mercury would be rich in gold, platinum, and other heavy elements. It is also the smallest planet in our solar system: it is only a little larger than the Moon, or one-third the size of the Earth. It has a diameter of 1,516 miles and a mass of $3.3 \times 10^{23}$ kg, making it 0.055 the mass of the Earth.

Mercury has long days and short years. One day on Mercury—in other words, the time it takes the planet to rotate on its axis—is the equivalent of 175.97 Earth days. A year on Mercury, the time required to complete its orbit around the Sun, is just 88 Earth days. Mercury travels at about thirty-one miles per second, faster than any other planet.

Mercury is a rocky planet with no moons or rings around it. It is the second most solid planet after Earth, with a large metal, partially molten or liquid core that has a diameter of about 2,480 miles, comprising approximately 80 percent of the diameter of the planet. Above the core is an outer layer about 250 miles thick, comparable to the outer layer of the Earth where Earth's mantle and crust are.

The surface of Mercury is rough and very like that of the Earth's Moon, marked by many impact craters and scars resulting from collisions with comets and asteroids. Because of these impacts, some important basins like Caloris (about 960 miles in diameter) and Rachmaninoff (about 190 miles in diameter) were formed on its surface.

There are very few features on Mercury that could shelter life as we know it on Earth. Life would have no chance to bloom, because we could not even breathe on Mercury: its atmosphere is too thin, consisting mainly of oxygen, sodium, hydrogen, helium, and potassium. In addition, the temperatures are too extreme to support life, ranging from minus 300 degrees F at night to 800 degrees F during daylight hours. Mercury has a gravity of 12.1 ft/s², meaning that a person who weighed 100 pounds on Earth would weigh only 38 pounds on Mercury.

Mercury has been visited by only two NASA missions: the Mariner 10 in 1974 and the Messenger in 2011.

## Venus

Venus got its name from the Roman goddess of love and beauty due to the dazzling beauty of the planet as seen from the Earth at night. Venus is the second planet from the Sun at 67 million miles or 0.72 AU. It is also our nearest neighbor and the second brightest object in our night sky, surpassed only by our Moon.

Venus is a rocky planet with a mass of 4.87 x 10²⁴ kg and a diameter of 7,521 miles. Its size is 80 percent that of the Earth. It has neither moons nor rings around it. Like Earth, Venus had a violent past because of its encounters with asteroids. It has an iron core with a diameter of approximately 3,800 miles. Although its iron core is like that of Earth, Venus does not have a global magnetic field because it rotates too slowly to generate one.

Venus and Earth at first were very similar in fact, they were called the twin planets of the solar system. While they are similar in size, in the material from which they are made, their mass, their density, and even their gravity, they evolved in very different ways. Those differences are so pronounced that, compared to Earth, Venus is a very strange planet.

Venus spins backward, so the sun rises in the west and sets in the east. And because the planet rotates so slowly, one day on Venus is longer than going around the Sun. It takes 243 Earth days for Venus to completely rotate on its axis, while it takes 225 Earth days to orbit around the Sun. The retrograde rotation of Venus causes the day-night cycle to be about 117 Earth days.

Venus is always cloudy. Its dense and toxic atmosphere consists mainly of 96 percent carbon dioxide, 3 percent nitrogen, 0.1 percent traces of water, and the rest other elements such as sulfur dioxide, carbon monoxide, argon, and helium. The atmosphere of Venus is so heavy that being there would feel like being 1 kilometer under the sea of the Earth. The atmospheric
pressure on the surface is ninety times more than that of the Earth. In fact, the pressure is so strong that it will crush even a hard metal ship after just a few hours on its surface.

Venus is the hottest planet in the solar system with an average temperature of 900 degrees F—so hot that small meteors burn in the atmosphere before they can reach the surface. It is a suffocating super greenhouse, resembling a hot hell, with heavy clouds of hydrogen sulfide. It has more than one thousand volcanoes measuring more than twelve miles in diameter belching continuous lava flows from volcanic peaks. All of this lava has been running for hundreds of miles on the planet's plains. Ancient volcanoes form layers of lava mountains cut by cliffs and valleys. The highest mountain on the surface is Montes Maxwell at 6.83 miles above the average elevation of the planet.

Venus has a gravity of 29.1 ft/s$^2$. A person weighing 100 pounds on Earth would weigh 91 pounds on Venus. The planet has been visited by more than forty NASA missions.

## Earth

Earth is the only planet in the solar system that does not owe its name to an ancient god or goddess. Earth is the third planet from the Sun at a distance of 93 million miles. This distance is the Astronomical Unit (AU), and it is the standard measure used to refer to distances in the universe.

A rocky planet with a metal center, it is the fifth largest planet in the solar system, with a mass of $5,972 \times 10^{24}$ kg and a diameter of 9,917 miles.

The surface of the Earth is composed mainly of water. Seventy percent of the planet is ocean saltwater with a relatively stable temperature and an average depth of about 2.5 miles. All the water in the oceans is salty. However, fresh water exists in the liquid phase only within a narrow temperature range of 32 to 212 degrees F. The presence and distribution of water vapor in the atmosphere are responsible for much of Earth's climate.

Earth is a geologically active planet. Its center is warmer than the surface of the Sun, and the Earth is constantly experiencing earthquakes, volcanoes, and climate changes. The outer rock layer of Earth, which is called the lithosphere, and which includes the crust and the upper mantle, is divided into huge plates that move constantly, zooming either in or out. When the plates approach and collide with each other, earthquakes occur; if those shocks are strong enough, they produce elevations and then form mountains like those we see on the surface along with the valleys, canyons, and plains.

The axis of the Earth, with respect to the plane of its orbit around the Sun, has an inclination of 23.45 degrees, which makes possible the seasons of the year and is the reason why there are vast expanses of ice at the poles. During a part of the year, the Northern Hemisphere is inclined toward the Sun, while the Southern Hemisphere sets away from the Sun, producing summer in the north and winter in the south. Six months later, the situation is reversed. When spring and autumn begin, both hemispheres receive approximately equal amounts of solar illumination.

The Earth rotates every twenty-four hours around itself, which we know as the day, while it orbits the Sun every 365 days, which we know as the year. The rapid rotation of the planet and its molten iron nucleus give rise to a magnetic field that protects us from the solar winds, the streams of charged particles expelled continuously from the Sun. When these charged particles are trapped in the Earth's magnetic field, these collide with air molecules above the Earth's magnetic poles. These air molecules then begin to glow, producing what we know as the polar auroras or northern or southern lights.

Planet Earth also had a violent past, but today it is a quiet place, with plenty of water and oxygen and an excellent balance of land, seas, and air. At first there was a lot of carbon dioxide in the Earth's atmosphere, but this was transferred to the rocks by small organisms that took that carbon dioxide to form their skeletons. The remains of these animals became sediments from which limestone rocks were formed.

Today the Earth's atmosphere is composed of 78 percent nitrogen, 21 percent oxygen, and 1 percent other elements. So far, Earth is the only planet in our solar system that harbors intelligent life. And it is precisely with the emergence of intelligent life, when we, the human beings, appeared to be part of the universe as well. Our planet is in perfect balance, so we can breathe and live on it, another unique characteristic of our planet within the solar system.

The atmosphere affects the Earth's climate; protects us from much of the harmful radiation from the Sun; and protects us from meteorites, as most of them burn before they can impact the surface. For more than three billion years, Earth has had the right temperature to maintain the pillar of life: water, which flows through the Earth, through the seas, and through the air forms the hydrological cycle or water cycle, which is part of the secret of the success of life on Earth. The average global temperature of the whole planet is 59 degrees F.

The Earth is the only known planet in the universe where life exists as we know it. On our planet, all the necessary conditions exist to survive under a thin layer of the atmosphere that separates us from outer space. Its gravity of $32.04 \text{ ft/s}^2$ keeps our feet on Earth. Our planet has a natural satellite that we call the Moon, a key piece in the flowering of life. See illustration above. The Moon formed when a rocky, Mars-sized body collided with Earth about 4.5 million years ago, and the resulting debris accumulated to form our natural satellite. The newly formed Moon was in a molten state, which solidified after about 100 million years with less dense rocks floating upward to form the lunar crust. At first, the Moon could have developed its magnetic field, as terrestrial planets do.

NASA has launched more than a hundred spacecrafts to explore the Moon. It is the only celestial body beyond Earth that has been visited by human beings. Twelve of them have walked on the surface of the Moon. The first human landing on the Moon was on July 20, 1969. During the Apollo missions from 1969 to 1972, twelve American astronauts walked on the moon and used a lunar vehicle to traverse the surface and expand their studies of soil mechanics, meteoroids, lunar terrain, magnetic fields, and solar wind. Apollo astronauts brought 842 pounds of rock and soil to Earth for study.

## Mars

Mars got its name from the Roman god of war. It is a rocky, dusty, dry planet with a mass of $6.42 \times 10^{23}$ kg and a diameter of 4,212 miles, making it about half the size of the Earth. It is the fourth planet from the Sun at 142 million miles or 1.52 AU; since its orbit is slightly elliptical, its distance from the Sun varies. The orbit of Mars around the Sun is about 1.5 times as far away as the Earth.

Mars is sometimes called the "red planet" because the iron minerals in the Martian soil oxidize, making the soil and dusty atmosphere look red. It is a bright object of the night sky and has been known since antiquity.

Like other terrestrial planets like Mercury, Venus, and Earth, Mars has a solid surface that has been transformed by volcanic eruptions, impact craters with other bodies, crust movement, and atmospheric effects such as dust storms. Volcanism on the Martian surface was very active more than three billion years ago. Some of the giant volcanoes are younger, having formed between one and two million years ago. Mars has the largest volcano in the solar system, Mount Olympus, which is three times higher than Mount Everest, the highest mountain on Earth. It also has A system of spectacular canyons called Mariner Valley goes across the equator of the planet and is a Grand Canyon almost the width of the United States.

About four billion years ago, Mars was also very similar to Earth, a blue planet that even had oceans. But some time ago Mars lost most of its atmosphere and became a dry and frozen world. Today Mars is a desert with big dust storms. There is plenty of frozen water under its surface and in the form of ice at the poles of the Martian globe.

On Mars, one day takes a little more than twenty-four hours. One year takes 687 Earth days. Like Earth, Mars has four climatic seasons due to the tilt of its axis of rotation. Its slightly elliptical orbit varies its distance from the Sun, which affects the length of the Martian seasons. The gravity on the surface of Mars is 12.2 ft/s$^2$. Consequently, if a person weighing 100 pounds on Earth would weigh 38 pounds on Mars.

Martian days are cold, with temperatures ranging from -225 to 70 degrees F. The air is mainly composed of carbon dioxide with a small amount of nitrogen and argon. There is almost no ozone, so the surface is not protected from the ultraviolet light of the Sun. Mars does not have a global magnetic field. However, it has been found that the areas of the Martian crust in the southern hemisphere are highly magnetized, which is an indication of traces of a four-billion-year-old magnetic field that remains. Currently the surface of Mars cannot sustain life as we know it. Poisonous air due to carbon dioxide makes Mars a dangerous place for humans. However, NASA missions continue to explore the planet to determine the potential for life.

Mars does not have a ring spinning around it, but it has two moons, Phobos and Deimos, which receive their names of fear from the horses that pulled the chariot of the Greek god Ares. Mars moons are among the smallest in the solar system. Phobos is a little larger than Deimos and orbits only 3,700 miles above the Martian surface. No known moon orbits closer to its planet. It rotates around Mars three times a day, while the more distant Deimos takes thirty hours for each orbit. Phobos gradually spirals inland, about 5.9 feet closer to the planet each century. Within fifty million years, this moon will either crash into Mars or break into pieces to form a ring around the planet.

Like our Moon, Phobos and Deimos always present the same face to their planet. Both appear to be asteroids captured with irregular surfaces covered with dust, loose rocks, and many craters. They are among the darkest objects in the solar system and appear to be made of rock rich in carbon mixed with ice. Phobos has only one-thousandth of the Earth's gravitational force. A person weighing 150 pounds on Earth would weigh only 2 ounces there. These moons are shaped like a potato and have very little mass, so gravity can make them spherical. Phobos, the innermost moon, has many craters, with deep grooves on its surface. The most outstanding of these is the Stickney, which is six miles wide.

## Jupiter

Jupiter, the fifth planet from the Sun, is named for the king of the Roman gods, since it is the largest of all the planets in our solar system. At 484 million miles or 5.2 AU from the Sun, it has a mass of $1.90 \times 10^{27}$ kg and a diameter of 87,000 miles. It is the largest and most massive planet in the solar system, containing more than twice the material of all the other bodies orbiting the Sun. It is so large that eleven Earths could fit in the diameter of it.

Jupiter is a giant gaseous planet and therefore does not have a solid surface. However, it may have a solid core the size of Earth. Jupiter is composed mainly of hydrogen and helium. It is the first of the giant gas planets with rings formed by fascinating arrangements of very fine particles that glide along its vast circumference. The small particles that form the rings of Jupiter are dark, which makes them very difficult to see unless the planet is illuminated by the Sun.

The clouds above Jupiter make it seem serene, but inside is the most spectacular storm in the solar system. The Great Red Spot, an immense swirl of wind of more than 15,000 miles wide, rotates at speeds of hundreds of miles per hour and has lasted almost four hundred years.

The composition of Jupiter is similar to that of the Sun, mainly hydrogen and helium. In the depths of the planet the pressure and temperature increase considerably, compressing hydrogen gas into liquid. This gives Jupiter the largest ocean in the solar system—though it is an ocean of hydrogen instead of water. Scientists believe that at depths near the center of the planet, the pressure is so immense that the electrons of the hydrogen atoms are compressed, making the liquid conductive to electricity. The rapid rotation of Jupiter is believed to be the push that originates the electric currents that generate the powerful magnetic field of the planet. It is not yet clear whether, at greater depth, Jupiter has a central core of solid material. The truth is that its center is extremely magnetic and has a force of gravity of 81.3 feet/$s^2$. Something weighing 100 pounds on Earth would weigh 253 pounds on Jupiter. This force of gravity is stronger than that of any planet in the solar system.

Jupiter is always sucking up asteroids, meteors, and comets in its way. Another feature of this planet is that it also has the shortest day and the longest year of the solar system. A day on Jupiter takes about 10 Earth hours, while a year is about 12 Earth years or 4,333 Earth days.

Jupiter has a total of sixty-nine satellites or moons: fifty-three of them are known, and sixteen are still awaiting confirmation of their discovery. Among the most well-known moons are Io, Europa, Ganymede, Callisto, Enceladus, and Mimas. The first four were first observed by the astronomer Galileo Galilei in 1610 using a rudimentary version of the telescope. These four moons are known today as the Galilean satellites. Io is the body with the most volcanic activity of the solar system. Its surface is covered with sulfur in assorted color type. Europa is a moon with a surface of water ice probably covering a warm ocean. It may have more water than the Earth, which makes it a candidate for habitability. Ganymede is the largest moon in the solar system with a size bigger than that of the planet Mercury. Its surface, furrowed and crumpled by craters, formed by ice tremors. It is the only known moon to have its own magnetic field. Callisto is a moon mistreated by cosmic bombardment with a surface featuring craters. Enceladus has a flatter and smoother surface. Mimas is a moon quite battered by ancient impacts.

The interior of the Io, Europa, and Ganymede moons has a layered structure like the Earth with a nucleus and other layers above. There is an interesting influence between these three moons. The time it takes for Europa to orbit around Jupiter is twice as long as Io, while Ganymede's time of orbit is twice that of Europa. In other words, every time Ganymede orbits around Jupiter, Europa makes two orbits and Io makes four orbits. All moons hold the same face toward Jupiter in their orbit, which means that each moon rotates once on its axis for each orbit around Jupiter.

Jupiter is not a place to visit—it is a gigantic gas ball with nowhere to land. Anything that passes through its colored clouds will be crushed and melted because of its intense pressure. Jupiter cannot sustain life as we know it. However, some of Jupiter's moons have oceans beneath their surfaces that could harbor life. There is an ocean of liquid water with the ingredients for life that might be below the iced crust of the moon Europa. This would be an attractive spot to explore.

## Saturn

The sixth planet from the Sun and the second largest in the solar system, Saturn takes its name from the Roman god of agriculture. In ancient times, Saturn was the farthest planet from Earth that could be observed by the human eye without the help of the telescope.

Like Jupiter, Saturn is almost entirely formed of gas, and its globe is a little flat due to its rapid rotation. Saturn is the second planet of the four gaseous giants, so it does not have a solid surface. Its atmosphere is composed mainly of hydrogen and helium. The winds in the upper atmosphere of the planet reach 1,649 feet per second in the equatorial region, almost five times stronger than hurricane-velocity winds on Earth. These super-fast winds, combined with the heat that comes from the interior of the planet, make yellow bands in the atmosphere visible.

Saturn has a mass of 5.68 x $10^{26}$ kg, which is 95.16 times greater than that of Earth; however, its specific density is 690 kg/$m^3$, the lowest in the solar system. It is even lower than that of water, which is 1,000 kg/$m^3$. Saturn has a diameter of 72,367 miles and is 886 million miles from the Sun, or 9.5 AU.

In the center of Saturn is a dense nucleus of rock, ice, water, and other compounds that was made solid by pressure and intense heat. This nucleus is enveloped by liquid metallic hydrogen within a layer of liquid hydrogen, like the center of Jupiter, but considerably smaller. Saturn's magnetic field is smaller than Jupiter''s but is still 578 times more powerful than that of the Earth. In Saturn, a day is 10.7 terrestrial hours, whereas a year is 29 terrestrial years or 10,756 terrestrial days. The gravity of Saturn is 34.3 ft/$s^2$, which is very similar to that of the Earth.

Saturn is famous for its beautiful rings, for which the planet is known as the "jewel of the solar system." Galileo was the first to observe strange bodies around Saturn with his small telescope in 1610; as technology evolved, these were confirmed to be the beautiful rings of the planet. This ring system is the most spectacular in the solar system. The system consists of seven rings with several spaces and divisions between them. The rings are made up of billions of very small bodies of ice chained around the planet. It is believed that those small bodies that make up the rings were formed when moons and other bodies like comets and asteroids were fragmented by the powerful gravity of Saturn. The largest of these bodies of ice is about ten meters wide. Saturn's ring system extends hundreds of thousands of miles from the planet, however, the vertical depth is typically about thirty feet in the main rings.

This planet has fifrty-three known moons with nine other moons awaiting confirmation of their discovery, totalling sixty-two moons. The largest of these is Titan, which resembled Earth before life began. Titan is a little larger than the planet Mercury and is the second largest moon in the solar system. Only the Ganymede moon of Jupiter surpasses it in size.

Each of Saturn's moons constitutes a fascinating world from Titan, with its clouded surface, to Phoebe, cratered and orbiting around the planet in the opposite direction. The first moon discovered was Titan; the next four to be discovered were Iapetus, Rhea, Dione, and Tethys. Hyperion and Phoebe were next. As the telescope's resolving ability improved, more moons, such as Epimetheus and Janus, were discovered to make a total of fifty-three. Each of the moons of Saturn carries a unique story. Two of those moons orbit within the spaces in the main rings. Some others, such as Prometheus and Pandora, interact with the material of the ring, following the ring in its orbit. Some small moons are trapped in the same orbits as Thetis or Dione. Janus and Epimetheus occasionally pass close to each other, causing periodic orbits to be exchanged.

Saturn cannot sustain life as we know it. However, some of its moons have conditions that could harbor life. The pressure of the planet is so powerful that it compresses gas into liquid that is capable of crushing anything that goes there. It would not be a possible place for human beings to live.

## Uranus

Uranus, named for the Greek god of heaven, is the third largest planet in our solar system and the seventh planet from the Sun at about 1.8 billion miles or 19.19 AU. It has a mass of $8.68 \times 10^{25}$ kg, about 14,536 times that of Earth, and a diameter of 31,518 miles. Most of the mass of Uranus is composed of icy materials such as water, methane, and ammonia that mostly extend above a small rocky core. Uranus is one of the two ice giants of the outer solar system; Neptune is the other.

The atmosphere of Uranus is composed mainly of hydrogen and helium, with a small amount of methane and traces of water and ammonia. The planet gets its blue-green color from the methane gas in its atmosphere. This is formed when the light of the Sun passes through the atmosphere and is reflected by the clouds. Methane gas then absorbs the red part of the light, resulting in a blue-green color.

Uranus, like Venus, rotates contrary to the rest of the other planets. In addition to that, it rotates on its side— almost on its equatorial line, which is almost at a right angle to its orbit around the Sun. Due to the unusual orientation of Uranus, the planet undergoes extreme variations in sunlight during each twenty-year season. This strange situation of Uranus is the result of a collision with a body of planetary size at its beginning. This impact took the planet almost to the brink of destruction. But gravity prevailed, and the planet managed to stay intact. As a reminder of that impact, the planet formed thirteen dark rings around its equatorial line. These rings seem to change from opaque to luminous when receiving light when the Sun begins to rise.

Uranus has twenty-seven moons, with Oberon and Titania being the largest and the first moons discovered. Next to be discovered were Ariel and Umbriel. After almost a century Miranda was discovered. Finally, the other moons were discovered, including Juliet, Puck, Cordelia, Ofelia, Bianca, Desdemona, Portia, Rosalind, Cressida, and Belinda. Perhaps the best known of these moons is Miranda, astrange-looking little moon with mountains and ice canyons. Ariel has a surface full of craters, but with enough brilliance. Umbriel is an old moon and the darkest of the five great moons, with many old and large craters. Oberon, the outermost of the five large moons, is old, full of craters, and has few signs of internal activity.

A day on Uranus takes about 17 Earth hours, while a year on this planet is about 84 Earth years or 30,687 Earth days. For humans, the time there would seem very long. Uranus cannot sustain life as we know it. Uranus is too cold, with an average temperature of -350 degrees F and many winds that are extremely poisonous to humans. It is a gaseous planet like Jupiter, Saturn and Neptune, so there is nothing on which to land. The air in the atmosphere becomes thicker and thicker until it is compressed into liquid. This gives us an idea of the existing pressure. Anything passing through the clouds of Uranus would be crushed. Due to its great distance from the Earth, Uranus is the first planet discovered with the aid of a telescope.

## Neptune

Neptune, named for the Roman god of the sea, is the eighth planet from the Sun at about 2.8 billion miles or 30.07 AU. It has a mass of $1.02 \times 10^{26}$ kg and is composed mainly of a very thick and hot combination of water, ammonia, and methane on a heavier and more solid core approximately the size of the Earth. It is believed that there could be an ocean of super-hot water under the cold clouds of Neptune; this ocean does not boil due to the incredible pressure of the planet. It is the fourth largest planet in our solar system with a diameter of 30,599 miles. It has the fastest winds in the entire solar system, which blow to about 1,200 miles per hour. It is a gas planet and extremely cold, with an effective temperature of -353 degrees F. Like Uranus, Neptune is an ice giant with an atmosphere composed of hydrogen and helium, mainly with a small amount of methane and traces of other elements. The bright blue color of Neptune is the result of methane in its atmosphere, like that of UranusNeptune is not visible to the naked eye due to its extreme distance from Earth.

Neptune, unlike the other planets, was the first to be located through mathematical predictions rather than periodic observations of the sky. Galileo had recorded it as a fixed star during his observations with his small telescope in 1612 and 1613. Neptune takes about 165 Earth years, that is 60,190 Earth days, to make a complete orbit around the Sun. A year in Neptune is quite long. However, one day in Neptune only takes about 16 Earth hours.

Neptune has six rings of dark ice fragments and thirteen known moons, with Triton being the largest moon. It passesthrough the rings. Triton orbits the planet in the opposite direction compared to the rest of the moons, suggesting that it may have been captured by Neptune in the distant past. This moon is the coldest body of the solar system. Triton contains liquid nitrogen trapped beneath its surface that bursts into snow. Other important moons of Neptune include Nereida, and Proteus. The planet cannot sustain life as we know it.

# The Asteroid Belt

Between Mars and Jupiter is a belt of probably a million asteroids orbiting, usually in an orderly way, around the Sun. These asteroids are rocky bodies, irregularly shaped and smaller than the planets. None of these bodies has atmosphere and none can harbor life as we know it. One of these asteroids, Chariklo, has a pair of rare rings around it. Some others have moons. To date, more than 150 asteroids with a small satellite are known.

Asteroids are thought to have originated from the remnants of the formation of the solar system 4.5 billion years ago. They could not unite to form a planet because of the enormous gravitational force of Jupiter, the largest planet, resulting in rocky residue that is observed today.

There are areas in the belt where no asteroids are found due to the great gravitational resonance with Jupiter, making the orbits of these asteroids very unstable. If any of them occupy these areas, the asteroid is expelled, usually outside the solar system— though occasionally the asteroid may be sent to some internal planet, such as Earth. The resulting collision, of course, would be a threat to life.

Asteroids can have a width ranging from 0.6 to 590 miles. Among the largest bodies of the asteroid belt are Ceres, Pallas, Vesta, Higia, and Juno. These asteroids constitute more than half of the total mass of the belt. The asteroid Ceres is the largest of all; it looks like a dwarf planet, has a diameter of 590 miles, and has double the mass of asteroids Pallas and Vesta combined. Most of the rest of the asteroids that make up the belt are much smaller. The total mass of the belt is barely 4 percent of the mass of the Moon, and it is scattered throughout the volume of the orbit, so it would be very difficult to hit one of these objects if something crossed the belt. However, two large asteroids can collide with each other, forming other smaller asteroids with similar compositions and characteristics.

The asteroid belt is not the only place in the solar system where asteroids can be found, since at least two other regions beyond the solar system also have similar bodies: the Kuiper Belt and the Oort Cloud.

# Beyond the Solar System

Beyond Neptune, where the light of the sun does not reach, is a very cold and melancholy region containing frozen bodies of rock and ice, possible remnants left behind when the planets were formed billions of years ago. In those depths of the cosmos are the Kuiper Belt and the Oort Cloud.

The Kuiper Belt, named after American astronomer Gerard Kuiper, is a disc-shaped region that lies beyond the orbit of Neptune. The Kuiper belt extends from approximately 30 to 55 AU. The belt probably fills with hundreds of thousands of icy bodies more than 62 miles wide with an estimated trillion or more comets.

Among the bodies of the Kuiper Belt is the famous Pluto, which was considered the ninth planet after being discovered in 1951. In 2006, it was excluded from the list of planets in the solar system. Approximately 3.7 billion miles from the Sun, Pluto is a very cold body with temperatures of -390 degrees F, a diameter of about 1,400 miles. It has five moons; Charon is the most important. Today Pluto is one more body of the Kuiper Belt; together with Ceres, Eris, Haumea, and Makemake, it is among the group of dwarf planets orbiting around the Sun. Other bodies like asteroids and comets also orbit the sun.

*Dwarf planets* are so named because they behave in many ways much like the planets. The dwarf planets are smaller than the Earth's Moon; some, like Pluto, Eris, and possibly Ceres, have very thin atmospheres.

The Kuiper Belt is considered a reservoir of comets located in the farthest region of the solar system. Comets are smaller bodies of ice and rock than asteroids, so they can travel faster. Like the planets, comets orbit about the same plane around the Sun, but the orbits of comets are more irregular. When comets approach the Sun and heat up, their gases evaporate, releasing solid particles that form the tail, which can be extended by solar winds. This is the famous long and bright tail that intrigued the ancient peoples. Once the comets move away from the Sun, they cool down, their gases once again freeze, and their tail disappears. When there is no more ice left, comets can become simple asteroids. Most Kuiper Belt kites are so-called comets with short orbital periods that take about two hundred years to make a full circle around the Sun.

Beyond the Kuiper belt lies the Oort Cloud, home to ice comets. These comets are at the limit of the Sun's gravity and the forces of other nearby stars. Although they are quite distant, they orbit around the Sun in an orbit that takes about a million years. The cloud is named in honor of Dutch astronomer Jan Oort, who in 1950 proposed that comets reside on a gigantic cloud in the outer zone of the solar system.

The Oort Cloud is between 5,000 and 100,000 AU. The outer measurement of the Oort Cloud is believed to be in the region of space where the Sun's gravitational influence is weaker than the influence of nearby stars. The Oort Cloud probably contains billions of icy bodies in solar orbit. Occasionally, some giant molecular clouds, or stars passing by, can disturb the orbits of some of these bodies in the outer region of the Oort Cloud, which can cause a comet to fall into the solar system. Many of the comets of the Oort Cloud are so far away from the Sun that they eventually disappear from the solar system.

# 1.5 DESTINY OF THE UNIVERSE

Today our universe is formed by a visible part that includes all the cosmic structures, surrounded by enormous empty spaces. The material that constitutes the visible universe is only 5 percent of the total. The other part of the invisible universe is dark matter that constitutes 27 percent of the matter of the universe. The rest of the universe, 68 percent, is comprised of dark energy.

Visible matter can form and hold together the cosmic structured by gravity, while dark energy would be responsible for the expansion of the universe. Edwin Hubble confirmed this expansion. The universe has expanded since its inception. Because it is expanding, that means it was smaller before. If we could go back in time, then, we would see the universe shrink to the size it was when it formed 13.7 billion years ago.

Like all things, our universe has a beginning and an end. The scientific consensus today is that the final destiny of the universe depends on its global form and how much dark energy it has. The shape of the universe depends on its density—in other words, the amount of mass and energy it has. In this sense, Einstein's theory raises three possible forms of the universe: flat, open, or closed.

Most scientists today accept that the universe has a flat shape. In a flat universe with the presence of dark energy, the universe expands at an accelerated rate and could end in a so-called "Big Freeze." This is the most likely scenario due to the shape of the current universe and considering that the universe continues to expand. In an open universe with the dark energy, the expansion is not only continuous but accelerating; the destiny of the universe would be a great freezing, or it may end in a "Big Rip." In a closed universe, all matter will eventually cluster, and the universe will collapse at one point, ending in a "Big Crunch."

For human civilization, however, the end will come with the death of the Sun, which would cause the end of the Earth. As the fuel runs out of the Sun, it will cool. This will cause it to expand and redden and get progressively closer to Earth. Eventually it will swallow Mercury, Venus, and then Earth. The Sun will finally throw a last breath of dust and gas, spreading ashes in the solar winds.

Before it dies and approaches its final stage, however, the Sun will unleash a hell on Earth. The atmosphere will become so hot that it will melt the surface of the Earth, and everything above it will disappear, including us humans. Billions of years after this, when the remaining heat of the Sun is extinguished, and its small, dark surface is at the same freezing temperature as the rest of space, the Sun will then be a black dwarf driven by the mysterious dark energy. That will continue in constant action until the end of our beloved universe. That will take billions of years, so let's look at the current universe.

## The Universe Today

The universe is everything that exists: matter, energy, space, and time. Our universe today is flat, formed in the Big Bang about 13.7 billion years ago; it may be infinite. The part of it that we have been able to see has at least 93 billion light-years in extension. It consists of a swarm of cosmic structures, including stars, galaxies, cumulus, superclusters, and other bodies called quasars. These quasars are distant objects that emit enormous amounts of energy. The radiations of quasars are similar to those of stars, but they are hundreds of billions of times brighter than stars and despite their enormous distances, some of them may have such intense energy that their brightness could be 60,000 times greater than that of the entire Milky Way. This entire system of cosmic structures is part of what we now know as the visible universe surrounded by huge empty spaces.

Within one of the galaxies that form the visible universe is our solar system, which orbits in one of its outer arms of the galaxy. That galaxy is the Milky Way, one of more than 125 billion galaxies that make up the visible universe. This gives us an idea of how immense our universe is. There could be 200 billion stars in this collection of stars called the Milky Way, and about 6 billion stars have planetary systems like ours. In addition to the planets of the solar system, more than 100 billion planets have been detected in the Milky Way and around $10^{24}$ planets have been discovered in the universe. Our solar system, with its central star and its eight planets, is spinning through space at 450,000 miles per hour, rotating as part of a vast collection of stars and star systems.

The material constituting the visible universe is known as visible or normal matter, which represents only 5 percent of the total matter of the universe. However, there are also enormous amounts of invisible matter called dark matter, which constitutes about 27 percent of the material content of the universe. Dark matter does not emit or reflect any type of light, nor does it give off detectable radiation. That is why we cannot see it, but we know it exists because of its gravitational effects, which we can detect thanks to current technology. The gravity of the dark matter is so intense that it moves the great galaxy clusters. The composition of the dark matter is still a mystery, although it is believed that it could be formed by neutrinos and other particles still unknown.

The other part of the universe, approximately 68 percent, is made up of dark energy. Dark energy seemed to be a characteristic of space as Albert Einstein had imagined when he realized that empty space was not a vacuum at all, but something filled with dark energy. While visible matter can form and hold cosmic structures together by gravity, dark energy tends to create more "empty" space between these structures, making them appear more distant from each other and part of a larger universe. Science today has admitted that the current universe is in a constant expansion and with greater acceleration than before as a product of dark energy.

## Expansion of the Universe

In 1929, Edwin Hubble proved that our universe is expanding. He measured redshift for numerous distant galaxies and measured their relative distances, determining the apparent brightness in each galaxy of a class of variable stars that change their luminosity cyclically and are called Cepheids. When he plotted the redshift versus the relative distance, he found that the redshift of distant galaxies increased in line with their distance. The only explanation for this observation was that the universe was expanding. The expanding universe is finite in both time and space. The reason why the universe does not collapse, as the equations of Newton and Einstein suggested should happen, is because it has been expanding from the moment of its creation and continues to do so. Once scientists understood the expansion of the universe, they immediately realized that the expansion must have been slower in the past.

Since its birth in the Big Bang about 13.7 billion years ago, the universe has expanded 156 billion years. If the universe is expanding today, it is because it was smaller before. In fact, if we could go back in time we would see the universe shrink to the size of our galaxy. If we keep going back, we would see it reach the size of our solar system. If we go even further back, we could get to the point where it formed 13,700 million of years ago—a point at which the universe was smaller than the smallest part of an atom.

## Final Destiny of the Universe

Now that we have understood the origin of the universe, we begin to formulate theories about its final destiny. So far, this is what we know or assume about the end of the universe, but of course that can change as we continue to discover more things. The scientific consensus today is that the final destiny of the universe depends on its overall shape and how much dark energy it has, which gives rise to several possible scenarios. The universe may continue to expand to infinity, its expansion may stop at some point and it may begin to contract, or it may reach a balance where it remains stable.

Currently, predicting the final destiny of the universe is possible thanks to Albert Einstein's 1916 theory of relativity. The shape of the universe depends on its density—in other words, the amount of mass and energy it has. In this sense Einstein's theory raises three possible forms of the universe: flat, open, or closed. Most scientists today accept that the universe has a flat shape.

In a flat universe, if the quantity of matter and energy are in equilibrium, the density of the universe will also be in equilibrium. This is called *critical density*. In a flat universe, gravity and expansion will be in equilibrium. Without dark energy the universe will expand, but it will do so much more slowly. With the presence of dark energy, the universe expands at an accelerated rate and the universe could end in a "Big Freeze."

This is the most likely scenario due to the shape of the current universe and to the fact that the universe continues to expand. In this scenario, on a time scale in the order of a trillion years, the existing stars will stop shining and most of the universe will become dark, cold, and chaotic. Later, after the passage of much more time, the galaxies will collapse into black holes and everything will disintegrate. At that time, the universe will be formed only of radiation. Expansion will continue indefinitely in a universe too cold to support life.

In an open universe, if the density of matter and energy is very high, the universe will curve outwards and take the form of a saddle on horseback horse's back. Without dark energy, the universe will be infinite and will expand forever, with gravity controlling the expansion. With dark energy, the expansion not only continues but accelerates; the destiny of the universe would either be the "Big Freeze," as in the flat universe, or the "Big Rip."

Under the scenario of the Big Rip, dark energy causes the rate of expansion of the universe to accelerate to the extreme. An acceleration of eternal or infinite expansion means that all the matter of the universe, beginning with galaxies and eventually including all kinds of structure, no matter how small, are disintegrated into disconnected elementary particles. The final state of the universe will be to return to a singularity or point from where it started with the Big Bang.

In a closed universe, if there is too much matter and energy, the density will be very high. The universe will curve inward and take the form of a sphere, and the universe will be finite. Without dark energy, gravity will be stronger than expansion, all matter will eventually cluster, and the universe will collapse at one point. The universe will end in a big collapse or ""Big Crunch."

In the presence of dark energy, the expansion will accelerate, and the great collapse will be greater. This theory postulates that the average density of the universe is sufficient to stop its expansion and begin the contraction. This scenario allows the Big Bang to be immediately preceded by the Big Crunch of a previous universe. If this happens repeatedly, there is an oscillating universe. The universe could consist of an infinite sequence of finite universes, each finite universe ending with a Big Crunch that is also the Big Bang of the next universe. In this way, the possibility of our universe coming from an earlier universe that was compressed and killed after a Big Crunch can not be ruled out.

So far, everything indicates that our universe will continue to expand even faster and to all directions on a large scale. Dark energy will condemn the universe to infinite expansion and a slow, cold death. The whole universe will experience great cooling. At the molecular scale, the expansion will overcome gravity, and everything will separate—not just galaxies, solar systems, and stars, but even atoms. Finally, the matter itself will be split in two. This would be the great final moment, the last great sigh of our universe Although we were not the center of the universe, we were always part of it. We are atomically connected to the universe, chemically connected to the Earth, and biologically connected among ourselves. As the Discovery Channel people said, we were in the universe and he was in us.

Perhaps with the passage of billions of years, in that cold and seemingly empty space, the formation of infinitesimal particles with some kind of matter will emerge. If the matter were to become very dense and were to warm to very high temperatures, the great energy generated could "bang" and give birth to another universe in the same way that ours was formed. Maybe we were not the first universe formed, and maybe we would not be the last one. Our universe was probably only one among others that existed in parallel.

Regarding the final destiny of our universe, it is important to emphasize that the most likely scenario that occurs, the great cooling, will occur in more than a million years, so we need not worry. By then we will have passed far from the end of human civilization and the lives of all creatures that lived on Earth. We will continue in our beloved universe for some five billion years more, until our Sun, the one who has given us life, runs out of all its nuclear fuel and finally dies.

# Death of the Sun

Nothing is eternal, for everything that exists in the universe has its time of death, and our Sun is no exception. Although the stars constitute the largest galactic structures hitherto known and their immense light illuminates huge spaces of the universe where they rotate, they eventually die. All stars are born and die, just like everything else, including people. The end of the Sun will be like the death of other stars that have existed in the universe.

The death of a star begins when the amount of available hydrogen in its nucleus begins to decrease. The star then begins to contract to raise its temperature and try to stop its gravitational collapse. In this process, the star increases its luminosity. When the hydrogen of the nucleus is finally exhausted, the star undergoes rapid transformations that lead to its death.

As it approaches its final stage, the Sun will become brighter and brighter. Its brightness will increase by 10 percent every billion years. Its hydrogen fuel will slowly deplete, but the nuclear reactor of the heart of the Sun will not slow its speed; on the contrary, its speed will increase.

The pressure in the core will drop as the fuel burns, the low pressures do not sustain the forces of gravity. Gravity will then compress the core, which will heat the hydrogen further by making the fuel burn faster, which will in turn increase core pressure until the two forces sway again. But this will be a cycle that will continue to burn more fuel as the Sun gets hotter and hotter.

As the fuel runs out, the Sun will cool. This will cause it to expand and redden as it gets progressively closer to Earth. Eventually it will swallow Mercury and Venus. On Earth, the water will evaporate, and the planet will melt when all the fuel in the Sun's core is gone. Sometime later, the Sun will swell and turn from yellow to red; it will appear as a red giant, and the old star will enter the last stage of its life.

Even then, the Sun will be more active than ever, even though it is already very old. After it consumes all the hydrogen, it will begin to burn the helium, which burns even hotter. The energy that will radiate from the super-hot core will push the top layer of the Sun out, making it bigger and bigger. As it grows, the Sun will cool until it turns red. Finally, the old Sun would throw one last breath of dust and gas, scattering ashes in the solar winds. From the storms of destruction, the seeds of newborn suns will emerge in billions of years to come.

The planets that will survive the Sun's death process, distance planets like Saturn and Neptune, will be completely changed by the outer expansive layers of the Sun. These outer layes, called planetary nebulas, will drift aimlessly through space like ghostly shards of bright gas. These planetary nebulae will absorb the gaseous atmospheres of these planets, leaving behind small rocky and metallic nuclei. The more distant planets that are no longer held by the Sun's gravity will drift in the immensity of space. Billions of years after this, when the remaining heat of the Sun is extinguished, and its small, dark surface is at the same freezing temperature as the rest of the space, the Sun will be a black dwarf driven by the mysterious dark energy that will continue in constant action until the end of our beloved universe.

## Final Destiny of Planet Earth

As the Sun approaches its final stage, it will unleash a hell on Earth that will be so hot that it will melt the surface of the Earth. First it will swallow the plants of the forests and the farms. Only the deserts will grow, and the surface would become a giant sand dune. Then it will take the animals. And things would only go from bad to worse.

The hot temperature will speed up removal from the atmosphere of carbon dioxide, which plants need to survive, and everything that feeds on the plant will perish. When the plants disappear, the oxygen they produce will also end, which will make it very difficult for us to breathe. It will end our food source.

We will be the last to leave.

After swallowing the entire Earth's life, the Sun will swell and turn from yellow to red, entering the last stage of its life. By that time the Sun will completely fill the Earth's sky during the day. In about 6.5 billion years, we will become cosmic dust.

For now, the Sun will continue to share its warmth with us and sustain us. And there will be at least five billion more years of beautiful sunrises before the end of our planet Earth.

# 2

# THE EARTH

Earth, our wonderful planet, is located at the precise spot of light and heat of the Sun that makes it conducive to life. The Earth is not as hot as Mercury and Venus, nor as cold as Mars. We are exactly where life can flourish. Our scientists have been exploring the Earth for more than two hundred years to discover its secrets, and with those discoveries we are able to write its history.

The planet Earth is unique. An immense rock ball that is 25,000 miles wide, it is 70 percent covered by water and 30 percent covered by outcrops of rock. Its atmosphere is rich in oxygen, and it is the only known place in the universe that serves as home to life as we know it.

However, this blue-green oasis has not always been so welcoming. Planet Earth bears the scars of its violent past in the form of extreme environments and catastrophes over its 4.5 billion years. It has been a world with many changes: a world of fire, ice, furious seas, and toxic skies. But life would eventually appear, live, and prosper in a climate of great tranquility, thanks to the changes that the Earth went through during its evolution.

# 2.1 ORIGIN AND EVOLUTION

Key events took place on the planet Earth that made life possible. Among these were the formation of the Moon, development of the magnetic field, the movements of the Earth, and the formation of water and atmosphere. However, our understanding of our planet begins with understanding the geological structures formed on its surface. For thousands of years, it was believed that these rocky structures had always been there, but then we discovered the actual process of how these structures were formed.

Misconceptions about the origin and formation of the Earth that persisted for thousands of years suddenly began to change about two hundred years ago. The discovery by James Hutton of a small outcropping of rock in 1788 in Scotland rewrote the history of the Earth.

James Hutton, who became the father of modern geology, was a very enthusiastic man with an extremely inquisitive and religious mind. During his explorations, he saw the rocks under the crust of the Earth and wondered how they had formed. After some analysis, he understood that the rocks were formed through extremely slow processes that created the layers of sediment, one on top of another. Hutton concluded that the rocks that resulted from these layers of sediments could take hundreds of thousands of years to form.

As a result, Hutton theorized that the geological structures on the surface of the Earth were not always there; instead, he demonstrated that they were formed by the Earth itself. Hutton also showed beyond doubt that the geological changes that occurred on Earth in the past continue to occur today. As he said, the present is the key to deciphering the past.

Hutton's radical ideas soon clashed with the Catholic Church's version of Earth's history, a version that had generally been accepted until then. For generations, the church had been the sole authority over all facts regarding creation, based on the biblical book of Genesis. Using biblical genealogy, church leaders pretended to know the age of the Earth; according to them, the Earth was created approximately seven thousand years earlier. But Hutton was convinced that Earth had been formed much earlier.

Finally, in a discovery unusual in 1788, Hutton found two layers of formations that were at right angles, parallel and vertical to each other. He noticed that these layers of rocks had been horizontally at the bottom of the ocean and that they were buried under great depths to re-crystallize. These layers of rocks must then have been erected by great forces from within the Earth and later eroded and truncated, which would take many millions of years. This discovery would change the conception about the origin and evolution of the Earth from there on. Now rocks would become the reliable guide to the distant past.

For the next two centuries, the study of rocks around the world would lead to the revelation that this planet of ours, like all things in the universe, had been undergoing a surprising process of evolution. James Hutton would allow the very rock from the bowels of the Earth to tell us the story about the origin and formation of the Earth.

# Origin and Formation of the Earth

The great contribution of James Hutton was crucial in understanding not only the formation of geological structures on the surface of the Earth, but also gave us a great understanding of how our planet really works from its heart to form any structure on its surface. Another great contribution to a better understanding of the planet would come from the more precise knowledge about when the Earth originated.

English scientist William Kelvin, an expert in thermodynamics, believed that the Earth first existed as a fireball but then started to cool slowly. The fire inside the planet, which is visible in volcanic eruptions, suggested that the planet was once completely molten. Radioactive particles of uranium, thorium, and potassium were already abundant in the newly formed Earth, and the heat produced by the decomposition of these particles kept the planet extremely hot for a long time. These radioactive particles, especially those of uranium, survived and could be harvested to create the first atomic weapons, but scientists had previously found a very different application: they used reactive particles to accurately calculate the age of the planet.

In 1911, Arthur Holmes used radiation to revolutionize our understanding of Earth. Radiometric dating was simple at first. It was based on the discovery that traces of radioactive elements found in the rocks of the Earth are broken down into other elements; for example, uranium is broken down into lead. By measuring the proportion of that decomposition of uranium to lead in the crystals trapped in the ancient rocks, Holmes could calculate their ages accurately. Thus, the Earth's age was calculated to be 4.5 billion years, an estimate that is fully accepted today.

The Earth has its origin in the formation of the solar system about 4.5 billion years ago. By then the surface of the Earth was an ocean of molten rock a few kilometers deep. During the initial stages of the Earth's formation, an immense rainfall of meteors that were also part of the solar system fell on the young planet in a relentless bombardment. From collisions with those other bodies, the planet combined with them to get bigger. It is believed that there were about ten collisions that led to the finalformation of the Earth. The Moon, which would have a profound effect on life in our world, formed out of the last collision.

## The Moon

The Moon, Earth's natural satellite, was formed from the impact of another rocky body against our planet shortly after its formation about 4.5 million years ago. That other giant rocky body was about the size of Mars; it rotated alongside the Earth around the Sun when it crashed in the center of the Earth to form in it the iron core that it has today. As a result of that collision, part of the crust of the Earth was fired into space, and the heavier elements of the other body were embedded in the center of the Earth. The lighter particles fired into space and then grouped in orbit around Earth.

For millions of years, the Earth had rings like those of the planet Saturn. Smaller collisions continued between these particles to form the rocky body we know tody as the Moon. The formation of the Moon has had a profound impact on life on Earth, because it also resulted in formation of the Earth's iron core, which later gave rise to its magnetic field: a protective shield for the life that would appear later.

The Moon has a rocky surface covered with crater dust because of the impacts of other space bodies reaching its surface. These impacts occur because the Moon does not have a strong atmosphere to protect it, as the Earth has. One of the outstanding craters of the Moon is the Tycho, which is more than fifty-two miles wide.

The Moon has a mass of $7.35 \times 10^{22}$ kg and a diameter of 2,159 miles; it is 239,000 miles from the Earth at 0.00257 AU. The Moon has a gravity of 5.32 ft/s$^2$. It makes a complete orbit around Earth in twenty-seven Earth days and rotates at the same speed as Earth does, which makes the Moon always show the same side or face toward Earth along its orbit.

The Moon is not a place fit for life as we know it because of its weak atmosphere, its lack of liquid water, and the absence of air to breathe. The temperature does not help much either: the Moon gets very hot and very cold. When it is hit by the Sun, the temperature on the Moon reaches 265 degrees F, and when the Sun goes down, the temperature falls to 170 degrees F below zero. In addition, the Sun's radiation, unimpeded by any atmosphere on the Moon, is very dangerous.

The Moon has an important influence on the cycles of the Earth, especially on the tides. The Moon moderates the nod of the Earth on its axis, which has maintained a relatively stable climate for billions of years. Another crucial event for life on Earth that was formed thanks to the formation of the Moon is the Earth's magnetic field.

## Earth's Magnetic Field

The magnetic field originates deep in the center of the Earth and acts as a protective shield for life against radiation and solar winds. Without this magnetic field, life on Earth would not have been possible.

The planet Earth is basically composed of three layers: the crust, a thin layer along the surface between three and thirty miles; the mantle, a layer of almost 1,600 miles of thickness; and the iron core, a huge metal sphere about the size of the planet Mars. The core consists of two parts: the inner core and the outer core.

Both temperature and pressure increase with depth within the Earth. The temperature at the boundary between the core and the mantle is sufficiently hot for the outer core to exist in a liquid state. The inner core, however, is solid because of the increased pressure. The core consists mainly of iron, with a small percentage of lighter elements such as nickel. Both iron and nickel are good conductors of electricity.

The outer core is in constant motion, due to the rotation of the Earth and the movement of the convection currents that are generated from the molten metals in the outer core. Convection is produced by the temperature difference between the top of the outer core at the boundary with the mantle, which is about 6.332 degrees F, and the bottom at the boundary with the inner core, which is about 10,832 degrees F. The currents are driven upward by the movement of the light elements and are driven downward by the heavier elements that precipitate toward the inner core. These ascending and descending currents of the liquid metal carry heat from the inner core to the mantle. The magnetic field is formed from the swirling flux mainly of the molten iron of the outer core, which triggers electric currents that generate the magnetic field of the planet through the same effect that any dynamo produces.

The magnetic field near the surface of the Earth is like that of a vertical bar magnet inclined 11.5 degrees approximately with respect to the axis of rotation of the

Earth. The magnetic south pole of this bar magnet would be pointing to Earth's geographic North Pole, so the compass needle points north toward geographic north.

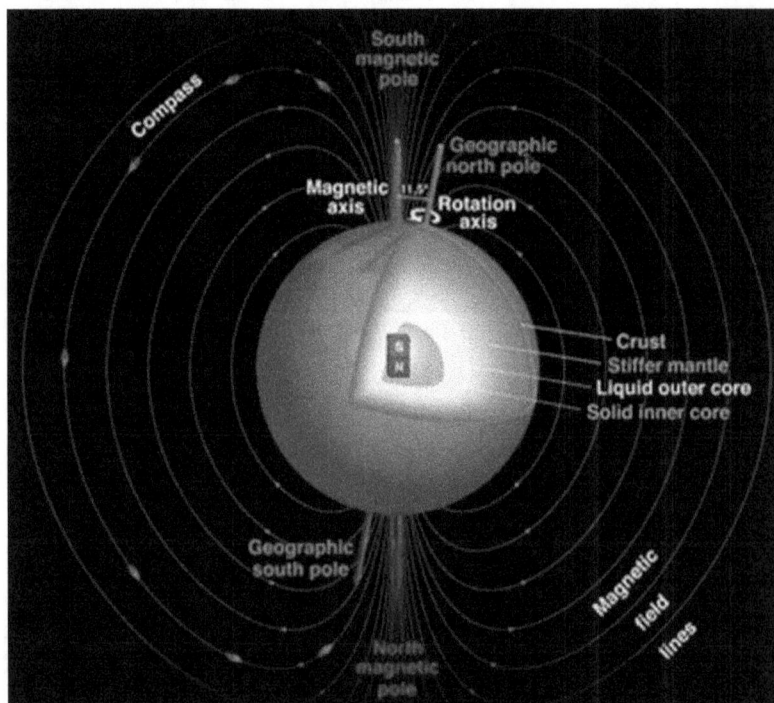

As you can see in the illustration, the imaginary lines of the magnetic field extend from the nucleus progressively attenuating in outer space, with known electromagnetic effects in the magnetosphere that protects us from the solar wind. The interaction of the Earth's magnetic field with the particles of the solar wind creates the conditions for the aurora phenomena near the poles. In addition, it allows very diverse phenomena such as the orientation of the rocks in the ocean ridges or submarine elevations that extend for thousands of miles in the bed of the ocean, the magnetic reception of some animals, and the orientation of people by means of compasses.

American physicist Walter Maurice Elsasser was the first to suggest that the rotation of the Earth creates, in its cast-iron core, slow eddies that rotate from west to east and generate an electric current. This process creates the equivalent of an internal magnet that extends north and south and that is responsible for the Earth's magnetic field. This internal magnet is oriented approximately along its axis of rotation so that the magnetic poles are located very close to the north and south geographic poles.

However, the movement of electrically charged particles in the atmosphere produces variations of the magnetic field, which makes the positions of the magnetic poles not constant. Every 960 years, variations in Earth's magnetic field include the change in the direction of the field caused by displacement of the poles. The magnetic field of the Earth tends to move westward at about 12 miles per year, which can eventually cause the field to reverse. There is evidence that the Earth's magnetic field has reversed 171 times over the past 71 million years and that the entire process could take thousands of years.

The magnetic field has an enormous impact on life on Earth. Without this, it would not have been possible to have the conditions required for life to be formed. Undoubtedly, the impact of the formation of the Moon gave the Earth both its Moon and its magnetic field. It also increased its mass and changed its axis of rotation by tilting it to 23.5 degrees. This inclination affects the way the Earth orbits the Sun and is responsible for the seasons of the Earth. Another event that also impacts life on Earth is the Earth's movements.

## Earth's Movements

The Earth is in constant motion as it rotates with the rest of the bodies of the solar system around our galaxy and along with the other bodies of the cosmos. At the same time, the Earth also has its own movements that directly affect life on it. Because of the Earth's movements we have day and night, which determine our schedules and biorhythms. We also have the terrestrial year with its changes of seasons.

The Earth has two main movements: one around itself, called the *rotation movement,* and the other around the Sun, called the *translation movement.* In its rotation movement, the Earth turns on itself or around an imaginary axis that passes through the poles and rotates in a west-east direction, or counterclockwise. Rotating on itself in this way gives us the feeling that the Sun and the sky revolves around us.

Currently, the Earth completes one revolution around its imaginary axis each twenty-four hour. During its rotation, part of it is exposed to the Sun and the other part is in the dark. We call it day when the Earth is illuminated by the Sun's rays; we call it night when the rays of the Sun do not reach us. Day and night together form the Earth day.

One trip around the Sun takes the Earth 365 days and about 6 hours, which we call a year. The difference of these six hours becomes twenty-four hours, or one day, every four years. To cover this difference, one additional day is included in February every four years to make twenty-nine days instead of twenty-eight; these are called leap years.

In its orbit around the Sun, our planet makes an elliptical trajectory of 578 million miles at an average speed of 62,300 miles per hour. In this elliptical orbit, the Sun is at a point called *focus,* which is not precisely at the center of the ellipsis. During its path around the Sun, the Earth's elliptical orbit describes a plane called the *ecliptic plane.*

The eccentricity of the Earth's orbit changes the distance between the Earth and the Sun over the course of a year. At the beginning of January, the Earth reaches its maximum proximity to the Sun at 88,700,000 miles. This point is called *perihelium.* At the beginning of July, the Earth is located at its maximum distance from the Sun at 94,400,000 miles, a point called *aphelion*.

In addition to the earth year, the Earth's translational motion around the Sunalso gives rise to the four seasons of the year, which are determined by the inclination of the Earth's axis with respect to its elliptical orbit. During this trajectory, there are times when the Earth is closer to or farther away from the Sun. Depending on the position of the Earth relative to the Sun, some areas of the planet receive more sunlight than others, and the seasons alternate depending on the proximity of each hemisphere of the Earth to the Sun. The closest points to the Sun are the *equinoxes*, which point to spring and autumn; the farthest are the winter and summer *solstices*.

Day and night have approximately the same duration of twelve hours at the equinoxes. During the spring equinox in March, it is spring in the northern hemisphere and autumn in the southern hemisphere. During the autumn equinox of September, it is autumn in the northern hemisphere and spring in the southern hemisphere.

The Sun's rays fall more directly on one of Earth's hemispheres and warm it during the solstice, indicating the summer; in the other hemisphere the rays fall more indirectly, providing little heat and signaling the winter. During the winter solstice of December, it is winter in the northern hemisphere and summer in the southern hemisphere. During the summer solstice of June, it is summer in the northern hemisphere and winter in the southern hemisphere.

The imaginary axis on which the Earth rotates suffered an inclination after the impact of the rocky body with the Earth from which the Moon formed. This inclination is now 23.5 degrees with respect to a vertical line, which is itself perpendicular to the plane of the ecliptic. This inclination of the axis of the Earth causes it to nod like a spinning top while rotating on itself. In addition to the rotational and translational movements we have already discussed, this nod causes the Earth to have a third movement called *precession* of the equinoxes, which is the circular motion of the inclined axis of the Earth. The precession movement completes one cycle every 26,000 years. However, due to the gravitational pull of the Moon, Earth's precession movement does not describe exact circles, but rather circles with oscillations due to the variation of the inclination of the Earth's axis. These periodic oscillations of the axis of the Earth are called *nutation*, the fourth movement of the Earth.

In addition, there is a fifth movement called the *Chandler Wobble*. Discovered by Seth Chandler in 1891, the Chandler Wobble consists of a small oscillation of the imaginary axis of the Earth that adds 0.7 arc seconds in a period of 433 days to the precession movement. The real cause of this movement has not been determined until now. However, it is believed to be caused by the fluctuation of the ocean floor caused by changes in the temperature and salinity of the water in the ocean and by the change in the direction of ocean currents.

The movements of the Earth make it practically in a constant dance around itself and around the Sun with a fascinating choreography. The series of events that occurred in the formation of the Earth and throughout its evolution to become what it is today is spectacularly surprising. It has resulted in the only planet where life could flourish and thrive. For this great feat to be possible, another pair of critical events had to occur so that Earth could continue its great evolutionary cycle: the origin of water and the formation of the atmosphere.

# Origin of Earth's Water and Atmosphere

When the Earth was only 100 million years old, 4.4 billion years ago, meteors still collided with it, but the gradual cooling of its nucleus had allowed most of the Earth to solidify in a crust of dark volcanic rock. In this early stage of the planet, water was forming on its surface.

No rock from this initial period of Earth survives today, but small zircon crystals do. The zircon-carrying uranium is one of the crystals that helped establish Earth's age, but these crystals can also retain the chemical traces of water molecules and are found on the oldest zircons. But that still does not represent all the water that existed on the planet back then. The origin of most of that water remains somewhat unknown.

It is believed that as the planet cooled the rock on the surface began to expel tons of carbon dioxide to form the atmosphere. During this process, some of the water vapors would also have been thrown into the atmosphere, but perhaps not enough to cover the surface of the Earth with water. In addition, the dust cloud and soil particles were probably too dry to form water. It is possible, then, that the large amount of water capable of covering the surface of the Earth came from outside the Earth, from an extraterrestrial source, or from asteroids and water-rich comets colliding with the Earth during the end of its process of growth. Regardless of its source, the water that arrived dramatically changed our planet.

The gases emitted by hundreds of millions of years of volcanic activity of the Earth combined with the water vapor that formed in the surface of the newly shaped planet to gave rise to the formation of the atmosphere. Enormous amounts of water vapor joined the carbon dioxide in the new atmosphere, forming thick sheets of clouds. About 4.2 billion years ago the atmosphere was composed mainly of carbon dioxide, water vapor, and nitrogen. In addition to its solid part called the *lithosphere*, the Earth now had a liquid part formed by all the water called the *hydrosphere* and a gaseous part called *atmosphere*.

About 4 billion years ago, condensed water in the atmosphere resulted in the most torrential rain the Earth has ever seen. As the lightning struck the sky, the rain began to fall on the rocky surface of the Earth. It continued to rain for millions of years. The result was a planet covered with water. By then, the Earth was about 500 million years old, and more than 90 percent of its surface was already covered with water. The planet had become a vast ocean with some small volcanic islands rising out of the water. This immense ocean was rich in iron, giving the waters an olive-green color. Carbon dioxide filled the skies so thickly that they looked red.

The dense atmosphere produced a lot of pressure and a lot of heat. The temperature exceeded 200 degrees F. This toxic and hostile water planet would continue for another 500 million years, but then a very convenient volcanic activity occurred to give the planet some dramatic transformations. This volcanic activity triggered the formation of continents, creating a totally new type of rock, turning the Earth into a mass of granite, and transforming it into the planet it is today.

# 2.2 TODAY'S BLUE PLANET

To become the blue planet we know today, Earth went through many transformations since its origin. At its beginning, Earth was completely covered by the great ocean for more than three billion years. Then a stronger mother rock was formed by a volcanic activity from the depth of the planet. This new continental mass raised up to the Earth's surface, forming the supercontinent Rodinia more than a billion years ago and bringing to an end the domination of the great ocean. The cyanobacteria flourished on Rodinia, producing elevated levels of oxygen. The oxygen produced in the ocean turned its waters blue, and when that oxygen went to the atmosphere, the skies also became blue. The oxigenation had profound consequences on the formation of the first and second glaciations, which turned Earth into a snowball. Rodinia's continental mass got fragmented to form continents, which millions of years later joined together again to form the supercontinent Pangea some 350 million years ago. Pangea eventually fragmented to form the continents we know today. As the continents separated, the cracks between them were filled with waters of the great ocean to form the oceans of today.

## Transformation of the Planet

Since its formation some 4.5 billion years ago, Earth has gone through many different episodes, from a fireball at the beginning of its birth to a world covered with water a few million years later. Earth's collisions with millions of meteors in the newly formed solar system increased the temperature of the planet so much that its surface became an ocean of molten rock and the planet looked like a ball of fire. However, even at that time, the Earth was starting to cool and the radioactivity that provided most of the heat was slowly diminishing, preparing the way for the first evolutionary change of the planet. That represented a radical change in which the planet was transformed from a world of fire into a world of water.

Proof of this world of water comes from a remote region of South Africa, where some of the oldest rocks on

Earth have been found in the rivers. These rounded rocks, called *pillow lava* because of their appearance, are about 3.5 billion years old. These rocks are formed by molten lava flowing into ocean water, similar to what happens today on the shores of Hawaii when volcanic windows burp into the Pacific Ocean. These rock pillows are formed only when molten lava solidifies under deep waters. All the rocks found dating to a period 3.5 billion years ago have been lava pillows. This indicates that water had existed long before a billion years after the formation of the Earth.

Throughout its evolutionary life, Earth would continue to undergo transformations. The rock of which the continents would be formed came after the world of water. The absolute dominion of the vast and immense ocean was over, for the continent had arrived. The slow expansion of the granite protocontinent changed the appearance of the planet. In addition, the shallow coastal lines between the first great ocean and the sunlit surface of the new continent brought new life in the form of cyanobacteria, which already existed some 2.7 billion years ago. It also helped trigger the production of oxygen in the water and then in the atmosphere.

The waste from the cyanobacteria went to the bottom of the ocean to form other microorganisms known as *stromatolites*, which pumped trillions of tons of oxygen. At first the gas dissolved in the oceans, where it oxidized billions of tons of iron that eventually filled the atmosphere and transformed the planet. Because of the oxygen produced by photosynthetic cyanobacteria about 2.2 billion years ago, the color of the oceans changed from olive green to blue.

The Earth was starting to look more like it does to us, but before it became the planet we know today a new cycle of cataclysmic events would take place. The Earth would enter a great volcanic activity because of the movement of tectonic plates, expelling large quantities of ferrous iron through fumaroles in the bottom of the great ocean.

Over time, that iron was deposited in the bottom of the ocean and further changed the color of its waters from olive to blue, dramatically altering the appearance of the planet. When the oxygen was moved into the atmosphere, it diluted the rest of the thick layer of carbon dioxide and cleaned the air. After almost 2 billion years of oxygenation, the blue planet was born.

With the oxygenation of the planet occurred another event of transcendental importance: the great oxidation. Earth now had blue oceans and blue sky. Relics of this great transformation can be seen today in the immense stratifications of bands of iron originally deposited in the bottom of the ocean.

Later, about 1.1 billion years ago, the Earth became a snowball and then returned to the planet of water with its primitive continents. Let's now see the details of all this transformation, beginning with the formation and fragmentation of the continental rock of the Earth produced by the tectonic plates.

## Formation and Fragmentation of the Continental Rock: The Tectonic Plates

Earth was dominated by an immense green ocean 3.4 billion years ago. But from beneath the great ocean, from the depths of the planet, there arose a great volcanic activity that created a stronger type of rock from which the continents would later be formed. In various parts of the globe, the heart of the first continental mass had raised up to the surface. As evidence of this, ancient rocks of this granite have been found in South Africa, which is a remnant of Earth 3.5 billion years ago, when granite was everywhere on the planet.

The rise of the volcanism of that time had fractured Earth's crust beneath the vast ocean, allowing water to enter the cracks along with molten lava. The mixture of superheated water and basaltic lava produced granite, which rose from the depths to form the first real crust of the continent. For the next few billion years, the granite protocontinent slowly grew. In various parts of the planet appeared the granite crust that would someday form the heart of a larger mass of earth.

One and a half billion years ago, when the planet was about three billion years old, for the first time in its history it began to resemble the planet we know today. The new oxygen that arrived made the oceans blue, and the exposed rock of the planet had grown to cover almost 25 percent of the surface. But beneath the ocean deep forces from the bowels of the Earth were working to break up the continental rock and later to form the continents.

The fragmentation of the rock formed rigid blocks of earth called *tectonic plates*, which would later form the continents. The study of the tectonic plates allows us to know the movement of the continents. Until 1960 the study of tectonic plates was very limited, and it was believed that the continents were fixed. The key to determining that the continents were moving was found in the geographic locations of some freshwater stromatolite fossils: some were found in the United States and comparable fossils were also found in salt water in Britain, on the other side of the world.

Another aspect of significant importance is the observation that the east coast of South America fits perfectly against the west coast of Africa. This could not be a coincidence, but instead indicates that these two continents were united in the past and subsequently separated.

Although the theory of tectonic plates for the study of the movements of the continents was established in 1960, it had actually started as early as 1912 when German climate scientist Alfred Wegener began conducting atmospheric investigations in Greenland. Wegener always sought evidence for his theory that the continents were moving. In 1930, he made his last expedition to Greenland, which ended in tragedy when he was lost in a snowstorm and died. But his theory of continental drift survived and came to life as submarines discovered gaps dividing the oceans into huge crust plates. These plates would be the building blocks of the new tectonic plate scienceand provided a solution to how continents moved by proving that the ocean floor is continually being recycled.

## Supercontinent Rodinia

Thanks to tectonic plate technology, it was possible to conclude that around some 1.2 billion years ago, there was a large mass of earth rising on the surface of the planet, a supercontinent, that scientists have named Rodinia. Using tectonic plate technology, it was possible to go back to the position the continents would have been in a billion years ago when the continental mass collided. As the oceans receded, they disappeared between continents, allowing them to know where the continents were before.

It is believed that a mass of land called Laurentia formed the heart of Rodinia a billion years ago. North America later arose from Laurentia, and the other continents as we know them eventually clustered around Laurentia.

But Rodinia was not like the continents of today. It was a desolate and lifeless place, like the Sahara Desert. There were no plants, no forests, or any other life forms on the continent. Although it was a lifeless continent, it would have a profound impact on ocean life, for in the oxygenated waters primitive life forms and stromatolites were flourishing. Rodinia also had tremendous impact because it entered the largest freeze the planet has ever had, which occurred because Rodinia's position at that time (about 700 million years ago) was blocking warm currents that should have flowed from the equator to the poles. Of course, without the warmth that these currents once carried, the whole Earth froze and became what is known as "the snowball." This event is also known as the second glaciation.

## The First and Second Glaciation: The Snowball Planet

The methanogenic bacteria kept the planet warm until the cyanobacteria appeared. With so much time passing without anything giving the planet heat and with the size of the Sun being smaller than it is today, the planet began to cool, causing the first glaciation. The cause of this great freeze was the Earth producing enormous amounts of oxygen as a product of cyanobacteria, which continued for millions of years, making the color of the atmosphere change from reddish to blue.

The first glaciation occurred about 1.1 billion years ago. The Earth became a snowball, a condition that continued for millions of years. But the forces of the Earth itself led it to break the immense ice shell that covered it. Then appeared a very timely volcanic activity: the bowels of the Earth itself let the immense power of heat escape to break up the cold.

About 400 million years after the first glaciation (in other words, about 700 million years ago) a second glaciation occurred when the position of Rodinia blocked the currents that brought the warm waters of the equator to the poles. Without that heat, the poles were frozen. As a result, enormous climatic changes took place over the next 50 million years and ice formed around the Earth. In a process of catastrophic snowball, the temperature dropped further and the ice advanced to cover the whole Earth. The temperature of the Earth dropped to -400 degrees F, and the oceans were covered by a one-mile-deep blanket of ice.

Rodinia was dying. But under the ice, the supercontinent revolted. Vast volcanic eruptions fractured Rodinia, and the resulting heat ended the snowball. After the rupture of Rodinia some 630 million years ago, the carbon dioxide released by volcanic eruptionscreated a temporary greenhouse effect; the ice sheets meltedand Rodinia fractured into large fragments. The elevated levels of oxygen that had triggered the explosion of life in the ocean formed a layer of ozone in the upper part of the atmosphere, which later allowed life forms previously confined to the ocean to escape to the surface. That was something, that was previously impossible since the powerful ultraviolet rays of the Sun would have destroyed any organism not protected by the water. We see then that the rupture of Rodinia gave way to another great supercontinent and to the formation of the planet that we know today.

# The Great Supercontinent Pangea and the Formation of Today's Continents and Oceans

There is evidence that about 200 million years ago the continents as we know them today were united in a single supercontinent called Pangea. The continents that separated about 650 million years ago after the fragmentation of Rodinia during the Ediacaran period eventually collided to form the supercontinent Pangea during the Devonian and Carboniferous periods Pangea began to fracture almost immediately, but the separation process took more than 250 million years.

The supercontinent Pangea was fragmented by volcanic activity that began about 180 million years ago and that divided the supercontinent into two large blocks of land: Laurasia to the north and Gondwana to the west. These were separated by a new ocean called Tethys, formed by the water of the great ocean as it filled the crack left by the separation of the two great masses of land. The Tethys Sea gradually reduced in size and finally disappeared with the subsequent movements of the continental masses of Pangea more than 40 million years ago.

This fragmentation continued for millions of years to form and position the continents as we know them today: America, Africa, and Europe. As the continents separated from Pangea, the cracks between them were filled with the waters of the great ocean to form the oceans we know today: Atlantic, Pacific, and Indian. The following illustration shows what the Earth looked like before and after fragmentation of the Pangea Supercontinent.

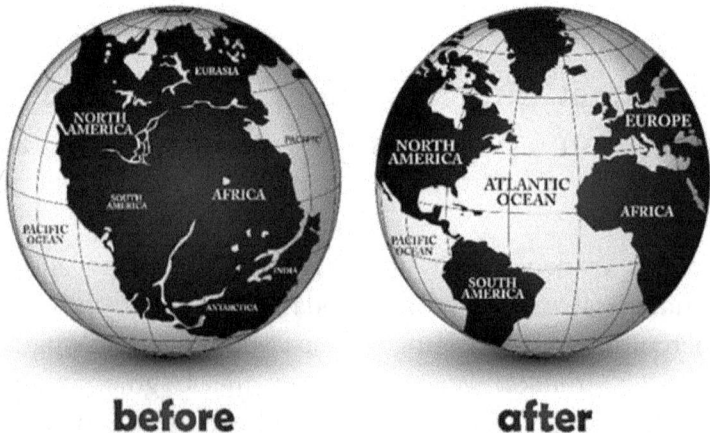

**before**          **after**

After the division that marked the end of Pangea about 100 million years ago, the dinosaurs and the volcanoes were distributed in each of the new continents. This is how the great transformation of the original Earth occurred in detail until it became our blue planet today. The divisions that occurred also provided us with the natural resources to sustain life and our economy.

# 2.3  FORMATION OF NATURAL RESOURCES

Our planet Earth has been so generous to us that it formed the natural resources essential to both our survival and the economy of our civilization. These resources include the formation of iron in bands, a vital mineral for the world economy, as well as the formation of the resources that provide us with all the energy we need, such as coal, oil, and gas. Another great and beautiful resource that the Earth gave us were the coveted diamonds. And of course it provided a natural resource critical to our existence: fresh water, indispensable for life on Earth.

## Banded Iron Formation

With the oxygenation of the planet about 2.2 billion years ago, the color of the ocean changed from olive green (due to iron dissolved in the water) to blue. The blue color resulted from the oxygen produced by the photosynthetic cyanobacteria that had already begun to make life in the ocean waters. Dissolved iron existed in the same waters; it probably came mostly from volcanic activities associated with movement of tectonic plates, which ejected enormous quantities of iron through fumaroles on the ocean floor. This iron dissolved in the waters of the ocean reacted with the oxygen produced by the cyanobacteria to form insoluble iron oxides, which precipitated the formation of bands or layers of sediments rich in iron. These wre converted into the solid minerals of magnetite and hematite, which were deposited at the bottom of the ocean in vast thin layers. This process continuously repeated, creating iron ore in large stratified formations.

After some 2 billion years of oxygenation, these iron bands spread all over the globe; they can still be found today around the world. These sedimentary formations that formed between 3.8 billion and 550 million years ago are unique. Constituted by bands of at least 15 percent iron, they are interspersed with bands of silica. Most of the iron we use today comes from these formations of 2 billion years ago, and they are vital to our current world economy. About 90 percent of all iron used in the world today comes from this type of iron.

# Coal Formation

Earth has always generated its own energy systems through the winds, the tides, or living organisms. About 300 million years ago, large coal deposits were formed on Earth. During the Carboniferous period, there existed a great vegetation with bark trees that grew in the vast forests in marshes of the low earth. The vegetation also included large mosses and giant ferns and trees. For millions of years, these organic deposits from the remnants of these plants formed the first deposits of carbon-rich coal. Hence the name of the Carboniferous period. Evidence of the dominance of these tropical marshes is present on all continents today in the form of coal.

The coal we use today as fuel was formed by millions of years of accumulated plant work and water in tropical marshes. Coal is formed in a unique process through which fresh water is trapped and decomposed. Fresh water prevents vegetation from degrading, allowing enormous quantities to be stacked over time. The vegetation and the mud of the marshes buried by sediments through millions of years and after undergoing great pressures and temperatures were decomposed to form the coal. Depending on the pressures and temperatures involved, any of several types of coal can result, such as peat, lignite, coal or bituminous coal, and anthracite. The higher the pressures and temperatures, the more compact and carbon-rich coal will be produced and the higher the calorific value.

Today coal is a great form of energy. Every year more than 5,000 megatons of this mineral are extracted and used in different sectors, mainly in the generation of electricity, the production of iron and steel, the production of cement, and as liquid fuel. Thermal coal is used to generate electricity, while coke coal is used to produce iron and steel.

## Oil and Gas Formation

Oil and natural gas were formed about 150 million years ago from millions of generations of dead marine microorganisms. When these organisms that lived in the oceans died, their remains fell to the ocean floor. With time, immense amounts of these organisms were deposited and buried in muddy sediments. Over the years, immense layers of sediment were deposited on the mixture of organic matter. The weight of these sedimentary formations at great depth exerted an intense pressure on the mixture of the organic matter and sediments. Additionally, the Earth's heat at that depth would raise the temperature of the mixture for millions of years to form oil and gas.

This mixture of organic matter was compacted to form the hydrocarbons oil and gas. Pressure caused these hydrocarbons to migrate through the pores of the rock until they reached impermeable areas where the hydrocarbons were trapped in oil or gas traps. In these traps, hydrocarbons were stored, forming the reservoirs from which they are extracted today.

Hydrocarbon is an oil substance of very dark color composed mainly of hydrogen and carbon; in its natural state, it is known as crude oil. Oil has transformed the lives of human beings along with their economy; its discovery created wealth, modernity, developed and prosperous peoples. From this crude oil, we obtain the products that move the economy of the world, including but not limited to fuels, lubricants, plastics, synthetic fibers, detergents, medicines, food preservatives, and fertilizers.

Natural gas constitutes another hydrocarbon of great importance for humanity. It can be found in the reservoir in the form of associated gas, accompanied by oil. When not accompanied by significant amounts of other hydrocarbons, it is known as non-associated natural gas. After being extracted from the field, the gas can be converted into liquefied natural gas and compressed natural gas for logistical and economic reasons. Today it is considered as the most compatible type of energy with the environment since it generates less pollution compared to other energy sources such as coal or oil.

Both oil and natural gas are the two most important energy sources used for the development of our civilization. Currently, about 35 billion barrels of oil are extracted each year; 3.5 billion cubic meters of gas are extracted. Coal, oil, and natural gas are the sources of energy that drove the industrial revolution in the world. Their importance is still vital in the survival of our civilization, despite certain controversies created by some ideologies.

# Diamond Formation

Coal, oil, and natural gas are synonymous with wealth—but another of the Earth's natural resources is also associated with beauty. About 100 million years ago, when planet Earth was still ruled by the dinosaurs, volcanic activity was also dominant. That volcanic activity also brought to Earth her most coveted resource: diamonds.

Diamonds were formed when volcanic magma compressed the coal on the rocky part of the Earth between the crust and the core known as the mantle. Between one and three thousand million years ago, unique conditions of pressure and enormous heat combined to form these precious gems. The temperatures in the mantle can be as high as 1,700 degrees F. When this temperature is combined with an extreme pressure of up to 725,000 pounds per square inch, carbon atoms are compressed and layered to form the diamond. These precious stones of crystallized pure carbon are then carried to the surface of the Earth through volcanic eruptions.

Today's diamonds spewed to the surface from the mouths of very old and deep volcanoes at speeds of more than 300 miles per hour. While not easy to find, they have been discovered for thousands of years around the world, embedded in rocks in mines or in the beds of some sandy rivers.

Today the diamond is the most precious jewel in the world. The exploitation of diamond formations is of significant importance for mining. In the operations of the diamond extraction process, the earth and stone covering the diamond formation is first removed, then the diamond is removed and washed. Because the diamonds are not abundant, these operations are very expensive

The carving and polishing of the stone is one of the most crucial elements in the diamond. Because it is the hardest element on Earth, the diamond can be cut and polished only with another diamond. The diamonds used in jewelry should be perfect. Any defect can detract from their value; those with defects are limited to industrial applications in which they are used to polish tools or cut all kinds of stones. They are also used in the manufacture of high-performance semiconductors, because they have conductivity characteristics of both heat and electrons that are much higher than those of silicon, the most common element currently used for these applications.

Today, synthetic diamonds are also made on a large scale. Their main used is industrial, although synthetic diamonds are also made for jewels that can then be purchased at a much lower price.

## Fresh Water Formation

Water is an indispensable resource for the development of human beings and their civilization.

All the water that formed on Earth about 4.4 billion years ago was salt water contained in the great ocean. Today, some of that water is transferred to the atmosphere in the form of vapor, where it forms clouds and then falls as rain. Evaporating ocean water leaves its salt content in the ocean, so the rain has been transformed into fresh water with only minimal amounts of dissolved salts, very different from sea water.

The same thing happened anciently. After the continents were formed, part of the rainwater fell to the ocean and another part fell to and flowed over the surface of the continents. Still another part of the rainwater evaporated and returned to the atmosphere; there it combined with the water that evaporated from the sea in a continuous water cycle call the *hydrological cycle.*

The water cycle is directed by the Sun, which heats the water of the oceans and causes it to evaporate into the air as water vapor. Rising air currents carry water vapor to the upper layers of the atmosphere, where the low temperature causes water vapor to condense and form clouds. The air currents move the clouds over the globe and the cloud particles collide, expand, and fall in the form of precipitation. Some of this precipitation falls in the form of snow and accumulates in layers of ice and glaciers, which can store frozen water for millions of years. In warmer climates, accumulated snow melts when spring arrives. The melted snow runs on the surface of the land as thawing water and sometimes causes flooding. Most of the precipitation falls in the oceans; the rest falls on the earth, where, due to gravity, it runs on the surface as what is called *surface runoff*. Some of this runoff reaches the rivers through depressions in the terrain; in the flow of rivers the water is gradually transported back to the oceans.

Not all rainwater flows into rivers, much of it is absorbed into the ground as infiltration. Some of this water remains in the upper layers of the subsoil and returns to bodies of water and oceans as discharge of groundwater. Another part of the groundwater finds openings on the Earth's surface and emerges as freshwater springs. Shallow groundwater is taken up by the roots of plants to the surface through the trunk; finally, through the leaves of these plants, the water returns to the atmosphere.

Another part of the infiltrated water reaches the deeper layers of the subsoil and recharges the rock to saturate it. These underground water deposits are called *aquifers*, and they store substantial quantities of fresh water for prolonged periods. Some of the groundwater that flows to the surface and some of the runoff water that does not go to the rivers accumulates and stores in depressions of the surface to form lakes of fresh water. Over time, fresh water from the rains continues to move. Part of it returns to the oceans, where the water cycle starts again.

More than 70 percent of the Earth's surface is covered by water. All this water, mainly salt water and fresh water, is known as the *hydrosphere* of the Earth. The total volume of all water on the planet is 1,386 km³. Salt water accounts for 97 percent of the planet's total water, or 1,338 km³, most of it in the oceans. Fresh water represents the remaining 3 percent, or 41.58 km³, found in glaciers, groundwater, rivers, lakes, and the atmosphere.

Fresh water regulates the climate of the planet, stores energy, forms part of the landscape, dilutes environmental pollutants, and is essential for living beings, who consume more than 7.5 trillion cubic meters of water per year. Water is also an essential resource for agriculture, industry, electricity generation, transport, and hygiene, among others. In the near future, water could be used to obtain hydrogen on a large scale and well as gas, which will be one of the essential energy sources for the development and progress of the planet.

Man uses mainly fresh water obtained from the flow of water in the rivers and from water stored in lakes; to a lesser extent, we obtain fresh water from underground aquifers. Now marine desalination plants are being built that will enable us to get fresh water from the oceans.

# 2.4 FORMATION OF THE CURRENT LANDSCAPE

The landscape of the Earth has been forming for billions of years. However, the landscape we can see today began to form about 400 million years ago, just after life left the great ocean to conquer the surface of the planet. The climate and the movement of the tectonic plates were crucial in the formation of that landscape. Water, ice, and wind eventually did the rest. However, the final touch was put in place by humans with their urban development, agriculture and breeding, and construction of their great engineering works.

Over billions of years, Earth's continents changed their positions due to the movement of tectonic plates, and the wind and water shaped their surface. The ice dug pathways along the face of the Earth, and the oceans continuously increased or decreased their levels over time. The tectonic plates formed the mountain chains of the Earth, while the erosion caused by snow, wind, and water continued the work of the landscape for millions of years. The formation of the mountains produced a colder climate. The ice in the Arctic grew, and sea level decreased to expose land bridges between Africa and Eurasia and between Eurasia and North America. Eventually South America moved northward and adhered to North America, forming the Isthmus of Panama.

Let's look now at the broad variety of landscapes found on our fascinating planet.

## Mountain Landscape

About 65 million years ago, the Earth's continents moved to where they are today. The continents continued to move and collide with each other until they merged. In In the process of colliding, great mountainous formations were created.

Slowly the landscape of the Earth was formed due to the movement of tectonic plates and erosion. This formed the landscape we see today. Some mountain ranges were formed by volcanic eruptions, but the largest were formed by incrustations of blocks of continents. These mountain ranges feature beautiful landscapes of glaciers, lakes, and rivers. The most important of these are the Himalayas and the Alps.

The Himalayas were formed 55 million years ago during the Cenozoic geological era, when the continents were still moving, colliding, and incrusting each other due to the movement of the tectonic plates. What is known today as the Indian continent collided with what is known today as the Asian continent to initiate the gigantic movement of continental rock upwards that would form the Himalayas. After the rupture of the last great super continent Pangea, the Indian continent separated from Africa and began to move north. As it approached Asia, the oceanic part of the Indian plate sank under the Asian. The Tethys Ocean between them disappeared and the two continents collided, folded the land surface, and made it rise. Today, the Indian plate continues to advance a little bit more than an inch per year, which indicates that the Himalayas continue to grow.

The Himalayas is a chain of mountains more than 1,500 miles long and 150 miles wide located on the Asian continent south of the Tibetan plateau and extending from west to east through Pakistan, China, India, Nepal, and Bhutan. With its name meaning "abode of snow" in the ancient Indian language, it is the highest mountain range on the planet, which is why it is called "the roof of the world." With an altitude of more than 26,200 feet above sea level, it is home to ten of the fourteen highest peaks in the world, the most famous of which is Mount Everest at 29,035 feet above sea level.

The Himalayas contain large reserves of fresh water in many glaciers, such as Siachen, Gangotri, and Yamunotri. These glaciers form and feed an important river system that supports several other rivers in Asia, including the Ganges, the Indus, and the Yarlung. This great mountain range also has hundreds of lakes, the most important of which are the Pangong Tso, the Gurudongmar, and the Tsongmo.

Another great mountain landscape formed about 45 million years ago is the Alps, now located in an area previously covered by the Tethys Ocean that separated Europe from Africa. The land mass of the south began to move toward the north. This movement bent layers of rock at the bottom of the ocean, and the heat and pressure transformed the rock and pushed the material upward. Today these regions are the highest parts of the Alps.

Most of the rock that formed in the Alps was granite, but some formations consist of limestone that also formed at the bottom of the Tethys Ocean. As the tectonic plates of Africa and Europe clashed, they overlapped. The plate of the African continent collided with the European plate, and the enormous pressure that forced the rock to rise upward formed this great system of arc-shaped mountain chains that are now about 745 miles long and about 124 miles wide.

The mountain range of the Alps covers the heart of central Europe, including parts of Italy, France, Switzerland, Austria, and Germany. It contains important peaks of more than 13,000 miles of altitude, including Mont Blanc, the highest at 15,000 feet above sea level and located on the Franco-Italian border. The part of the alpine range located in Switzerland is a natural wonder because of its famous peaks with their pointed peaks and steep gorges.

Among the best-known peaks of the Swiss Alps are the Matterhorn and the so-called Pennine Alps. The Matterhorn is possibly the best-known mountain in the Alps for its spectacular pyramid shape with four faces that point to the four cardinal points. It is located on the border between Switzerland and Italy. It has an altitude of 14,691 feets and is above the city of Zermatt. The Pennine Alps are noted for having the highest peak in Switzerland, Mount Dufourspitze, located in the massifs of Monte Rosa and Jura.

During the Ice Age of about one million years ago, the Alps were covered with a thick layer of snow from which the glaciers of the mountain range formed. These glaciers moved down into the valleys, making them wider and deeperand dragging rocks and other materials with them. When the glaciers began to melt, they filled the natural depressions and levees with rocks to form the alpine lakes. The water that continued flowing formed rivers.

The largest of the Alpine glaciers is the Aletsch in Switzerland, which is about fifteen miles long. Other glaciers of importance are the Gorner glacier in Switzerland, seven miles long, and the Pasterze in Austria, which is about five miles long. Among the most important lakes are Lake Leman and Lake Constance in Switzerland, which are the largest in the region. The most important rivers are the Rhine, the Rhone, the Danube, and the Po.

The movements between the rock within the continents also produced alterations of the Earth's crust. The formation of the Pyrenees mountain range took place on the European continent, the Rocky Mountains and the Sierra Nevadas formed in North America, and the Los Andes formed in South America.

The Pyrenees mountain range is located on the European continent on the isthmus of the Iberian Peninsula, between the Mediterranean Sea and the Cantabrian Sea. The Pyrenees mountain range emerged from the seabed between the continental masses of Iberia and Europe, raising the stratified sedimentary rocks accumulated in them to more than 9,842 feet. The Pyrenees were formed about 65 million years ago through a long and complex process.

The elevation of the mountain range originated during the formation of the Alps. During that period, the Iberian plate that had been drifting for a prolonged period moved to the north, and its edges collided with those of the European plate, which had been separated until that moment by an intracontinental basin in which a great amount of sediment had accumulated. During the collision, a subduction process was initiated that caused the Iberian plate to sink under the European plate. After its formation, the mountain range continued to change. The cold periods of the Quaternary modeled its surface, forming sharp ridges, valleys, glaciers, lagoons, and rivers.

The Pyrenees covers an area of 21,380 square miles, extending from west to east about 270 miles long and 100 miles wide. They constitute the natural border between Spain and France, housing the Principality of Andorra, a small independent country between Spain and France.

The highest peaks of the Pyrenees include the peak of Aneto, the highest in the mountain range at 11,167 feet above sea level, followed by the Posets, the Monte Perdido, the Perdiguero, and the Maladeta peaks.

There are about fifty Pyrenean glaciers between France and Spain. On the Spanish side, the largest of all is the Aneto glacier in the Aneto massif at more than 80 hectares. Its neighbor, the Maladeta glacier, measures more than 40 hectares. On the French side, the most important is the D'ossoue glacier in the Vignemale massif, measuring more than 50 hectares.

The Pyrenees is also the cradle of a number of important rivers. On the Spanish slope are the Bidasoa, Aragón, Gállego, Cinca, Ésera, Segre, Ter, Llobregat, Muga, and Fluvia rivers. On the French side are the Adur, Garona, Nivelle, Tec, Têt, and Aude.

Among the mountainous formations of North America are the Rocky Mountains and the Sierra Nevada. The Rocky Mountains are an important mountain chain also known as "the Rockies." It is made up of a system of almost flat elevated surfaces linked together that runs parallel to the west coast of North America. The Rocky Mountains extend from Canada in the northwest, passing through the states of

British Columbia and Alberta, through the American states of Montana, Idaho, Wyoming, Utah, Nevada, Colorado, and New Mexico. The Rockies occupy a total area of more than 2,982 miles with a width from 68 to 298 miles.

The Rockies formed between 80 and 55 million years ago, when the Pacific plate began to slide under the North American plate at a shallow subduction angle, resulting in a wide belt of mountains. Its formation took place for the most part by upheavals of the terrestrial crust at the end of the Cretácico period and the beginning of the Tertiary; they were re-molded in the Pleistocene epoch of the Quaternary period. Since then, erosion by water and glaciers has carved the Rocky Mountains into peaks and valleys to further embellish the landscape. Among the highest peaks is Mount Elbert in Colorado at 14,438 feet above sea level.

The Sierra Nevada is a mountain range in the western United States. The vast majority of the mountain range is in the state of California, while a minor part is in the state of Nevada. The Sierra extends about 397 miles from north to south, with a width of approximately sixty-eight miles. Among the most notable features of the system are Lake Tahoe, Mount Whitney, and Yosemite Valley, which was sculpted by glaciers.

The formation process of the Sierra Nevada began in the Cretaceous period, when a subduction zone was formed on the edge of the continent when the oceanic plate began to get under the North American plate. The magma formed through the process of subduction was raised in plumes deep underground. Around 10 million years ago, the Sierra Nevada began to form a block of crust that began to lean to the west. The rivers began to cut deep canyons on both sides of the mountain range. The lava filled some of these canyons, which have subsequently been eroded, leaving a kind of tepuis that follow the old river beds.

Around 2.5 million years ago, the Earth's climate cooled and the ice age began. The glaciers carved characteristic U-shaped canyons along the Sierra. The combination of river and glacial erosion exposed the upper parts of the plumes formed millions of years ago, leaving only a remnant of metamorphic rock at the top of some peaks of the Sierra.

While the granite of the Sierra Nevada was formed in the subsoil more than 100 million years ago, it was exposed when the mountainous system began to rise about 4 million years ago. Glaciers eroded the granite, forming the mountains and cliffs of the system. The upheaval produced a wide range of elevations and climates of the Sierra Nevada. This upheaval continued due to geological faults caused by tectonic forces, creating spectacular escarpment of fault blocks along the eastern edge of the southern Sierra

Another of the large formations produced by the movement of tectonic plates is the Andes Mountain Range in South America. The Cordillera de los Andes was formed about 100 million years ago at the end of the Cretaceous period as a result of the movement of tectonic plates. The Nazca Plate that lies under the Pacific Ocean moved toward and underneath the Plate of South America, pushing up its western edge. The tectonic forces that were generated by this collision triggered volcanic eruptions and earthquakes, which had an impact on the configuration of the relief of the area. Volcanic activity is still active today.

The Cordillera de los Andes is the largest mountain range in the American continent and one of the longest in the world, some 4,660 miles long and 150 miles wide. It is located in South America and extends almost parallel to the Pacific Ocean coast from Chile and Argentina, serving as a natural border between these two countries. Then it crosses Bolivia, Peru, Ecuador, and Colombia until it reaches a part of Venezuela. The average height reaches 13,123 feet, with points that reach 19,685 feet above sea level. Its highest point is Aconcagua, Argentina. Among the volcanoes in the Andes are Tungurahua, Cotopaxi, and Chimborazo in Ecuador; the Nevado de Tolima in Colombia; and the Llullaillaco between Argentina and Chile.

## Jungle Landscape

The formation of the mountains produced significant changes in the climate of the planet that would have a profound impact on the formation of other types of landscape. The climate has shaped the diversity of the landscape. In the higher areas, such as in the mountains, temperatures are cooler than in the lower areas. In the mountains the clouds collide, making them discharge the water they contain so the precipitations are usually abundant and frequent to maintain life in this ecosystem or biome.

In addition to altitude, climate also depends on latitude. This is because of the Sun's radiation. In the equatorial zone, the Sun's rays heat more because they arrive more directly in that area. The inclination of the Earth's axis produces the temperature difference that in turn causes the three climatic zones of the planet: the warm, the temperate, and the cold. The warm zone is found along the equator and between the tropics. Within the warm zone are different climates, such as the equatorial, the tropical, and the desert. The temperate zone is between the polar circles and the Tropics of Cancer and Capricorn. One temperate zone is in the northern hemisphere and the other in the southern hemisphere. In this area are the oceanic climate, the Mediterranean, the continental, and the desert climate. The cold zone is at the poles and in the high mountains. In these areas, the landscape is transformed by external geological processes that result from water, ice, and wind.

The jungles, also called "tropical forests" or "rainforests," are bioclimatic landscapes or biomes formed by abundant rainfall in a warm climate. These occur mainly along the equator, where the abundant rainfall maintains the great diversity of life of these areas. In these forests there is an important environment of living beings or biomass, which includes plants and animals, with the greatest range in the variety of species.

The equatorial jungles generate much of the oxygen on the planet—an estimated 40 percent of the total oxygen on earth. In addition, these jungles are great sources of medicines for human consumption, which are made with sylvan plants.

In these areas, constant humidity is essential for the decomposition of organic matter in the soil to form the nutrients that serve as sustenance for plant and animal species. The annual precipitation in these jungles ranges between 1,500 and 2,000 millimeters on average but can reach up to 3,000 millimeters. Since the rains continue throughout the year, rivers and lakes in the jungles are formed and maintained. The average temperature in the jungle areas of the tropical zone is between 80 and 84 degrees F to 1,312 feet in elevation.

In addition to the equatorial jungles, other jungles also exist in the region between the tropics, above the tropics, and in the temperate and subpolar forests. Other types of jungles also exist at eleveations generally below 3,280 feet above the sea level. These are known as lowland jungles and are prone to flooding, which tends to turn them into swampy areas. Other jungles of this type are the mountain jungles or cloudy jungles and the gallery jungles around the rivers or lagoons in the plains of the Savannah.

The jungles cover 6 percent of the total surface of the Earth and are located mainly in the intertropical zone. The most important are the Amazon Rainforest in South America and the Congo Rainforest in Africa.

The Amazon Rainforest or Amazonia is the largest forest on Earth and covers almost 7 million square km. It extends along the Amazon River, which with a length of 6,400 km is the second longest river in the world and represents one-fifth of all the fresh water that flows into the oceans. The Amazon is spread across nine countries in South America: Brazil, Bolivia, Peru, Ecuador, Colombia, Venezuela, Guyana, French Guiana, and Suriname.

This jungle is a critical factor in the regulation of carbon dioxide in the atmosphere, since much of the carbon cycle is produced there by what is also known as the "lung of the planet." The Amazon is a rich source of biodiversity and contains about a quarter of all terrestrial species.

The Congo Rainforest, with approximately 700,000 square km, comprises an important area of Central Africa that extends around the Congo River and its tributaries in Central Africa. It is an area where a great diversity of flora and fauna coexist that give a great ecological richness to this tropical jungle. In the Congo it is possible to find dry forests, meadows, savannahs, high mountain forests, and coastal forests. The tropical rainforest of the Congo is the second largest tropical forest in the world spreading through six different countries: The Democratic Republic of the Congo, the Republic of the Congo, Gabon, Equatorial Guinea, Cameroon, and the Central African Republic.

The fauna of this African jungle is varied and abundant. This includes gorillas, elephants, crocodiles, and insects such as termites, ants, flies, and mosquitoes. Its flora is also very rich and varied and includes oil and coconut palms, bananas, teak, cedar, mahogany, orchids, ferns, and bromeliads.

# Landscapes of the Great Lakes of North America and the Niagara Falls

About 2 million years ago, after the appearance of humans in Africa, the Earth's climate progressively cooled and a large part of the planet was covered by glaciers. The Ice Age, which would last for tens of thousands of years, had arrived. The cause of this cooling was the outcrop on the surface of a land mass that was previously under the sea, an outcrop that was caused by volcanic activity about 3 million years ago. This land mass was a bridge that united North America with South America and separated the Atlantic Ocean from the Pacific. It is what is known today as the Isthmus of Panama. It radically altered the ocean currents, having a huge impact on global environmental conditions.

Because of the snow that fell on the high zones during the Ice Age and that later was compacted, the glaciers of the last glaciation were formed. These huge blocks of ice were dragged down by the force of gravity and moved like a slow-moving river, but they moved faster if the temperature dropped. During the period of these glaciers, the climate fluctuated and the ice sheet finally disappeared.

The geological structure of the Great Lakes of North America was formed by the action of glaciers during the Pleistocene era. Before that period, there were wide valleys and a group of rivers in the area that today occupies Lake Superior, while in the current location of the other four lakes there was probably a plain. During the glacial period, the glaciers moved southward, deepening the valleys of the Lake Superior area and excavating the plains where the beds of the other lakes formed.

The glaciers retreated about 10,000 years ago, exposing the rocks that the glaciers once dragged with them. The great depressions on the surface of the Great Lakes could then be seen. The five lakes on the border between the

United States and Canada include Superior, Michigan, Huron, Erie, and Ontario.

The largest group of freshwater lakes in the world, they cover a total of about 94,595 square miles, contain 84 percent of the fresh water in North America, and contain 21 percent of the world's fresh water.

When the glaciers were disappearing, there remained in these depressions arms of ice that formed the Great Lakes when the ice melted. These lakes were interconnected through rivers. Four of the Great Lakes use the thirty-four-mile-long Niagara River to pour their waters into Lake Ontario. However, due to the unevenness of this river of about 100 meters between Lakes Erie and Ontario, the famous Niagara Falls between the United States and Canada are formed.

Today, more than 170,000 cubic meters of water per minute pass over the falls during the spring and summer. The falls are composed of the "Velo de Novia" waterfalls on the American side and the "Herradura Falls" on the Canadian side (so named because of its *u* shape). The American bridal veil falls have a drop of 111 feet, while the Canadian horseshoe falls fall from a height of 170 feets. The natives named the falls *Niagra*, a word that means "thunder of water."

# The Grand Canyon of the Colorado Landscape

Tectonic plates lift the mountains, and years later erosion gives them form. But the movement of the plates and the erosion by the waters can also create structures totally opposite that of the mountains. Under certain conditions, the crust of the Earth's surface can sometimes be sculpted spectacularly with wonderful depressions such as what we see at the Grand Canyon of Colorado in the United States.

The Grand Canyon is more than a mile deep, 10 miles wide, 277 miles long, and still growing. Over the past six million years, this spectacular canyon has been sculpted by the Colorado River while the Colorado Plateau has been rising. Volcanic activity pushed up the plateau to about 8,000 feet above sea level when the Pacific plate entered North America and compacted the crust to form the plateau. Although the Colorado River seems too small to dig such a deep canyon, its high altitude above sea level causes the force of gravity to give the river immense power. Other rivers, such as the Amazon River and the Mississippi River, do not dig large canyons because they are not as high above sea level as the Colorado River.

# Desert Landscape

A desert is a landscape of the Earth that supports little or no life, whether human, animal, or vegetable. The deserts are dry and desolate regions with very little rainfall and, as a result, a scarcity of water. (Rain almost never falls in cold or polar deserts and may only fall once in a number of years in the central parts of the great warm deserts.) The largest are the polar deserts, followed by the warm deserts, which constitute the majority of deserts on earth.

The polar or cold deserts are formed when snow falls on the poles, freezing and compacting with temperatures below zero, leaving the region with practically no way to sustain any kind of life. In the cold deserts below the poles, where temperatures may climb above zero, vegetation forms a type of landscape known as the *tundra* with a fauna and flora very well adapted to the cold.

Warm deserts are formed over the centuries, in a slow process driven by the constant decrease in rainfall and increased evaporation of water on the surface of the region, caused mainly by atmospheric pressure. These desert areas are subject to great pressures that reduce the humidity of the environment and soil, further promoting the aridity of the region and making it difficult for any vegetation to grow. . Most of the warm deserts are around the tropics, where the trade winds originate; these are hot and dry winds caused by solar heating in the equatorial region. When these winds rise in the atmosphere they absorb any humidity in the air and produce clouds, which then cause it to rain over the tropics. After this, the already dry winds dissipate the clouds that are in the way, reducing the possibility of rain. As they descend toward the surface, they cause the ground of the region to be heated by direct radiation of the Sun.

Other deserts occur when large mountainous barriers prevent water clouds from getting to regions in the lower part of the other side of the mountain. As the air rises on one side of the mountain, the water rushes in the form of rain. The air then loses its moist content and is hotter and less humid as it descends on the other side of the mountain to the surface A desert is then formed on the opposite side.

The deserts cover more than 50 million square kilometers, which constitutes approximately 30 percent of the Earth's surface; 53 percent of these are warm deserts and the rest are cold deserts. In most of the warm deserts, the average annual rainfall ranges from 25 to 250 millimeters. The temperature in these zones is very variable between day and night. Warm deserts can register average temperatures of 77 degrees F but can reach up to 135 degrees F during the day and fall below zero at night. In the polar deserts formed by large areas of ice with almost no annual rainfall, the average temperature is about 104 degrees F below zero.

Depending on the rainfall, a desert region is classified as arid or semi-arid, which is known as a *steppe*. The steppe is a landscape in a region more humid than the warm desert and is usually a transition zone on the desert side. Its flora consists basically of grasses and some trees, while its fauna is made up of grazing animals such as the bison and the horse. In the steppes, rainfall ranges from 250 to 500 millimeters per year. Warm deserts and steppes are concentrated in the subtropical regions around the Tropic of Cancer in the north and the Tropic of Capricorn in the south.

Most of the warm deserts are in the desert belt of the dry trade winds near the Equator. This belt extends from the Gobi Desert between northern China and southern Mongolia to the deserts of the Great Basin in the southwestern United States and the Sonoran Desert between the United States and Mexico.

The cold deserts are located at the poles, the Arctic Desert of 5.3 million square miles at the North Pole and the Antarctic Desert of 5.339 square miles at the South Pole. The Antarctic desert is the largest in the world. There it rains very little, only about 50 millimeters per year. The Antarctic flora consists of some fungi, mosses, and algae. Its fauna includes penguins, seals, sea lions, seagulls, and other similar species. The Arctic desert is by far the second largest desert on the planet and extends across Alaska, Greenland, Canada, Iceland, Norway, Sweden, Finland, and Russia.

The Sahara Desert is also located in the great desert belt, covering the northern part of thre African continent and extending from the Red Sea to the Atlantic Ocean. It is the third largest desert on the planet after the polar deserts and is the largest sand desert in the worldwith an area of 3,500,113 square miles, almost the size of the United States. From northt to south it extends from the tropical savannah belt of the Sahel to the Mediterranean Sea.

The Sahara Desert is made up of sandy and rocky soils. The sand is transported by the wind to form accumulations called dunes. Some of these dunes can measure more than 623 feets in height. The wind can also sculpt rock formations and transform them into the well-known *yardangs*, which are a kind of aerodynamic ridges with a parallel orientation to the wind that forms them. In addition are the *ventifacts*, rocks with surfaces cut and polished by the action of the sand transported by the wind. Sometimes the wind becomes aggressive enough to cause the so-called desert sand storms, which can make visibility and breathing impossible.

The desert has seasonal rivers. The only exception is the Nile River, which crosses the desert from its source in the eastern part of Africa to its mouth in the Mediterranean Sea. The desert also has a system of underground aquifers that can sometimes reach the surface in the form of an oasis. The aquifer system of the Sahara occupies an area of 1 million square kilometers, has a volume of more than 30 thousand cubic kilometers of water, and receives an annual contribution of almost 1.5 million cubic kilometers of rainwater.

The flora of the desert consists basically of thorny and resistant plants, like the cactus and some small bushes. Around the oases with their water grow date palms and shrubs. As for the fauna, in the Sahara there are snakes, insects, scorpions, spiders, the famous camels, and other animals. The Sahara records maximum temperatures of up to 135 degrees F in the day during the summer and minimums of up to 70 degrees F below zero at night during the winter. Though it is rare, it occasionally snows.

The Sahara Desert is extremely fascinating because it moves from pasture to desert and back again in a cycle every 20,000 years. What is today the driest, hottest, and most inhospitable desert on Earth, the Sahara was once a region of savannahs and leafy meadows with some forests. Between 5,000 and 10,000 years ago, the "Green Sahara" was home to hunters and gatherers who lived from a variety of animals and plants, supported by lakes permanent and substantial amounts of rainfall.

Today, the Sahara Desert has an annual precipitation of only 35 to 100 millimeters, while a few thousand years ago it received rains up to twenty times more intense when the seasonal monsoon winds brought the cyclical rains that kept the land fertile.

What happened?

The history of the Sahara is fascinating. It all started when the supercontinent Pangea was fragmented by volcanic activity and was divided into two large blocks of land. As mentioned, Laurasia went to the north and Gondwana to the west, separated by the Tethys Ocean. As the continental masses moved, the Tethys Ocean got progressively smaller until it became the Sea of Tethys. This happened more than 40 million years ago when the African tectonic plate collided with the European plate.

The African plate continued moving toward the north, further reducing the Sea of Tethys. The Mediterranean, Black, and Caspian seas formed from the remnant of the Sea of Tethys. The disappearance of the Sea of Tethys caused a change in the climatic patterns of Africa, substantially weakening the winds that produced torrential rains or monsoons in the north of the continent, causing the conditions of aridity to extend towards that part of the continent and leading to the formation of the desert about 7 million years ago.

Where before there was a large green meadow with lakes and swamps, today there is a large warm desert. The Sahara began to become a desert for the first time about 7 million years ago, and since then it has changed from desert to green meadow every 20,000 years due to the variation in the orbit of the Earth around the Sun. As the Earth's trajectory is further away from the Sun, the southern monsoons move to the north of Africa, causing the rains to fall on the Sahara Desert; as a result, it becomes green again. The system of interconnected aquifers of the desert helps in the formation of the humid climate necessary for the formation of the green meadow. The last time the Sahara went from green pasture to desert was only about 5,000 years ago, so according to its cycle it would again become green in about 15,000 years. That, of course, depends on the desert aquifer system still having enough water to favor the humid conditions required to return to prairie.

In addition to the cold deserts at the poles and the hot deserts in the desert belt, other deserts include the Arabian Peninsula Desert; the Great Sandy Desert and Simpson Desert in Australia; the Gobi Desert between Mongolia and China; the Kalahari Desert in the south of Africa; the Atacama Desert on the coasts of Chile and Peru (the driest desert in the world, where it rains only once every fifteen years); and the Patagonian Desert in Argentina.

As we have seen, the tectonic plates, the climate, water and wind erosion, and glaciers have sculpted the landscape of the Earth for millions of years. However, the finishing touches have been applied by man, another magnificent force of nature took his first steps on Earth two million years ago in what is today East Africa. May God grant that we may preserve for a long time the beautiful landscape of our planet Earth and that we may prolong its inevitable destiny.

# 2.5 DESTINY OF THE EARTH

Previously we talked about the final destiny of planet Earth based on the end of the universe. Now let's address what in theory would be the final destiny of the Earth based on other natural events. It is likely that we can survive some of those natural events, but we will face several battles to survive as our planet follows its pattern of normal changes. Life depends on Earth, and we will have to adapt to changes in the Earth if we hope to survive.

Our civilization has already existed on Earth for more than 10,000 years in what has been a very pleasant environment. There has been some concern about global warming, but even if industrial activity is affecting global warming for the next two centuries, this would put off only slightly the inevitable: another ice age. Within about 15,000 years, such an event will inescapably occur.

Why? In the pleasant period of 10,000 years in which we have been living, we are only in a stage between glaciations. In other words, we are between the past and the next glaciation. This current period—one of stability—has been a gift.

Even if we survive the next ice age, there will be other challenges to overcome. In about 200 million years, some coastlines will likely disappear, and entire continents will no longer exist as the tectonic plates move at the end of that future glaciation. The planet will then be very different from what it is today, as a single continent will once again dominate, and everything will change.

In that scenario, the Earth would become a place of turbulence. Oxygen levels and temperatures may swing dramatically, pointing to another mass extinction. But none of this will be as catastrophic as in an estimated two billion years when the tectonic plates finally stop moving. When tectonic plates cease to move, it is because the planet would no longer have the force that originated its movement from its nucleus. That is, the nucleus would be cold and solidified. Without the active core of the Earth, the magnetic field will disappear, leaving the surface of the Earth without its protective shield. When this happens, death would dominate life on the surface, and the history of our planet would come to an end. Without its burning heart, Earth would have consumed the fuel that kept it alive, and it would look like the planet Mars: no more atmosphere, no oceans, and nothing but a huge desert. The planet would be dead.

However, it is possible that humans today will continue to develop innovative technologies that will allow their generation to leave planet Earth before they face a massive extinction as did our ancestors. They may be able to go in search of another planet as blue and green as the one that gave us life and was our home for so long. Thus, our beloved planet Earth would end its glorious history without us. However, it may be possible for its glorious seed to follow the universe to continue our Mother Earth's mission on life: to survive regardless of the odds.

# 3

---

# LIFE

The story of life on our planet is obtained from reading the very life that preceded us: it is imprinted on the rocks that were once at the bottom of the sea and were eventually transported to the surface of the Earth to tell its history. The first forms of life on Earth evolved through a long and slow period to form human beings capable of deciphering our past. Our lives today are tied to that long chain of struggles to survive.

# 3.1 ORIGIN OF LIFE

Life on Earth could form only under certain events that include the formation of water, atmosphere, oxygen, the Moon, and the magnetic field. With these required elements in place, the first living cells originated in the great ocean of the Earth, where they transformed into bacteria. These first forms of life went though a great odyssey as they faced different challenging living environments and still managed to survive.

## What Made Life Possible on Earth?

The formation of life on Earth began with a series of key events, such as the formation of water, atmosphere, and oxygen, all of which are essential to life. It continued with what seemed almost miraculous processes. One of those was the formation of the Moon, which is directly related to the Earth's magnetic field. Both are key to stabilizing the climate and essential for the development of life on Earth.

From the impact of the rocky body that collided with Earth to form the Moon, *magma*—or molten rock from the center of the Earth—formed. By rotating this fluid in the nucleus and interacting with the convection currents in the heart of the planet, the Earth's magnetic field was formed, acting as a protective shield of life. Without its magnetic field, the Earth could not have hosted any type of life. With it, Earth received the key conditions for life not only to form but also to survive.

The melted rock core of the Earth remains very agitated until it produces volcanic activity, releasing the gases that help to form the atmosphere. The same restless heart also makes possible the movement of the tectonic plates, which allow part of the earth's crust to surface. Without water, atmosphere, magnetic field, and the Moon, life on Earth would not have prospered.

After its formation, the Earth was under thick layers of clouds of gas because of the heat of the melted rock produced at the time of formation. It had a dense, rough atmosphere and a great ocean. Originally, the Earth was only about one-tenth the size it is today. But the planet grew as a result of rather violent events, which was crucial for the story of life and for who we are today.

Somehow, somewhere on the planet life began to exist. The first form of life probably emerged on Earth about 4.3 million years ago, just after the great ocean had formed on the new planet. By then the conditions for the existence of life were already present. The Earth, because of its size, had sufficient gravity to sustain its great ocean, which would be vital for the formation of life.

Life not only needed to be formed, but also needed to survive in order to evolve. And survival required that the Earth have an atmosphere balanced in essential elements. It also needed something to protect its atmosphere, and that's where its magnetic field comes in. The Earth's magnetic field protects it from the flares emitted by the Sun in all directions. Of all the other planets in the solar system, only the Earth has this protective shield against the rays of the Sun. The magnetic field force lines are compressed against the solar winds, which causes those winds to be swept over the globe and protects us by deflecting particles charged with solar matter. And although we cannot see it, we can see its effects.

Most lethal particles emitted from the Sun at speeds of one million miles per hour pass over Earth leaving our planet's atmosphere, water, and life intact. While some of these solar particles do reach the atmosphere, they ride on the magnetic field; as a result, we have the beautiful auroras with their light shows that form at the poles. The Earth's magnetic field is so critical to the survival of life on Earth that if we did not have it, our atmosphere would be swept away by the solar winds. Without atmosphere, the earth would become a desolate, icy body very much like the Moon.

The Earth is the only planet in the solar system with enormous amounts of liquid water. Water has always existed on Earth in one form or another. It was present on the rocks that formed the planet, and then more water came from the bombardment of large numbers of water comets. Without the Earth's magnetic field, water would not exist in its liquid form, and without water there would be no life. Put simply, it is the magnetic field that allows us to exist.

The gases that were emitted over hundreds of millions of years by the volcanic activity of the Earth gave rise to the formation of the atmosphere, which was composed mainly by nitrogen and carbon dioxide. It is believed that about 4.2 billion years ago the atmosphere was saturated with steam and became so heavy that the first rains began to fall. Large storms with vast amounts of electricity were unleashed in the sky over the Earth. These intense rains that fell for millions of years gave rise to the formation of the great ocean, thus creating the necessary conditions for life to originate.

Almost immediately after the arrival of the first ocean, which covered the entire Earth, it is believed that primitive life forms made up of unit cells had already appeared deep within the great ocean. These organisms lived in the heat produced by the volcanic fissures at the bottom of the ocean and then spread upward to the continental shores to transform the planet by filling the atmosphere with oxygen. These organisms were the cyanobacteria. Using the energy of sunlight to obtain their food, they produced rocks as waste, which precipitated to form very thin layers of those microorganisms that were deposited slowly, layer after layer, year after year. These formations are known as stromatolites, and they would eventually fill the atmosphere with oxygen. For more than two billion years, innumerable generations of stromatolites have pumped trillions of tons of oxygen. At first the gas dissolved in the ocean, where it oxidized billions of tons of iron; eventually it also filled the atmosphere and then transformed the planet.

With the oxygenation of the planet about 2.2 billion years ago, the color of the ocean changed from olive to blue, because of oxygen produced by photosynthetic cyanobacteria. By then the Earth looked more like it does now—but before it became the planet we know today, a new cycle of cataclysmic events would take place. The Earth would enter into a great volcanic activity as a result of the movement of tectonic plates, expelling large quantities of ferrous iron through fumaroles in the bottom of the ocean. As the iron left the ocean waters to sink to the bottom of the seabed, the ocean shifted from olive green to blue, thus altering the appearance of the planet dramatically. When the oxygen was transferred to the atmosphere, it diluted the rest of the thick layer of carbon dioxide and cleaned the air. After about two billion years of oxygenation the blue planet was born.

Earth now had its ocean and blue sky. Remains of this great transformation can be seen today in the immense layers of iron deposited on the seabed. Now that we have seen the series of events that made life on Earth possible, we can go into the issue of how life originated.

# How Did Life Originate?

After the formation of the great ocean of the Earth and its atmosphere, the key ingredients for the origin of life would be formed: carbon, methane, ammonia, and water vapor. It is believed that when the energy from the solar radiation, the electrical activity of the atmosphere, and the volcanic activity of the Earth was added to the mixture, these elements would create life. This would be the magic recipe that combined the original elements into unique chemical reactions.

For life to be formed, all elements were required to be in place at the right time and in the right combinations. Of the ninety-two elements that appear naturally on Earth, life requires only a fistful of them: carbon, hydrogen, oxygen, and nitrogen are the raw materials required to form life. Today we know that carbon can be combined with other elements to form at least ten million compounds called *organic compounds* and that water contains hydrogen and oxygen. We also know that to convert these elements into life requires a very special chemistry—a chemisty so special that until now only Mother Nature has been able to accomplish it. The energy that activated that chemistry has been able to create the fundamental structure of life: a living cell from a few elements and compounds.

Since the formation of the Earth, the elements of life were already present. Water already existed on the surface, and when the planet achieved relative calm, water provided the ideal place for the first life forms to flourish. Life on Earth began about 3.8 billion years ago, just after a period of prolonged bombardment of asteroids and meteors crashing against Earth. At that time there was still no oxygen in the atmosphere, just a mixture of nitrogen and carbon dioxide.

After the formation of the Earth and the later formation of its great ocean, the conditions for life existed. It is possible that somewhere on Earth some chemical reactions would convert inorganic molecules to organic molecules. Of course, that would require the proper conditions to carry out that miraculous process. Over time, these organic molecules could interact with one another to miraculously form other more complex organic molecules such as amino acids, fatty acids or lipids, and sugars. But the complexity for these molecules is very natural and very spontaneous between them.

Of the chemical reactions between these organic molecules, it is possible that what was more difficult to form were the first amino acids, because from them proteins can be formed without problems. However, it is likely that the amino acids arrived on Earth in the meteorites that constantly bombarded Earth at the beginning of its formation. Today, amino acids have been discovered in bodies of the extraterrestrial world. But whatever the case, amino acids form the basis of all living matter, so that when united with the fatty acids or lipids, the sugars could form a kind of bubble of microscopic size that we could call the first cell.

## The First Cells

The first cells were formed from the union of complex molecules and or clusters of organic molecules. The amino acids connected to each other to form molecules of long chains called proteins; that connection took place in a long and random process, but in the correct sequence. Proteins are highly complex molecules from which DNA molecules are formed, allowing reproduction or copying of themselves.

The components of the cell were bound by a membranous cover formed by the lipids or fatty acids, as they are commonly called. This membrane would protect the internal contents of the cell from the external environment where the cell lived. The cell contains in it an aqueous medium in which the components of the cell reside. Sugars or carbohydrates are the source of energy that allow the cell to perform all its processes. The cell then went through a certain chemical evolution and became a living cell that absorbed nutrients, produced waste, reproduced, and moved.

# First Forms of Life: Bacteria

About 3.8 billion years ago, life existed in the form of microorganisms from a single cell that were drifting in the water, eating a little, and reproducing, finally slowly dying and falling to the bottom of the great ocean. The only option for these organisms was simply to survive. Although the hope for life to thrive in this time was very remote, it was on the right path. The key to survival is nutrition, just as the key to evolution is survival. Put another way, if we do not eat we do not survive, and if we do not survive then we do not evolve. It's as simple as that.

Since its arrival on Earth some 3.8 billion years ago, life remained in microbial form for another 3 billion years, or 77 percent of the Earth's existence. But over time these tiny organisms would break their long lethargy and evolve to change the world. It is true that organisms are affected by the environment, but it is also true that the environment is affected by the organisms. Once an organism is formed, it explores its environment, perceives the various aspects of that environment, and fine-tunes its genetic formula to increase the chances of survival. When that relationship between the organism and the environment is favorable, then life can thrive.

The first forms of life on Earth survived in a very simple way, because they were simple single-celled microscopic organisms that spread through the great ocean and perhaps through the atmosphere. Bacteria, a form of these organisms, survive to this day. Bacteria are the most primitive life forms on the planet and represent the vast majority of living beings. Bacteria evolved before Earth had its oxygen atmosphere and generally lived on the bed of the great ocean eating and digesting stone to obtain its chemical energy.

Bacteria use the DNA mechanism to replicate or copy their single cells to ensure the survival of the species. Not all copies were identical, as some mutations or variations occurred due to the environment, but that was not negative as a whole. Mutations can give an organism the skills to survive. For example, some bacteria can survive in cold, hot, humid, or dry environments. Over time the mutation produces a variety of organisms from a single cell that are different enough to allow it to survive in any environment. The great adaptability of life once it has been formed has allowed it to survive throughout the great odyssey of its evolutionary process.

## The Initial Great Odyssey of Life

Our planet Earth was born in fire and grew up amid violent events. After its birth, the planet was baptized with a lot of water and life began, but after a great asteroid bombardment, the planet became a fireball. This is where the odyssey of life begins to survive.

Life must have escaped unscathed from the fire, for it continued when the water returned to the planet. Sometime later, the water froze, and the Earth remained covered by a blanket of ice for millions of years. Still life not only persevered, but also prospered. Over time, microorganisms evolved into thousands of creatures. Eventually one of them left the great ocean to walk on the surface and settle on it.

Billions of years ago, creatures from which we descended began their great odyssey on Earth, but life must have been very minute by then. However, it was only a stage of the amazing journey of life on our planet from unicellular organisms to humans. All of life is connected over time to those simple cells that lived adrift in the first great ocean of our planet. Therefore, the small cell must have survived all the obstacles that it faced, such as the fire and the ice.

After its formation about 4.5 billion years ago, the solar system was still a very violent site with some asteroids wandering through space. During that time, Earth was hit by a massive wave of these asteroids. This intense impact turned the Earth into an immense fireball. Despite episodes as violent as these, life continued. If life was destroyed at that time, it must have started again, for it obviously exists today.

When the Earth became a ball of fire, the great ocean disappeared. Everything evaporated. But life would find its refuge away from the sweltering heat, perhaps in salt. Life could be preserved in layers of salt and could then return to its animated form when conditions were favorable for it. It seems that life is indestructible, because even if the entire planet is sterilized, once life is formed it will seek a way to survive. Life could also have taken refuge under the Earth where it was not susceptible to heat from either the outside or the inside.

There is evidence that some 700 million years after the formation of the Earth, there was already ocean water where life would have formed. These life forms have been found in Earth formations today as layers of fossilized carbon in which life could exist, since carbon constitutes the building blocks of life. If life existed 3.8 billion years ago, then the life we have today on Earth would be descended from life that was living in elevated temperatures without photosynthesis. However, primitive life needed water, and water had evaporated on the surface of the planet. Would it have been possible to keep another kind of life beneath the surface deep in the rock?

Evidence has now been found of organisms or bacteria living about three miles below the Earth's surface in gold mines in Africa. Classified as anaerobic bacteria, they do not use oxygen for their energy. However, they still carry in their genes the capacity to breathe oxygen. This is evidence that these microorganisms possibly once lived on the surface and then migrated to those depths to escape the heat and impact of total evaporation. This may have been the refuge of life for billions of years. Perhaps after surviving in the depths, life came back to the surface when conditions were right.

Even as our planet became a fireball, the rock vapor began to dissipate, and temperatures began to fall. Due to the size and gravity of the Earth, the evaporated water could not escape the space out of the atmosphere, and in only a few thousand years the water vapor would cool and condense and then fall to Earth like torrential rain. Once again, the great ocean began to fill, for those rains would be as heavy as the rains of today's tropical storms. The oceans would have regained their original depths in just three thousand years, providing optimal conditions for the return of life from the depths.

The organisms that survived the fire lived in very hot places and then became the lifelong ancestors on Earth. These organisms survived the immense heat to once more re-colonize the great ocean from the depths of the Earth through tiny cracks and fissures of the mother rock. The life of the subsoil returned to the ocean and remained in it for the next two billion years, living adrift in its waters, eating, reproducing, and dying.

The next challenge to life came almost two billion years ago, when the planet slowly became an immense ball of ice. For millions of years, the planet was covered by a thick blanket of ice, and life was able to withstand this as well. Life on Earth managed to survive the fire that covered our newly formed planet and then the two great glaciations that turned the planet into huge snowballs.

# 3.2 FIRST ORGANISMS AND EVENTS IMPACTING LIFE

About 2.3 billion years ago, life on Earth was still purely bacterial and resided in the ocean, but then a substantial change occurred: the planet's atmosphere, which was once a redish color, became blue. The reddish color was caused by methane gas produced by bacteria called *methanogens*, which were prokaryotic organisms. But with the arrival of another type of prokaryotes called *cyanobacteria*, the color of the atmosphere turned blue. These cyanobacteria would not only change the color of the skies but would also change life forever by oxygenating the planet.

## Prokaryote Organisms

Prokaryotic organisms are unicellular microorganisms such as bacteria that are made up of prokaryotic cells—in other words, cells that have no nucleus. The prokaryote is structurally simpler and smaller than other cells. Like any cell, it is delimited by a cellular membrane that folds toward the interior. The outside of the membrane is surrounded by a wall that protects the cell. The inside of the cell is called *cytoplasm*; inside the cytoplasm, around the center in a dense region called the *nucleoid*, is the genetic material or DNA (*Deoxyribonucleic acid*), which is not separated from the rest of the cytoplasm.

DNA, a molecule composed of the nucleic acids, contains the genetic code or instructions for the formation and reproduction of the cell. When reproduced, the entire genetic contentof the cell is copied to the other cell. This genetic information is transmitted to the next generation and thus ensures its survival.

In the transmission of genetic information, DNA needs another nucleic acid molecule called RNA (*Ribonucleic Acid*). These two molecules composed of nucleic acids control the synthesis of proteins that the cell needs to live, providing information about what proteins must be and do to make the vital processes as well as the basic functions of living beings. The cytoplasm of the cell also contains *ribosomes*, structures that make proteins. The ribosomes can be free or grouped forming sets called poly-ribosomes, as shown in the following illustration.

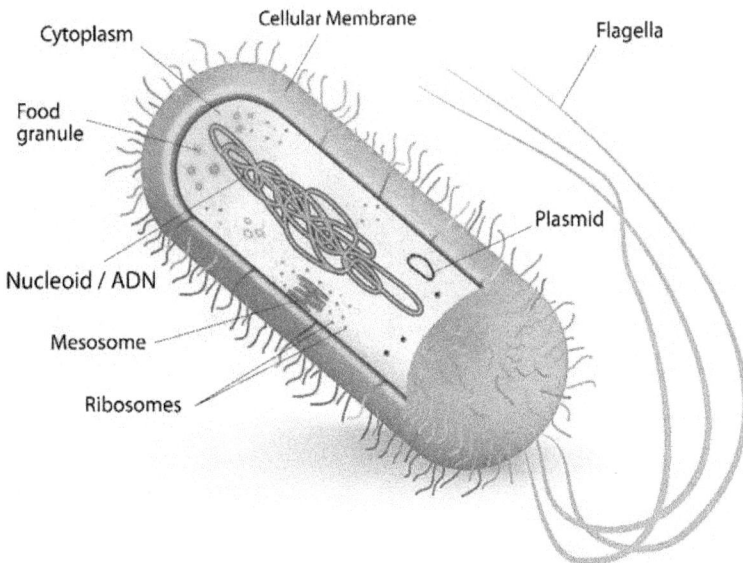

Prokaryotic cells may have different structures that allow locomotion, such as *cilia* and *flagella*. Cilia are numerous short hairs, while the flagella are scarcer longer hairs. Among the most important bacteria constituted by prokaryotic cells are methanogens and cyanobacteria.

*Methanogens* are a type of bacteria that process nutrients and then produce methane as a waste product. They are unicellular organisms that are part of the group of archaea. Methanogens do not depend on sunlight for their energy; they get it by decomposing their nutrients and producing methane gas as a byproduct or waste product. It is likely that this methane will keep the planet warm, because when the methane began to bubble to the atmosphere, it raised the Earth's temperature and filled the whole atmosphere, turning it red. Over time methanogens evolved to form a new type of bacteria called cyanobacteria, which would not only change the color of the planet but would have an enormous impact on life.

*Cyanobacteria* are microscopic organisms of a single cell formed by changes or cellular mutations. Cyanobacteria were the dominant form of life on earth for over two billion years and are the lifelong ancestors on Earth. These cyanobacteria, as illustrated on the right, were the first organisms to use sunlight to obtain their energy through the photosynthesis process. These bacteria get the energy to survive and reproduce from the elements and molecules around them. The microorganisms absorbed the carbon dioxide that was very abundant by then in the great ocean

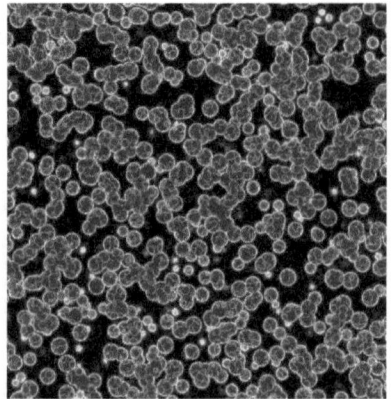

and turned it into carbohydrate, which provided them with food.

Cyanobacteria filled the atmosphere with oxygen as its waste product, which made other types of life flourish. This was possible once the light of the sun had become stronger. The oxygen produced by the cyanobacteria was released into the atmosphere in massive quantities. This oxygen reduced the amount of methane in the atmosphere produced by the methanogens until eventually the methane was completely eliminated. About 2.4 billion years ago, the entire atmosphere was full of oxygen.

Organisms that evolved after cyanobacteria used oxygen as energy and are called *aerobic organisms*. This new form of energy sought to take control of the power of sunlight through the biochemical process known as *photosynthesis*. This magnificent event would later form much more complex cells from which the first plants would form. This would open the planet for life.

In photosynthesis, the cyanobacteria produced rocky debris that sunk to the bottom of the ocean to form very thin layers of unicellular microorganisms. These were deposited slowly, layer after layer, over a period of years to form *stromatolites*. These are the oldest known fossils in the world and can still be found today. In Western Australia, you can see living stromatolites in shallow waters. Ancient fossils contain many fossilized stromatolites.

The discovery of the formation of stromatolites ignited scientific interest in fossils. From these fossils, it is concluded that the planet Earth was already occupied by life 3.5 billion years ago. Rock records show that 2.5 billion years ago stromatolites bloomed around the globe. As the stromatolites filled the coastal waters, they in turn filled the atmosphere with oxygen and new forms of life appeared, as shown in the following illustration.

# Oxygenation Effects on Life

For about two billion years, the cyanobacteria were oxygenating the planet to definitively change the world. With the abundance of oxygen, the unicellular organisms evolved to multicellular organisms. In addition, oxygen began to bubble to the atmosphere; when it reacted to the ultraviolet light of the Sun, part of that oxygen became ozone, which deflected the harmful ultraviolet rays of the Sun. But it would take a billion years more for these microorganisms to completely change the Earth's atmosphere.

Cyanobacteria not only changed the atmosphere but also changed the way of life of organisms living on Earth at that time. Before cyanobacteria, no life form used oxygen to live, so they are called *anaerobic organisms*. Oxygen was lethal to almost all of these organisms, and as a result a large number of them perished. However, some others were able to adapt and survive oxygen. The new organisms that would use the oxygen to live are called *aerobic organisms*. One of the most successful in this process was the *mitochondria*, which managed to oxygen it as a fuel for its energy.

Over time, single-cell aerobic organisms very spontaneously began to come together to form colonies of several cells, in which the individual cells combined with each other to incorporate other organisms into them. These captive organisms remained intact and thus managed to contribute their special abilities to the captor. The new organisms became larger and adopted specific functions. The first plants evolved from cells that incorporated a green-blue organism called *chloroplasts*. The chloroplasts gave this new cell the ability to make photosynthesis, with which it expanded its chances of survival. In the same way, the first animals evolved from the cells that incorporated the mitochondria. The mitochondria gave the new cell the ability to breathe to ensure its survival.

The production of oxygen continued, and the atmosphere became very rich in it, resulting in the formation of ozone that protected the life of the rays of the Sun. The organisms depend on a balance between oxygen and carbon dioxide in and out of the ocean. About 2 billion years ago, Earth began a process of dramatic changes that would make life in the next 1.3 billion years become more complex, diversified, and abundant. From a simple cell like the prokaryotic organisms, larger and more complex organisms like the eukaryotic organisms appeared.

# Eukaryotic Organisms

The first cells, called prokaryotic cells, were very simple and lacked a nucleus. Through a slow evolutionary process over billions of years, these cells managed to develop a nucleus to form eukaryotic cells. Eukaryotic cells derived into larger and more complex microscopic cells to later form organisms of several cells or multicellular organisms, probably by the combination of two or more cells.

Eukaryotic cells evolved after oxygenation of the planet. In addition to the *membrane* and *cytoplasm* with the *ribosomes*, as in prokaryotic cells, the eukaryotic cells also have within the cytoplasm a spherically shaped *nucleus*, separated from the rest of the citoplasm by a membrane. Within this nucleus is DNA genetic material. The nucleus also contains another cellular structure of spherical form called the *nucleolus*, which is formed by proteins and whose main function is to synthesize the ribosomes. The ribosomes in turn are sent to the cytoplasm to translate the RNA that transfers the genetic code of the DNA from the nucleus to the ribosomes of the cytoplasm.

Within the cytoplasm are also other small cellular structures called *organelles* that fulfill specific functions. The organelles were formed by other cells, organisms, or bacteria when one ended inside another in what is known as the endosymbiosis process. Among the major organelles of eukaryotic cells are the *mitochondria* for cellular respiration, the *endoplasmic reticulum*, and the *Golgi apparatus* for the management of proteins.

In the Golgi apparatus are formed organelles called *lysosomes* that contain enzymes for cell digestion. Mitochondria was one of the bacteria that ended up as part of another, which was a very fortuitous event, since mitochondria had already learned to handle oxygen for energy. A similar process occurred in plants when the chloroplast ended up being part of other bacteria to allow photosynthesis. Mitochondria still retain their own DNA and RNA, and their ribosomes are very independent of the cell in which they live. See the following illustration.

cell membrane

nucleus

nucleolus

vacuole

lysosome

cytoplasm

mitochondrion

endoplasmic          golgi
reticulum           complex

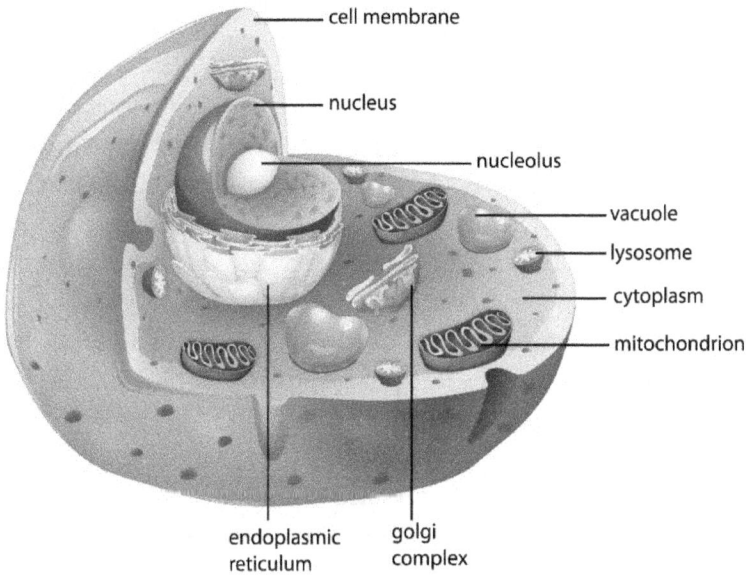

Eukaryotic cells were much larger and had more DNA than prokaryotic cells. This made the level of complexity of life become greater to form two types of more advanced organisms: those that give off oxygen like plants and those that absorb oxygen like animals. From these organisms, plants, animals, and fungi evolved after billions of years as eukaryotic cells clustered into larger complex multicellular organisms. Unicellular eukaryotic organisms that did not evolve into plants, animals, or fungi are called protists.

## First Glaciation and its Effects on Life

Life continued its course without major changes until the first glaciation occurred. The production of oxygen over millions of years cooled the planet during a time when nothing was producing heat; as a result, the planet froze, giving way to the first glaciation 1.1 billion years ago. At that time, life almost died out.

The planet turned into an ice ball and continued in that form for millions of years until a great volcanic activity from the heart of the Earth broke the ice. In its obsession to continue existing even in the ice, life sought refuge in the thermal cracks of the ocean bottom and evolved into new heat-loving microorganisms called *thermophiles*. Thermophilic bacteria are microorganisms that live and develop under extreme temperature conditions in places with volcanic activity, where they can live peacefully in bubbles of water so hot that it would kill any other type of life.

After the ice began to melt from the heat that came from the center of the Earth, life gradually began to change, even though the size of organisms remained very small. At that time appeared tiny organisms called *choanoflagellates*, shown in the illustration at left. The choanoflagellates were organisms that lived together in colonies and are the ancestors of all animals, including man. They lived without major changes for the next billion years. But then another freezing period on the planet caused the second glaciation, which was a consequence of the first and that introduced very important changes in life.

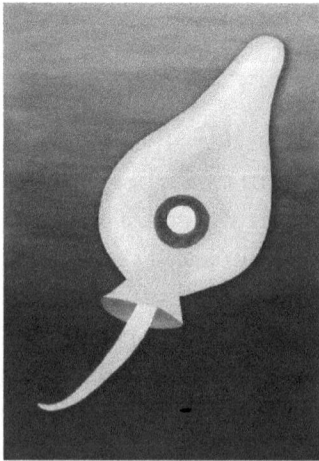

# Second Glaciation and Its Effect on Life

Had it not been for the two glaciations, life on Earth might have continued as bacteria, and Earth would be nothing more than a planet of muddy oceans containing stromatolites. Both glaciations were crucial to the evolution of lifeby allowing the evolution of eukaryotic organisms.

The second glaciation occurred about 700 million years ago; at that time, the planet became an immense snowball. The only life on Earth, the marine bacteria, were trapped under the dark. This event resulted in the largest glaciation ever experienced on Earth. The result was disastrous. Everything but a small fraction of organisms became extinct. Even the marine organisms, the only life on the planet, had almost completely disappeared. The future of life on Earth hung by a thread. Finally, the heat of vast volcanic eruptions fractured the supercontinent Rodinia and melted the glaciation.

After the rupture of Rodinia some 630 million years ago, the carbon dioxide released by the eruptions from the heart of the Earth created a temporary greenhouse effect and the ice sheets melted. Rodinia fractured into large fragments and the ice sheet broke. As the ocean thawed it opened; the oxygen level increased and the primitive organisms were free to take the next step in the evolutionary process. These organisms would become larger, much more complex, and even very aggressive later during and after the Cambrian Period.

After the thawing of the snowball, life thrived like never before. The carbon dioxide produced by the volcanic activity while the Earth was frozen began to be released from the mantle of the Earth to the bottom of the seabed; from there, the carbon dioxide went to the atmosphere. Carbon dioxide was stored in the atmosphere until it reached sufficient levels for global warming.

As the Earth warmed, the ice began to melt, and the temperature reached about 110 degrees F, forming patterns of the climate never seen before. The temperature differential caused massive hurricanes to form. These huge hurricanes generated giant ocean waves. All this activity increased oxygen production. The nutrients that were dumped into the ocean from within the Earth during volcanic activity would either go back to the ocean floor or be consumed by bacterial life.

The life of bacteria on the ocean floor would not be directly impacted by hurricanes, but many of them were transported from the bottom to shallower waters. When the winds settled down and the calm came, the sun bathed the shallow waters with its light and nutrients, causing the bacteria to multiply tremendously, producing more oxygen. The algae bloom began. The ocean then turned green.

More and more oxygen was pumped into the environment. The life that had survived two glacial periods had changed the planet, adding a new chapter in its history—this time adding a lot of oxygen, which changed the world and introduced *collagen*, which in turn tremendously impacted the growth and development of the first forms of life to form the first animals.

# 3.3 THE FIRST ANIMALS

Since its beginning 3.8 billion years ago, life on Earth evolved from a living cell without nucleus or prokaryote to another with nucleus or eukaryote; from these would arise the multicellular organisms. Some 580 million years ago, life underwent some very important changes after a long lethargy of more than 3 billion years, thanks to the second glaciation.

At that time appeared on Earth the first forms of multicellular animals that could be visible to the naked eye. These animals were the first invertebrates, soft-bodied specimens similar to some plants and the first forms of jellyfish and worms. When they were first discovered it was not known whether these organisms were plants or animals. The very rare specimens we found did not resemble modern animals at all, and were up to two meters long.

It is believed that these earlier forms of larger animals were formed of the collagen that resulted from the large amount of oxygen on Earth. Collagen is a kind of support substance used by cells in the pre-Cambrian period to keep their body structures united and stronger. This allowed these cells to multiply quickly and then become part of every living creature. It was the collagen that gave shape to life after the second glaciation.

Thanks to the help of collagen, organisms of larger and more complex bodies were later formed during the Ediacaran period and even later during the great Cambrian explosion. Animals, including humans, still produce collagen to help form the tissues of their bodies. The trillions of cells that form a human being are held together by collagen. Collagen is the most abundant protein in the human body and an essential component of bones, ligaments, tendons, cartilage, and skin. It also forms part of the walls of the blood vessels, ocular cornea, dentin (the main component of the teeth), gums, and scalp, as well as connective tissue that wraps and protects our vital muscles and organs. Like all proteins, collagen is made up of long chains of amino acids. These chains coil and bond together to form thick strands called fibers that provide strength and flexibility to our tissues.

Evidence of the existence of the first animals appeared in the fossils found in Australia's Ediacara Mountains; the site of this discovery is called the "Fauna of

Ediacara" and is the only clue we have so far about life in the Precambrian period. In 2004, the Fauna of Ediacara was officially accepted as a geological period by the International Union of Geological Sciences, extending from about 635 until 542 million years.

Some of the animals from this period were similar to today's ferns, while others were a form of disc that remained crushed at the bottom of the ocean. It is believed that they were not plants but animals, because they lived in a very deep environment in the ocean where no plant could accomplish photosynthesis. They were the first animals to start the race for food in the history of Earth life and are our modern ancestors. Among these animals are Pteridinium, Yorgia, and Kimberella (shown in the illustration below).

*Pteridinium*, the first great step of evolution on Earth, were organisms that appeared after the second glaciation and lived in the bottom of the ocean, half buried in the mud. These did not appear to be fish or leaves but were the first living organisms larger than microorganisms or bacteria. Pteridinium have been found as a fossil in deposits of the Precambrian period in various parts of the world. They have a body consisting of three rounded parts, each consisting of several parallel grooves extending to the main axis where the three parts meets. Even well-preserved specimens do not show any sign of a mouth, anus, or any other organ. Specimens found indicate that the animal lived in the sediments of the ocean floor, but it is not known if it moved, was fed by photosynthesis, extracted its nutrients from ocean water, much less if it had any obvious way of ingesting or removing salt water.

*Yorgia* was another creature belonging to the fauna of Ediacara that appeared after the second glaciation. Yorgia has a bilateral symmetry—in other words, the two halves of the body are equal. You can also see a focal point on which the head was formed. Yorgia appears to be the first creature to move in a certain direction and with a purpose. The body was like a soft, flat, elongated disk; it had a broad and short head in an elongated body divided into two parts by a depression. Each side of the body had segments that gave a symmetrical appearance to the animal. Between the body and the head was a segment wider than the rest of the body segments that allowed the animal to bend to move better. The fossils indicate the Yorgia moved with a curved back.

Another animal that appeared in this era was *Kimberella*, which had a body protected by a shell. An elongated trunk with a mouth at the free end allowed the animal to feed from the ground. The Kimberella may have been the first creature that had to dig in the oceanic mud in search of food. It was the size of the small finger of the human hand; had a kind of backbone, making it the predecessor of vertebrates; and had bilalteral symmetry. Kimberella was the first creature that would have been visible to the human eye.

For about thirty million years the animals of the Ediacaran Period dominated the life of the great ocean. After that, they disappeared with the arrival of the new creatures of the Cambrian explosion.

# 3.4 THE CAMBRIAN EXPLOSION

The animals of the Ediacaran period disappeared because of new creatures born in the Cambrian explosion, a new evolutionary event about 540 million years ago that that changed life on Earth forever.

## What Was the Cambrian Explosion?

The Cambrian explosion marked a period of transcendental changes in life on Earth: life went from a prolonged period of more than three billion years without major evolutionary changes to a period where an immense variety of creatures appeared in the ocean over a time span of just ten million years or so. This great evolutionary leap of life in that relatively condensed period of time is considered somewhat explosive.

Today the "Burgess Shale" of the Canadian Rockies is a clear example of what happened in the Cambrian explosion, marking the highest concentration of oxygen and greatest variety of animals in the Earth's existence. The Burgess Shale, the site of the most important fossils in the world, contains a fossil mine that represents a window into the evolution of life as it existed some 500 million years ago. The first fossils there were discovered in 1909, and since then more than 100,000 fossils have been excavated there. These fossils reveal that about 500 million years ago life exploded with diversity and staggered complexity. In the ocean of the

Cambrian, the oxygen-rich waters were filled with organisms and creatures that fed not only on plants but ate among themselves.

When it comes to the diverse types of animals, the Cambrian period is the most special in the history of life. During this period the creatures became quite complex animals that developed hard shells, skeletons, eyes, mouths and teeth, stomachs, and guts; they were even the first to experience sex as we know it today.

## What Caused Such an Explosion?

It took a long time for the earliest forms of life on Earth to become the complex creatures of the so-called Cambrian explosion. It is believed that the cause of this explosion could have been the oxygen in the atmosphere that resulted from the work of cyanobacteria and its photosynthetic process. The high oxygen level would be the fuel required to boost the development of more complex creatures with the help of newly formed collagen.

It is also believed that the new creatures began to eat each other, which helped them to develop larger bodies. However, they not only had an appetite for food, but for sex. Sex is a better way to reproduce because it guarantees variations and ensures that each generation will be a variation of the latter. Thus, organisms mix and combine their genes to form other organisms with variations. And the variations that best adapt to the environment evolve in a process called natural selection.

*Evolution* is an organism's ability to change over time, and natural selection is the application of that change in a natural environment. This made the Cambrian explosion possible. It was a burst of sex rather than of animals. It is important to note that life does not come by spontaneous generation, so certain conditions must be present for life to form and prosper.

## Life Prosperity

The chapter of life during the Cambrian explosion represents the most important period perhaps in the history of evolution. Predator animals started the arms race by developing sophisticated teeth, giving them the means to eat and chew things. Other animals began to develop traits that would help protect themselves from predators. Unlike the pre-Cambrian, the Cambrian period produced the most intense evolutionary outburst ever known with the Cambrian explosion, from which emerged the greatest diversity of life, including the two large groups of animals known as invertebrates and the vertebrates.

The Cambrian atmosphere provided much more hospitality with warm weather and rising ocean levels, which flooded the low land and created shallow marine environments ideal for nesting new life forms. During the Cambrian explosion, invertebrate animals with hard bodies proliferated, including the brachiopods (like today's clam) that lived in shells. There was also a proliferation of trilobites, invertebrate animals that were the ancestors of insects, spiders, and crustaceans.

# First Invertebrate Animals: Trilobites and Predators

Among the first invertebrate animals appeared the trilobites and the predators in the Cambrian period. The *trilobites* left an immense number of fossils. These animals, belonging to the group of arthropods, were invertebrate animals with an articulated external skeleton. These animals had strong bodies, giving them better defense against predators as well as better structural capacity to support even larger bodies.

These creatures had crushed, and segmented bodies protected by hard shells as seen in the illustration below. Some of them swam, while others crawled on the bottom of the ocean. The trilobites eventually began to change their appearance; some developed a stronger shell to protect themselves from the predators that had already appeared in the ocean. The trilobites varied in size between much less than an inch to more than one and half feet long, and they were among the most successful primitive animals until their extinction at the end of the Permian period about 250 million years ago.

The first predators appeared in the Cambrian period and included the *anomalocaris* and *opabinia*, invertebrate animals belonging to the group of arthropods with shells or external skeletons. These predators had huge, supposedly compound eyes.

The great predator of the Cambrian was the anomalocaris, a creature more than three feet wide. Its body was very long but narrow, similar to that of today's shrimp. It caught its prey with its fearsome gags, which also carried them to a circular mouth with teeth that was almost always open. It is shown at left in the illustration below.

The other important predator of the Cambrian, perhaps stranger than the anomalocaris, was the opabinia. This creature was small in size, no larger than three inches, with a head that had five eyes, giving it a very wide visual sweep of perhaps 360 degress. Under its eyes the opabinia had a kind of elongated, flexible trunk that ended in a kind of pincer with which it captured its prey and then carried the prey to its mouth, as shown below on the right. Its body was segmented and had a kind of tail at its end that served to propel it. To the sides of the body were fins that allowed it to turn quickly

# First Vertebrate Animals: The Fishes

One of the earliest primitive chordate animals or dorsal cord animals from which vertebrate animals later emerged was the *pikaia*, a kind of fish resembling a flattened worm (seen in the following illustration). Pikaia swam in the waters of the Cambrian and had a premature vertebral column, a very

significant step in the evolution of vertebrate animals. Its dorsal cord gave the pikaia great speed and elasticity that the other animals did not have. This advantage allowed it to escape predators and survive. The pikaia was less than two inches long and seems to have fed by sucking particles from the seabed. According to fossils found in Canada's Burgess Shale, pikaia lived in the bottom of the great ocean about 500 million years ago.

Later appeared one the first real fish: the *arandaspis*, which could be our nearest ancestor. This is the oldest fish with a spine. See illustration at right. This fish might have been feeding on microbes from the corals at the bottom of the ocean, as it had not yet developed jaws. It lived about 470 million years ago during the Lower

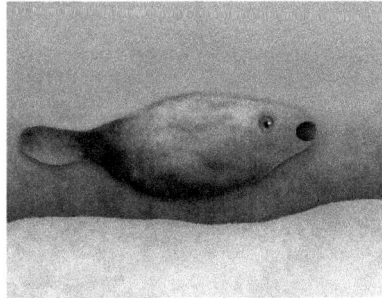

Ordovician period. Its fossils have been found in Australia. The arandaspis was about six inches long and had a hydrodynamic body covered with scales, but no fins. It had a flattened tail that served to propel itself. His head was reinforced with relatively small eyes.

Over time, fish became faster and began to eat any smaller creatures they could find. The world had split between predators and prey, marking the path of a new stage of life on Earth: competing for survival. Only the strongest and best-prepared animals would survive, and in order to do that, they had to develop the mechanisms that would help them survive.

# 3.5 EVOLUTION FOR SURVIVAL

The need to survive has been a constant in all species. Billions of years of changes, mutations, and natural selection enabled animals to develop the things they needed to survive, such as a digestive, circulatory, and respiratory system; a nervous system and the first sensory receptors; and the ability to see and reproduce in the water.

Fundamentally, life depends on the environment. All living creatures must feed to survive and then evolve. They must also reproduce to ensure the survival of the species.

The matter on which the organism feeds provides the energy to fulfill its basic life functions. This exchange of matter and energy between the organism and the environment in which it lives is responsible for the growth, development, reproduction, and maintenance of the species. Apart from energy, food also provides the matter and elements necessary to build, repair, and maintain the parts of organism's body. To metabolize food—convert it into energy—the body must develop various physical and chemical processes such as digestion, circulation, respiration, and excretion, hich evolve as the organism grows and develops.

To ensure their survival, organisms also develop the capacity to capture information from their outside world, so they can generate appropriate responses to the situation presented to them. This means that animals would have to develop the necessary organs and processes to maintain a continuous supply of oxygen and food to fulfill their mission.

# Digestive System

Every organism on Earth needs energy and food to move forward. Animals take energy and food from the oxygen of the environment where they live and from the food they eat—including plants, microbes, or other animals. Food is the raw material they need to grow and develop. To get that sustenance, the animals must decompose the food; for most, that decomposition happens in the digestive system.

The earliest ancestors of the animals that existed some 700 million years ago did not even have a mouth or stomach. These animals were microorganisms that simply absorbed each other to obtain the energy necessary tofeed and reproduce. Later animals of the Ediacaran period—such as the plants, jellyfish, and worms that lived in the bottom of the ocean—began the race for food. These animals did not move, have any type of muscle, have any bone, nor have any digestive system, much less a brain. They simply absorbed their food from the water and transmitted it to the rest of the body. Fixed on the ocean floor, these animals grew larger by absorbing more nutrients.

After the Cambrian explosion, the animals of the Ediacaran period disappeared, possibly because they were absorbed or devoured by other new types of animals who were equipped with a new way of eating. Animals with guts appeared on Earth for the first time in its history. However, in addition to guts, predatory animals needed some other help to digest food, and that help was obtained from other animals so small that they were invisible to the naked eye: bacteria. Bacteria, the first form of life on Earth, long ago developed enzymes to break down all types of organic material. When the first animals emerged, the bacteria took refuge in their intestines to aid in the digestion process. As a reward, the bacteria also benefited from the banquet by breaking down the foods that the animals could not digest by themselves.

More than 500 million years later, bacteria are still essential in the digestion of almost all animals. Humans carry about 10 trillion of these organisms in our guts, which help us extract the nutrients from our food. Bacteria have been very important in digestion in each of the lineages of the animal kingdom with guts.

The first animals with guts were species of jellyfish, which still had no mouth, no digestive tract, and no anus. They had a kind of sac where they put the food on one side; after extracting the nutrients, they put the waste on the other side. As this evolved, life in the ocean became much more complex. The predatory animals of the Cambrian explosion started the arms race by developing sophisticated teeth and means to eat and chew things. Other animals began to develop traits that would help protect them from predators. This outbreak of new types of animals also brought a new radical way of digesting. The creatures of the Cambrian period were too aggressive compared to the passive creatures of the Ediacaran period. One of the most notable features of the Cambrian was mobility, which allowed animals to feed differently.

Active hunter animals needed efficient digestive systems, mechanisms that allowed them to take food on one side of the body, store it, digest it, absorb it, and excrete the waste on the other side. In these animals evolved a kind of digestive tube with an entrance and exit at its ends that constituted the initial basic design of our own digestive system. But the digestive tract alone was not enough to digest food from the new food chain.

The first fish, creatures with a spine that evolved into the fastest predatory swimmers, by then had powerful eyes and other senses that allowed them to hunt other fish. They also developed a more sophisticated digestive system that had the first real stomach instead of a simple sac. With the stomach, digestion became more efficient in extracting more nutrients. This powerful digestion machine opened the way for the evolution into larger and more complex animals.

This innovative design of the digestive system allowed animals to ingest their food, digest it, absorb it, and then discard the waste. It also allowed more efficient transformation of the complex substances from food, so nutrients could pass through the membranes of the digestive tract and be incorporated into the circulatory system. As a result, nutrients were transported to the body cells as sustenance for maintenance and growth.

## Circulatory and Respiratory Systems

The first single-celled microorganisms that lived in the great ocean of the Earth some billions of years ago were fed the water of the ocean where they lived. Water provided the oxygen and nutrients the microorganism needed to survive. Both the oxygen and the nutrients were filtered within the microorganism, where they were absorbed. When the water came out, also by diffusion, it took the microorganism's waste into the ocean. Microorganisms and some simple multicellular animals use this diffusion mechanism to exchange oxygen, nutrients, and waste with the environment in which they live.

Later, as animals evolved into larger and more complex organisms, the distance between their body cells and the environment became too large for each cell in the body to get the required oxygen and nutrients directly from the environment by diffusion. Consequently, a sort of "part of the ocean" developed inside the body of these large animals, something like a kind of internal sea, whose nutrient-carrying liquid and oxygen would feed the organism and then take the waste away. From this primitive system of circulation, circulatory apparatus, and evolutionary brackish liquid evolved the blood and its nutrients. From the channels through which the blood circulated, blood vessels emerged; from those blood vessels the heart in turn developed. The contracting vessels produced a natural pumping of blood.

In fish, the first vertebrate animals, the heart evolved into a muscle with cavities that contracted in series, with a single atrium that communicated with a single ventricle. Blood pumped from the ventricle first passed through the capillaries or blood vessels of the gills, where it took in oxygen and released carbon dioxide as waste. From there the blood traveled to the rest of the body, supplying oxygen to the tissues and collecting carbon dioxide. By taking oxygen and releasing the carbon dioxide in the gills of fish, there is an exchange of these gases, which is known as respiration.

Gills are respiratory organs, one on each side of the head, to improve gas exchange compared to diffusion. In this system, water enters the mouth of the fish; as it passes through the gills, they absorb and send oxygen to the heart. The rest of the water leaves the gills and returns to the ocean. The force of the heart drives the blood flow through the blood vessels of the gills.

As fish developed, their gills became more efficient. But to make the big leap to the surface, the fish had to turn their gills into lungs. The lung formed as an extension of the fish's esophagus, which was a kind of bladder with capillary vessels to absorb oxygen and make gas exchange.

The next step in the evolution of the circulatory system and its relation to the respiratory system occurred when the first fish became an amphibian on the Earth's surface. Another mechanism that these animals had to develop to survive was the nervous system and the first sensory receptors.

# The Nervous System and the First Sensory Receptors

The nervous system evolved along with life itself. From the primitive processing of information from the first unicellular microorganisms such as bacteria to the development of the cerebral cortex in humans, the nervous system has been in a constant evolution to help ensure survival.

Like all beings, bacteria are microorganisms that seek to survive. They can perceive their environment, investigate it, and memorize it in ways that help them feed and reproduce. These microorganisms have chemical type receptors, usually composed of protein chains, which are able to detect their food. They also have a mode of locomotion originated by their flagella; these chemical receptors are composed of chains of proteins that are moved by the chemical reactions of the flagella to the environment. By moving toward food or moving away from toxic environments, bacteria process information to survive just like us. From these chemical receptors would develop the senses of smell and taste, with which animals could then find food.

From unicellular microorganisms, information processing continued to evolve in multicellular microorganisms of different cell types with distinct functions. Among them appeared the first cells dedicated to the transmission and processing of information. These primitive nerve cells of the multicellular organisms connected the external part of the body through the skin with the inner part, allowing them to feel their external environment and respond to tactile and chemical stimulations. These cells are the precursors of the nervous system. According to the record, the first organisms with these cells are the marine sponges. After a long evolutionary process, these primitive nerve cells became the first neurons in a very primitive nervous system. The first beings with this nervous system were the jellyfish.

With time, the primitive nervous system developed ganglia or nuclei, which acted as processing centers, allowing faster contact between neurons of the same nucleus. This type of nervous system is the one that the annelids (like the polychaete worms of the great ocean) have. Later, the ganglia evolved to form the brain ganglion and then the brain, becoming the main nerve center of information processing.

When the first vertebrate animals appeared about 500 million years ago, their column included neurons forming several nuclei. The vertebral column began in the brain ganglion in the head of the animal and extended through the body, housing in its extension the groups of neurons that transmitted information to the rest of ganglia or organs. Among the information transmitted to the brain were the pressure and vibrations in the water, which is a progression in the sense of touch. The main ganglion from the beginning has been in the front of the animal so that it could capture the information of the environment as the animal moved, which is why the center of the nervous system is always in the head.

# Vision

Eyes began to form in animals some 600 million years ago in the calm waters of the great ocean of the Earth, where there were not yet any predatory creatures to disturb the calm of the environment. About 545 million years before the arrival of the Cambrian period, the animal kingdom was living a time of transition. Animals that existed before this period were passive creatures drifting or anchored at the bottom of the ocean. Within a period of 50 million years came profound changes. Life underwent an explosive transformation, and thousands of new species formed during the resulting Cambrian explosion. During this period the animals were formed with a structure much more complex than that of their predecessors. These animals were larger, had better mobility, and developed weapons to attack and defend themselves. For the first time, the creatures developed the natural weapons they still use today: jaws, claws, shells, and, most importantly, developed eyes.

The first eyes were very simple, but they evolved over time to become much more complex. Life at that time was also simple. Animals had no skeletons, no heart, and no brains. They were very small, had very soft bodies with very little protection, and were very slow. A group of these creatures began to develop the same kind of vision that still exists in the jellyfish today.

These animals had something like a network of loose nerves and a ring of small dark spots aligned at their base, with which they could perceive the light. These black spots became light-sensitive cells that helped these animals detect some changes in light, enabling them to move toward food and away from threats. This type of cell was a kind of light receptor or photoreceptor that later developed the primitive eye and formation of a simple type of vision that helped these organisms survive for about 600 million years.

About 500 million years ago, the calm waters of the ocean filled with a great diversity of creatures, and enormous progress occurred in their eyes, which would change the way they saw life forever. Simple eyes had evolved into compound eyes in a group of invertebrate animals called trilobites.

The eyes of the trilobites were round structures in their heads, formed by small circular bodies in a series of rows. Each row had several circles. They were like eyes with many lenses. These were rigid eyes made of calcite rock, the same mineral that the trilobites secreted on their skin to form their ruled shell. This same matter also formed its outer skeleton, or exoskeleton.

The eyes of the trilobites were crystalline eyes and were better than the light-sensing cells that existed before. These eyes perhaps gave the trilobites their advantage to survive, turning these animals into great visionaries who then diversified and lasted for about 300 million years until the mass extinction of the Permian period 250 million years ago.

Though the trilobites were swept into extinction, other arthropods survived, and a group of them, the insects, took the compound eye to a more sophisticated level. The eyes of the trilobites, as well as those of the vertebrates, evolved from different ancestors.

The vertebrates, another group of animals from the Cambrian explosion, also developed their own eyes. The vertebrate eye consists of a camera with a simple lens made of soft tissue. These eyes began as simple detectors of light, but they later evolved and became a system of very sophisticated vision.

The common ancestor of the first vertebrates was a primitive fish that lived in the great ocean during the Cambrian explosion. Genes to form eyes passed through the entire vertebrate chain. From the first fish to sharks to shallow-water swimmers, they finally brought their eyes to explore the surface of the Earth and then evolve into reptiles, birds, and mammals.

The other mechanism of significant importance to survival developed by the animals of aquatic environment was reproduction in the water.

# Reproduction in the Water

About 700 million years ago, life in the great ocean was limited to single-cell organisms. They did not have to mate to pass their genes to other cells. Instead, they reproduced by themselves through an asexual reproduction process that made copies of themselves and sent those copies to the environment. In this way the cells were limited to their genes and not those of someone else.

This type of reproduction guarantees that all genes are passed in their entirety to others, but it could have serious problems in the battle of evolution. When each organism shares exactly the same genes, they also share the same weaknesses. If the body has a virus, for example, that virus is shared and can attack all other organisms because they all share the same DNA or genes.

Sexual reproduction increases the possibility of life of the organisms. The secret to surviving longer, then, is sex. The first animals to adopt sexual reproduction did it about 600 million years ago, but it was a rare sex. These creatures, from which modern corals descend, lived anchored to the bottom of the ocean. They did not move, but ejected sperm and eggs into the ocean in the hope that they would cross. This is known as *external fertilization*. Each summer billions of coral polyps simultaneously released their reproductive cells, each releasing sperm and eggs. But instead of combining with each other, they hoped to meet the seed of another coral. Amazingly, they did. Throwing both sperm and eggs at the same time increased the chance of survival for the offspring even amid the latent threat of being depredated in the attempt.

Throwing their DNA into the ocean might be the only way for stationary animals to reproduce sexually. But a new creature evolved, and sex evolved with it. Some 570 million years ago in a very short period we see the origin of many different and complex forms of bodies. Some of them still walk among us, such as the modern, cretaceous vertebrates. We also saw the first fish moving as no creature had moved before. They no longer depended on the current to direct their destiny but could move on their own to bring their sperm to the eggs of another fish. But even this method of pairing still had its problems. Once fertilized, the eggs were not only small and fragile, but were also exposed to much depredation. This forced the parents to be constantly on guard or to abandon the fertilized eggs.

It would take many millions of years for evolution to develop a new strategy with the participation of sharks. With them, a new mechanism developed where the male deposited his sperm directly inside the female. These were one of the first vertebrates to physically connect during sex. These animals developed a penis and a vagina that fit perfectly into each other. They also invented copulation and became pregnant, a process known as *internal fertilization.* This new stage in biological reproduction not only protected the eggs from predators, but also allowed new, fully formed pups to develop. For millions of years the penis proved to be of so much value that it evolved independently in each of the animals, including insects, birds, and reptiles.

# 4

# LIFE CONQUERS EARTH'S SURFACE

For more than three billion years life remained confined to the great ocean. However, after the Cambrian explosion, life continued to evolve until one of these creatures developed the necessary mechanisms to leave and continue its evolution on the surface of the Earth. During the Ordovician period, a wide variety of life that flourished in the great ocean began to appear on the surface. Thanks to the protection against the ultraviolet rays of the ozone layer formed by the large volumes of oxygen in the atmosphere, life was free to leave the great ocean and conquer the surface of the Earth about 400 million years ago.

The first to surface were the plants followed by the insects, which evolved from the trilobites. The plants evolved in such a way that they eventually grew into vast, dense forests and marshy tropical forests with a completely different atmosphere on the face of the Earth. Both plants and insects were making and establishing their life on the surface. Plants over time developed seeds, which drastically accelerated their spread. The insects adapted and thrived because of the reliable source of food provided by terrestrial plants.

Meanwhile about 350 million years ago, fish living in marshy waters near the surface shore turned their fins into paws through an evolutionary process, forming the first tetrapod or vertebrate animals with two pairs of limbs. The legs allowed this new type of vertebrates to raise their heads out of the water to breathe air, allowing them to survive in oxygen-poor waters or chase small prey in shallow water. Later tetrapod could venture on the Earth's surface for short periods of time. Some of them came to adapt so well to life to land that they progressively spent most of their life on the surface, despite being born and having to lay their eggs in the water. This new form of life gave rise to the amphibians, of which the reptiles later evolved. Over time the reptiles managed the miracle of evolutionary engineering: the amniotic egg, which could be laid on the ground, giving an advantage in the survival of reptiles.

# 4.1 EVENTS TOWARD THE CONQUEST OF SURFACE

Before life from the ocean could adapt to the Earth's surface and conquer it, certain necessary events had to take place.

These events include formation of the ozone layer in the Earth's atmosphere, formation of the first freshwater environments and the first plants, the adaptation of fish to freshwater environments, the emergence of the first amphibians, and the great initial step of amphibians to the surface.

## The Ozone Layer

After the first and second glaciation, the high oxygen levels triggered by the explosion of life in the ocean would also make a final modification in the atmosphere. For about 100 million consecutive years, oxygen reached today's elevated levels, a level dense enough to allow an ozone layer to form at the top of the atmosphere. This layer allowed life in the ocean the necessary protection to survive on the surface. Before then, powerful ultraviolet light would have destroyed any organism not protected by water. Now the ozone acted as a protective shield against ultraviolet rays for life that took the next step to dry land.

## The First Freshwater Environments and the First Plants

As the ocean level rose, waters flooded the shores of the continent to form large tracts of wet land along the coasts. Ocean water formed shallow lagoons, in which several types of small aquatic plants with tolerance to salt water began to grow. These plants tried to scatter to the surface as if escaping from the destructive effect of the tides, which always tended to remove them from the mainland and return them to the ocean. There they decomposed to form rich nutrients that would benefit many other organisms living in the ocean.

The salt water in some of these lagoons mixed with fresh water from rain or rivers, which diminished their salinity and turned the water into brackish ponds. They eventually formed aquatic environments of fresh water, which favored the development of more productive plants. From marine lagoons formed marshes where the plants progressed and continued their upward race to survive.

Eventually, one of these plants became strong enough to become trees with stems, branches, and leaves. The *archaeopteris* were the first real trees to emerge on Earth about 370 million years ago; while some types of plants had emerged from the water about 130 million years earlier, they did not become real plants as we known them today. When these first plants managed to overcome the biochemical problems that prevented them from supporting additional weight, they became real trees.

Archaeopteris developed a more extensive root system that supported thicker trunks and larger branches. Its bark better protected the conduction of water and nutrients from the earth to the last branches. But it would take about a hundred million years for these changes to take place. The archaeopteris reproduced when they shed their spores, since they had not yet developed seeds. These trees grew in freshwater environments around the shores of lagoons formed by the ocean as they invaded the mainland. These plants were conifers with well-developed roots, stems, branches, and leaves. As the leaves and branches eventually fell to the bottom of these lagoons, nutrient-rich sediments formed.

The roots of the archaeopteris were so strong and so well formed that they were able to support a trunk of more than sixty-five feet with branches and leaves. These trees scattered the surface along the shores of the ocean and formed the first forest on Earth. The first forest changed the ecosystem by producing shade and shelter and shaping the surface landscape; it also helped the land retain moisture, which was beneficial for the development of other plants.

The archaeopteris were the trees that ultimately changed the planet to a freshwater environment. Other forms of life, such as the fish, also made appropriate adaptations to this new environment.

## Fish Adaptations to the Freshwater Environments

The first plants that grew on the banks of the freshwater environments later helped to change the environment inside the water as well. The parts of the plants that fell into the water decomposed and formed rich nutrients. These plants provided protection and food to the animals in the aquatic environment, making it attractive for our ancestors. The fish explored the environment rich in nutrients, but these animals would have to make some modifications to live in an environment of fresh water.

First, these fish would have to get used to living in a low-oxygen environment. To begin, they had to develop lungs to store extra amounts of oxygen, and they had to develop legs for walking instead of swimming in this shallow and marshy aquatic environment. These fish faced very interesting challenges in taking the next step and conquering the surface, as plants and insects had already done. When freshwater environments flood, the water level rises, and substantial amounts of nutrients are formed, causing a great diversity of fish to grow. When the level goes down, the waters recede, leaving their nutrients in the soil to produce more plants. Remains of the plants decomposed in the water. By that time, about 370 million years ago, bacteria that broke down all that organic matter consumed oxygen, which made levels of precious gas drop in that shallow freshwater environment. To manage this situation of low oxygen the fish developed a special organ to store oxygen: the lung.

The lung formed as an extension of the fish's esophagus, which was a kind of bladder with capillary vessels to absorb oxygen. The lung became larger by worsening the low oxygen condition of fresh water. Today's fish are descendants of those fish that developed lungs in freshwater environments. In modern ocean fish, the lung was transformed into a bladder of air to help them maintain balance when they changed their level of depth; over time this bladder was extinguished.

Fish that stayed in freshwater environments along the coast would use their lungs to breathe air by lifting their heads out of the water and storing oxygen. These fish highly perfected the ability to breathe in the air. From these fish evolved the animals that later emerged from the water to the surface.

For our ancestors to take this great step, they needed to walk in addition to breathing—and the other important development that emerged in fish about 360 million years ago was the development of legs. From the lobed fleshy fins of the lunged fish evolved the four legs of these animals, with which they adapted to become one of the primitive forms of terrestrial life. With functional lungs and two pairs of legs, to the fish could move its body and support its own weight without depending on the buoyancy of the water. The body of these lunged and pawed fish was flattened, and from them the first amphibians evolved.

# The First Amphibians

The first vertebrates that came to the surface of the Earth were the amphibians. These animals were fish with lungs, broad legs, and a flattened body and head that could live in and out of the water. These first amphibians appeared in the Devonian period of the Paleozoic Era, about 350 million years ago. These animals represent a great evolutionary step of the vertebrates to conquer the terrestrial surface. From these evolved the reptiles; modern amphibians, such as the anurans group, which includes today's toads and frogs; and the group of urodele, which includes today's salamanders.

One of the earliest amphibians was the four-legged acanthostega; each leg had eight fingers instead of five, its tail was formed by a series of fins, and it was about three feet long. It was something between a fish and a reptile: it looked like a fish, but it had legs instead of fins, its skull was more crushed and strong than that of the fish, and it could move its neck. This animal evolved from fish that got into the freshwater environment and developed lungs to breathe and then legs to walk.

About the same time and in the same place was hyneria, a fish that was one of the most ferocious predators and that was always harassing the acanthostega. As the Discovery Channel reports, when the hyneria was in pursuit, the acanthostega was forced to take its head out of the lagoon where he was living, because of the low level of water. When that happened, the acanthostega managed to breathe air and found a new way of obtaining oxygen—leading to the beginning of a new life outside the water.

These animals could live both in the water and on the surface. The first amphibians, such as those seen in the above illustration, had arrived to take the big step to the surface.

## The Amphibian's Great Step to the Surface

The step of the vertebrates to the surface of the Earth was a great evolutionary process of adaptation. Before leaving the water, many transformations took place in the fish over millions of years. Apart from developing lungs and legs, its skeleton became more robust and more flexible; in the process, it developed muscles to support its weight without relying on the buoyancy of the water, enabling it to walk on the surface of the land.

The acanthostega was not the first to walk on the surface. Instead, another animal named pederpes, a descendant of the acanthostega, was the first tetrapod (four-legged animal) to walk on the surface of the Earth about 348 million years ago. Since then these amphibians have undergone long processes of adaptation and evolution. To live on the surface, the amphibian had to develop eyelids to protect its eyes from dryness. Life on the surface freed them from predators in the water and provided them with abundant food: the insects that had already arrived to settle the surface.

It is believed that amphibians had to abandon aquatic life because of droughts d. To overcome that threat, some of these animals were able to adapt to survive on Earth for short periods of time and began the search for new ponds. In one way or another, the transition of these animals meant a very important aspect for terrestrial life. From here, natural selection was in charge of the evolution of these creatures.

During the Carboniferous period, the amphibians grew and diversified. They were a species of crocodile like those seen today. Some of these amphibians developed thicker scaly skins to avoid dryness when they were out of the water for long periods.

After some time, the amphibians were basically terrestrial animals. However, they were still linked to water by their reproductive and developmental mechanisms. Later they were able to cut off dependence on aquatic environments when they developed the amniotic egg. This would protect the embryo inside the egg with a membrane that retained fluid, allowing even the passage of air. This event would lead to the formation of reptiles.

# 4.2 REPTILES AND THEIR EVOLUTION

Of the amphibians that had left the water to settle on the surface evolved the reptiles, animals that were better equipped to colonize the Earth. The first reptiles developed the amniotic egg, which helped them break their bond with the aquatic spaces to better colonize the Earth's surface. These reptiles spread across the surface to change the planet until the great permean massive extinction came to kill most of them. After some million years the planet recovered, and the surviving reptiles evolved into the rest of the reptiles, including the dinosaurs. The mammals also evolved from the surviving reptiles.

# First Reptiles

Reptiles evolved from the first amphibians that managed to live on the surface of the Earth. Of course, this evolutionary process included a series of adaptations and changes that protected the reptile in its new habitat. Among the most significant changes were development of the eyelids to protect their eyes; development of scaly skin that resisted dehydration; and development of the amniotic egg.

The amniotic egg has a calcified shell to protect the contents of its interior, where the embryo is surrounded by a series of membranes that feed and protect it. The embryo is connected to a bag of reserve substances for feeding during its stay in the egg. The embryo is also connected to another compartment where waste substances are deposited into the egg. The entire interior of the egg is protected by the amniotic membrane. There is also a small space of air inside the egg between the shell and the membrane.

The appearance of the amniotic egg gave rise to a new species of animals called *amniotes* that in turn gave rise to the reptiles about 325 million years ago. The amniotes developed a waterproof skin and a pair of kidneys to filter the blood and release the debris. This process was more efficient than that of its predecessors.

With the appearance of the reptiles on the surface, the colonization of the planet began, since these animals had made several adaptations to avoid dehydration when living outside the water. In addition, the amniotic egg allowed them to break their bond with aquatic spaces.

A great vegetation existed during the Carboniferous period, of which large forests were developed. This event removed enormous amounts of carbon dioxide from the atmosphere, resulting in a surplus of oxygen. Oxygen levels in the atmosphere reached 35 percent, compared to 21 percent that exists today. This abundance of oxygen triggered an exponential increase in both plants and insects. There were centipedes measuring up to seven feet, gigantic cockroaches, and scorpions up to three feet long. Dragon-like flies the size of swallows with a wingspan of more than three feet darted through the air.

During the Permian period, the new supercontinent Pangea emerged with a climate of extreme environments where the Carboniferous swamps were gradually replaced by coniferous plants, seed ferns, and other plants more resistant to adverse climates. Since animal reptiles are *ectothermic*, or cold-blooded, they can't regulate their body temperature and would have find it difficult to stay warm in an environment with temperatures that range from freezing at night to very hot during the day. In time, however, cold-blooded reptiles evolved into a type of reptile that was better able to regulate its body temperature, with many becoming *endothermic*, or warm-blooded animals. The most successful hot-blooded reptiles later evolved to become the ancestors of mammals and birds.

All fish, amphibians, and reptiles, other than the reptiles from which later mammals and birds evolved, are cold-blooded. The warm-blooded animals are mostly mammals and birds. These animals use the heat generated by the food they ingest to keep warm. As a result, they could survive in the supercontinent Pangea and become the dominant animals of the planet at the end of the much later Permian period.

At the end of the Carboniferous period, the first reptiles followed the movements of the mass of the Earth, which eventually formed the Great Pangea. For the next 100 million years, life spread throughout the surface of the Earth, which changed the planet. For the first time the surface of the Earth had been populated with a new biosphere, until the first great mass extinction came about 250 million years ago. At that time, the poor creatures on the planet experienced a real hell as forces from the depth of the Earth resulted in immense volcanic eruptions that caused the first mass extinction on the Earth's surface.

# The Great Permian Massive Extinction

Between the end of the Permian period and the beginning of the Triassic period, about 250 million years ago, one of the worst mass extinctions on the planet occurred. Normally this episode is known as the Permian massive extinction; it is estimated that 90 percent of ocean life and 70 percent of the animals on the surface perished along with much of the vegetation. The life of some ocean species, such as the trilobites, disappeared completely. It is believed that only about 10 percent of the planet's life survived. Considered one of the greatest catastrophes of life on Earth, this extinction was also called "the Great Death."

    Life on Earth had faced many challenges for millions of years, but nothing on the scale of this cataclysm. A great eruption that melted the earth's crust came from its mantle. This eruption continued for more than a million years, throwing immense amounts of molten rock to the surface and scattering large volumes of toxic throughout the atmosphere. The resulting hostile environment was too much for the species that had just come to life on the surface of the Earth. Most of it became extinct. It was the most catastrophic event the Earth had experienced to that date.

Scientists believe it took more than 10 million years for the Earth to recover. Gradually, the landscape, which had turned into an almost uninhabitable desert without vegetation, began to recover.

There has been significant debate about the cause of the great extinction, but most agree it was a massive volcanic eruption along with some additional factors.

# Causes of the Extinction

Three hundred million years ago the Earth hosted a single supercontinent named Pangea. This vast mass of rock was surrounded by a huge gap in the depth of the ocean. From that gap, the rocky plates that had formed the continent rushed slowly toward the core of the Earth. This resulted in a flow of molten lava to the crust; that lava was forced upward to break into the surface at what is now known as Siberia. This massive eruption formed a lava dome that rose from the center of the Earth. The first cause of massive extinction, then, was tremendous volcanic activity that came from the very bowels of the Earth. However, there is another cause of significant importance: methane hydrates.

This massive eruption of Earth was an event of unprecedented scale, but this event alone could not have destroyed most of the planet's life. Perhaps all of life in immediately around the volcanic eruption may have been eliminated, but not throughout the globe. Another factor had to have existed. And it did.

The evidence for that factor came from drilling a deep well into Japan's ocean waters in 2002 as scientists were looking for methane hydrate as an alternative energy source. Methane hydrate is formed when methane and water combine. When this gas is buried deep in the ocean it is frozen, and it is very stable at low temperatures. When the temperature rises, the methane hydrate melts and generates methane gas, increasing 150 times the volume than when the gas is interlaced with water and becoming very volatile.

In China in the formations that demarcate the mass extinction, evidence was found that enormous amounts of methane hydrate had begun to melt at the same time as the eruption in Siberia. Scientists also found an increase of the carbon 12 element—an element found in large levels in methane hydrate. There's an obvious connection between these two elements.

Perhaps the methane hydrate was to blame for the mass extinction. As the methane hydrate melted, the methane gas began to escape upward and was then released into the atmosphere. The eruption at Siberia produced enormous amounts of carbon dioxide, which caused the temperature to rise. As the temperature of the water rose, the methane hydrate began to melt.

Methane is twenty times more effective as a greenhouse gas than carbon dioxide. As the temperature rose higher, more methane hydrate was produced, creating immense heat. Once that process starts it is hard to stop. The temperature at the poles was 80 degrees F. This had a devastating effect all over the globe. The ecosystem disappeared, and oxygen levels dropped. This was a critical element in the maximum extinction initiated by the volcanic eruption. Firm evidence of this arises on the frozen continent of Antarctica, where they found an element called *berthierine*, a very rare mineral that forms in conditions of low oxygen. The low oxygen condition suffocated animals that needed it to live on Earth. With an oxygen level in the atmosphere as low as 10 percent, life would be almost unsustainable, especially when it has been accustomed to living in abundant oxygen. Before mass extinction, the oxygen level was 35 percent, while the level in the atmosphere today is 21 percent.

Of course, several other factors came together to produce extinction. For example, when the plants died they stopped producing oxygen. In addition, the methane released from the ocean floor reacted with molecular oxygen, greatly reducing oxygen levels in the atmosphere. Fortunately, some life was able to survive.

## The Surviving Reptiles

After the great extinction of the Permian, Earth began to recover slowly. The plants returned and the animals that survived thrived. The animals that survived perhaps did so by chance or because they were able to successfully live with little oxygen. The great survivors were the reptiles, which dominated all life on the planet after the great extinction. It is believed that the reptiles got used to living with little oxygen, which made them active compared to other animals.

Of those reptiles that survived the great extinction, the *sauropsida* and the *synapsid* reptiles descended. From the sauropids evolved turtles, lizards, snakes, crocodiles, dinosaurs, and birds. From the reptilian synapsid, currently extinct, the *cynodonts* evolved from the order of the therapsids; in turn, mammals evolved later in the Late Cretaceous period.

The cynodonts were advanced animals that had better locomotion than the reptiles because their limbs were longer and were more attached to the body. That in turn allowed them to rise higher off the ground and move more easily on any land with less consumption of energy. The bone structure of the head already separated the mouth and nasal canal in these animals, which allowed them to eat and breathe at the same time. They had also developed an ear that would later be perfected in mammals.

Another of the animals that thrived after the mass extinction were the dominant archosaur or reptiles of the early Triassic period, which had a remarkable success in their evolutionary and diversification process. This type of reptile, descendants of sauropids, includes crocodiles, birds, and extinct dinosaurs. Dinosaurs grew to become giant creatures spreading to inhabit all available space on the surface, because the planet that emerged from the chaos of mass extinction would be very different. A planet in which an immense mass of land had surfaced formed a new supercontinent, the Great Pangea, which housed these new animals that would evolve and become the most immense and imposing creatures ever to walk the surface of the Earth.

## Dinosaurs

Some 200 million years after the great extinction, oxygen and carbon dioxide reached high but balanced levels. Under these new conditions, the life that survived extinction evolved into a very different species. From the sauropod reptiles evolved the archosaurs, and from these evolved the famous dinosaurs, gigantic creatures that ate enormous amounts of food to achieve their enormous sizes.

Like all the reptiles from which they evolved, the dinosaurs were oviparous animals, which means they laid eggs to reproduce. Regarding the food they ate, there were two types of dinosaurs. Most of the dinosaurs were *herbivores*, plant-eating creatures with a large stomach that allowed them to store up to 450 pounds of vegetation per day. Their teeth served to tear off and chew the leaves of the trees. To help digestion, some species swallowed small stones, or *gastroliths*, to help grind food in the stomach. Among these herbivorous dinosaurs were a wide variety of species from the small to the big ones like the *apatosaurus* with its four legs, small head, and long neck that allowed them to reach the leaves in the highest trees. These animals reached a weight of more than 27 tons and stood more than 88 feet in length; they lived in what is today North America, about 150 million years ago at the end of the Jurassic period.

There were also *carnivorous* dinosaurs, which ate meat from the prey they hunted. Although some of these carnivorous dinosaurs came to be scavengers and fed on animals they had not hunted, they also came to feed on eggs, fish, and even insects. Carnivorous dinosaurs basically walked on two legs. They had sharp teeth curved back that allowed them to better tear the flesh of their prey. They had a large skull, which suggests that their brains were also large enough to develop strategies for hunting. Their lateral eyes allowed them to have an overall view of almost all their surroundings. Among the carnivorous dinosaurs were the terrible predator *allosaur* and the famous *tyrannosaurus rex*, which is now believed to be more scavenger than hunter.

Both herbivorous and carnivorous dinosaurs lived very happily, because they lacked nothing. The abundance of oxygen favored the formation of large forests with much food in the form of plants and animals for the formation of large bodies of dinosaurs. Many of them grew to almost fifty-six feet in height and eighty-nine feet in length and weighed more than seventy tons.

The dinosaurs evolved in a wide variety of species including the flying dinosaurs, of which the birds evolved; the first specimens of these appeared crossing the skies at the end of the Jurassic period. *Archaeopteryx* lived in the Upper Jurassic period about 150 million years ago. It is generally considered one of the first birds. These birds later diversified to form the ancestors of modern birds. Insects were also abundant at that time, as were early mammals that slipped between dinosaur feet in fern forests and cyan and coniferous plants. These mammals would be the dominant species on Earth after the dinosaurs.

Dinosaurs lived and reigned on Earth for about 150 million years until they were swept from the face of the Earth at the end of the Cretaceous period 65 million years ago. It was a time when Earth seemed a huge paradise and life seemed to prosper. But something terrible happened to upset the ecosystem of the entire planet, and the dinosaurs—along with 75 percent of the rest of life on Earth—disappeared.

This second mass extinction was caused by a huge meteor more than six miles in diameter that fell on Earth in what is now the Yucatan peninsula in Mexico. This impact caused what we know today as the Gulf of Mexico.

How could a meteor that fell on one spot cause such widespread destruction? Tons of terrestrial crust were excavated by the impact of the meteor, and all that material evaporated into the atmosphere, combining with the iridium that had brought the meteor to Earth. *Iridium* is a rare mineral found on Earth that usually originates in rocky space bodies. All this matter formed a thick cloud of dust containing particles of earth.

In addition to the impact of the huge meteor, a parallel extinction caused by currents of molten lava occurred at the edge of what is now India, though it was likely not as catastrophic as the meteor. Folowing these two events, the dinosaurs became extinct, paving the way for the era of mammals and later the world of humans.

# 4.3 MAMMALS

Mammals are four-legged vertebrates that evolved at the end of the Triassic period, some 200 million years ago, from the surviving reptiles of the great Permian mass extinction some 250 million years ago. Among the surviving reptiles there was one called *cynodonts*, shown in the illustration on the following page, which is believed to be the common ancestor of all mammals. The evolution of this new species was a long, slow, and gradual process of about 100 million years.

The new species had managed to control its body temperature; along with birds, also descendants of reptiles, it became one of the few warm-blooded animals. To keep their

bodies warm in a cold environment, the cynodonts generated energy or heat from their food; as a result, they had to eat greater quantities and more often than the cold-blooded animals (like the reptiles) from which they evolved. Because these reptiles did not generate much energy from their food, they could go lengthy periods without eating. Another feature of warm-blooded mammals that helps them control their body temperature is the hair covering their skin.

Like warm-blooded animals, mammals could adapt to cold climates and adapt to the temperature of the night to take advantage of food resources without greater danger. Their vision adapted to allow them to see in the dark. While it was difficult for mammals to perceive colors, they managed to develop very efficient night vision as well as extraordinary auditory and olfactory systems.

Mammals also introduced improvements in their digestive system, making them able to digest their food more quickly and better utilize their food. Their circulatory and respiratory systems also became more efficient, increasing their ability to better oxygenate the blood and realize more energy. This led to the development of a more efficient heart with four chambers and the complete separation of oxygenated blood from deoxygenated blood.

The brain continued to evolve, giving mammals a more efficient central nervous system to better perceive the world and process information to respond more appropriately to external stimuli. This nervous system also allowed them to develop their olfactory system to perceive the odors and thus have better information about their environment, enabling them to make better decisions that contributed to their survival. The mammals also developed a more efficient hearing system formed by the three bones that we still have today in the middle ear: the hammer, anvil, and stirrup. Essentially, the constant evolution of the mammals produced great transformations in all their organic systems.

Initially the mammals were very small animals, about the size of a mouse, but they had a well-developed brain and were very active. They had jaws that enabled them to chew with developed and specialized teeth such as the incisors to cut food, canines to tear, and molars to grind. During the time of the dinosaurs, mammals lived as nocturnal creatures of low profile, staying half hidden among the trees and the bushes to survive, where they ate fruits and some insects. They occasionally descended from the trees and were surrounded by other animals, including giant dinosaurs. In doing so, they were extremely careful not to be prey or end up being trampled by the giant creatures.

After the extinction of the dinosaurs, the mammals that existed were still small, perhaps because they had not gotten used to or adapted very well to low oxygen levels. But that would soon change. Mammals developed improvements in their breathing system, eventually making physical changes in their bodies so they could store more oxygen. Although this change was not as efficient as those made by dinosaurs when they adapted to living with little oxygen, it proved very advantageous later so that the mammals could adopt comfortable positions from which to feed their young.

Mammals are peculiar in that the young gestate inside the mother. The mother develops mammary glands from which she feeds her offspring—and the name *mammals* comes from those glands. These glands secrete milk, a very complete food with high nutritional value. With this new modality, mammals began a new way of life in which they nursed and fed their young with breast milk. It is believed that low oxygen levels continued for more than 100 million years, playing a significant role in the evolution of real mammals.

Another major event in the evolution of mammals occurred about 125 million years ago with the appearance of placental mammals, as was observed in fossils discovered in China. From this finding, we can deduce that placental mammals originated in the Upper Jurassic period, when dinosaurs were at their peak. This would be the ancestor of all mammals with a placenta, including humans. Placental mammals are generally viviparous animals—that is, following fertilization, the embryo forms and develops in the womb of its mother. There it is fed by a placenta, hence the name of placental mammals.

It is believed that the low oxygen level favored the development of the placenta, since the placenta allowed the mother and the fetus to share the oxygen and enabled the mother to feed the fetus in her womb. This system was more efficient than laying eggs. In addition, the new modality encourages development of a better relationship between mother and child, which was later perfected by humans and is unique in the mammals of the planet.

The placenta evolved from the membrane that covered the inside of the shell of the egg in the reptiles from which the mammals evolved. It is the placenta that makes possible the live birth of the placental mammals. It envelops the developing embryo and regulates the flow of nutrients and gases between the fetus and the mother through the umbilical cord. Feeding in the placenta allows faster and more efficient transfer of nutrients from the mother to the baby, allowing for faster brain development, a larger adult brain, and a more efficient metabolic rate. These characteristics had important repercussions on the evolution of mammals.

Placental mammals have spread and diversified widely around the planet to reach a variety of more than five thousand species today. Most of these species live on the surface; however, some species of placental mammals swim and others fly. One of the most interesting species of placental mammals is captivating because of its enormous size: the whale weighs about 160 tons and evolved from placental mammals on the surface before venturing to the ocean, perhaps during the Paleogene period. By this time the ocean was full of fish, which provided a reliable source of food and a strong stimulus to stay.

The other species of placental mammals evolved in an interesting way. One of the rarest and the smallest was the bat. This is the only mammal that flies; during its development, its front limbs evolved into wings. Bats feed mostly on insects, although they also feed on other vertebrates such as frogs, mice, birds, and fish. They hunt their prey with a system they developed not only hunt but to orient themselves. This system is a kind of biological sonar that emits ultrasounds that bounce when they reach the prey; in return, their echoes transmit signals to the brain that help them detect the location of the prey.

But one species of placental mammals on the surface would follow the evolutionary path to bring the species that would later emerge to dominate the world. This species would be able to feel and see the world as never before. Our ancestors, the primates, had arrived.

# 4.4 PRIMATES

After the disappearance of the dinosaurs, mammals began to occupy every available space on Earth. Among those mammals was a group that appeared about 70 million years ago at the end of the Cretaceous period. These animals, the primates, evolved from mammals, lived in treetops, developed an astonishing ability to survive, and started a new life on the path of evolution.

The life and evoluation of the first primates became obvious from appearance in the United States of a fossil of the skeleton of a primate called *carpolestes*, a primate that lived some 56 million years ago. These primates apparently spent most of their time in trees, where they felt more secure than on the forest floor; their diet may have been leaves and fruits, and they were probably nocturnal mammals.

The fossil of the carpolestes indicates an animal with some characteristics of the primates, including the same kind of body and long tail. The hands had fingernails that would allow the animal to grasp branches and climb between them, as well as to take leaves and fruits to the mouth and chew with teeth designed for this purpose. However, the eyes of this animal did not have looking forward, which is a characteristic of primatestes, as seen in the illustration below. The carpolestes also lacked another characteristic of the primates: its bone structure did not allow it the specialized jump of the first primates. Some studies suggest that

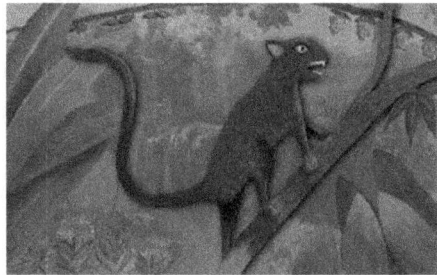

these characteristics developed later.

Primates form the animal group that evolved from mammals. They have the same characteristics as mammals. However, they developed some other features that helped them adjust to their lifestyle. They developed a superior brain that allowed them to coordinate their sight and movement of their body and the movement of their hands. In fact, the way they moved from branch to branch or from tree to tree and even jumped to look for their food is an outstanding feature in primates. With the movement developed in their hands they could grab their food and take it to their mouths; they could also grab and discard or remove any other object that prevented them from reaching their food. The position of the eyes looking forward at the front of the skull allowed a three-dimensional view.

The primates also managed to develop other characteristics: hands and feet with five fingers with nails; plantigrade feet, allowing them to walk leaning on the soles of the feet; thumbs that protruded on hands and feet; clavicles; flat nails instead of claws; color vision in the vast majority of species; binocular vision in different degrees; well-developed shoulder and elbow joints; and well-developed brain hemispheres. The primates' sight evolved to be more precise, so they could calculate the distance of objects around them. The brain also expanded sensory perception. As a result, the primate managed to better develop the senses of touch, smell, and hearing. Later in time, the primates began to walk on two legs, as humans later would. This and other continuous evolution of the species provided primates with the things necessary for their survival.

# 4.5 EVOLUTION FOR SURVIVAL AT THE SURFACE

The improvements and adaptations that creatures that made to life on the surface had introduced to the mechanisms that ensured their survival and allowed them to continue evolving until they became humans. Among those improvements and adaptations are those made to the central nervous system and the senses (especially the vision) as well as the digestive, circulatory, and respiratory systems. Changes also had to be made in how these creatures reproduced on the surface.

## Central Nervous System and the Senses

The small brain of the fish that evolved about 500 million years ago brought the first amphibians out of the water to make life on the surface. This small brain evolved over time as amphibians evolved into reptiles and eventually into humans.

The brain of the reptiles developed some 200 million years ago was formed by the brainstem and the senses, which were still very precarious. However, this brain allowed reptiles to perform the basic functions of automatic movements, as well as the functions of respiration and metabolic reactions. In addition, the brain was responsible for basic survival instincts such as the pursuit of food, the desire to mate, and aggressive responses to fight or flight.

As reptiles evolved during the Permian period some 260 million years ago into species like the mammals, a significant difference can be seen between the development of the mammalian brain compared to that of reptiles. The brain mass in mammals became much larger and more complex than that of reptiles, which fortunately resulted in intelligence. From this large, complex brain mass, our nervous system developed.

Through millions of years, the nervous system has been able to evolve from the primitive brain we inherited from fish and reptiles to the nervous system we have today, capable of feeling and thinking. The nervous system of early mammals began with the development of the brainstem or primitive brain inherited from their ancestors. This primitive brain is the one that regulates the basic vital functions to assure the survival of the being, such as breathing, the cardiac rhythm, and the metabolism, besides controlling the reactions and the movements of the body.

With the primitive brain the first mammals could feel, but perhaps they would not come to think. This brain was rather emotional. With the passage of time in the first mammals, the limbic system was composed of the thalamus, hypothalamus, hippocampus, and amygdala. These new brain structures developed about 60 million years ago as the structure of the primitive brain formed around the brainstem. As it evolved, the limbic system developed learning and memory. This allowed mammals to remember an experience of the past and determine whether to repeat it in the present. These two powerful tools allowed an animal to be much smarter in choosing a more appropriate response as it adapted to the changing situations around it. For example, if a food caused discomfort, it could be avoided the next time. Decisions such as knowing what to eat and what to dispose of were still largely determined by smell. Thanks to the interrelated work between the olfactory bulb and the limbic system, odors were distinguished and recognized and then compared with past odors to determine good and bad.

With the limbic system also came initial emotions like fear and pleasure. The emotional brain had arrived. However, evolution would continue its work, and later mammals would evolve into primates, whose nervous system would grow enormously. The humans who descended from the primates about five million years ago had a nervous system that was even more astonishing. Throughout evolution, the brain continued to grow from the bottom up. From the brain from which the emotional centers emerged, additional layers of tissue were formed about two million years ago. This new part of the brain from which the thinking brain evolved is known as the neocortex. In this part of the brain reside the higher cognitive abilities, such as language, analysis, abstraction, problem solving, and planning. These abilities allowed humans to develop will and thought.

After forming the neocortex, the brain continued to evolve over time. In the Homo Sapiens that lived about 200,000 years ago, the neocortex was much bigger than in any other species. The neocortex is the seat of thought, containing the centers that compare and understand what the senses perceive. In addition, it allows us to have feelings about ideas, art, symbols, and imagination. It is the neocortex that makes us human. In its evolution, the neocortex was creating mechanisms that would help us survive in the face of adversity. Thus, the neocortex came to design strategies and long-term planning to conquer the world.

One of the determining factors in the development of the nervous system of humans was improvement in the senses, especially in the sense of smell and touch introduced by mammals. Once the nervous system of mammals became larger and more complex, the sense of sight also made improvements that allowed the mammal to see in color. The senses in mammals would evolve as never before in some other species. In mammals many sensory receptors were developed to capture much better information about light, smell, sounds, heat, and even the taste of their world to know it better and to have a better chance of surviving in it.

With your sense of vision, you can see all your surroundings, including the size, shape, color, and location of the things around you. The eye, the organ of sight, can distinguish and perceive very small variations in shape, color, luminosity, and distance. It then converts the electromagnetic waves or vibrations of the perceived light into a certain type of nerve impulses transmitted by the optic nerve to the brain, which processes it to convert it into the image we see.

With the sense of smell, you can smell and differentiate odors from things in the environment. One of the most primitive senses of the nervous system is the sense of smell, which detects chemical compounds in the environment. It is believed that the improvements in the sense of smell were the initial step of evolution and the enormous development and complexity of the nervous system in mammals. The smells of things around us come wrapped in the air we inhale through the nose, the organ of smell. Inside the nostrils, odor particles dissolve in the mucus. Then the olfactory receptor cells or neurons detect the odors and transmit the information to the olfactory bulb in the brain, where the olfactory sensations are associated with memories of people, places, or situations related to those odors.

In primitive times, detection of odor became the supreme sense for survival. After analyzing the odors, the existence of other living species can be detected. The brain can distinguish between something nutritious, such as prey; something poisonous or dangerous, such as a predator; and something desirable, such as a sexual partner. The old centers of emotion began to evolve from the smell, which was initially composed of thin layers of neurons to analyze the smell. One of those layers of neurons took the smell and classified it—food or toxin, sexual partner, friend or foe. At second layer sent messages to the nervous system indicating to the organism how to act: approaching, biting, or fleeing.

In addition to smell, the sense of taste is also a chemical sense. In the first animals, the sense of taste allowed them to detect something was food or might be toxic, helping the animal continue to survive. Early animals could also use their tongue to lick scented marks on objects to get information about other animals. The sensory cells of those first animals to detect the flavors were not only on the tongue; some were also on the skin, the legs, the whiskers and other parts of the body.

In mammals and especially in humans, the sense of taste has evolved a lot. This sense allows you to perceive the taste of the things in your environment, especially the food that is brought to your mouth. , When the food enters the mouth, its flavor is a combination of sensory information that originates with the senses of taste, smell, and touch. In addition to the flavor of a food, you also know its smell, its texture, and its temperature.

The initial function of the sense of taste has been to protect the being from not eating foods that can cause any harm to the body. However, the sense of taste also allows for a sense of enjoyment.

The tongue is the main organ of taste. In the tongue of humans are thousands of taste buds with receptor cells; when stimulated by the chemicals in the food, these cells send nerve impulses to the brain. The tongue can detect the four basic traditional tastes: sweet, salty, bitter, and acidic. A fifth and recently discovered flavor, umami, distinguishes the flavor of proteins, such as meat.

With the sense of hearing you can hear the sounds as well as perceive the volume, tone, timbre, and the direction from which the sound comes. The ear is the organ responsible for hearing. This organ picks up the sound waves and transmits them through the external auditory canal toward the eardrum, which processes the sounds saves and sends vibrationsto the middle ear. There the vibrations move the chain of ossicles, formed by the hammer, the anvil, and the stirrup. The resulting vibrations enter the inner ear, where the fluide-filled, snail-shaped cochlea transforms vibrations into nerve impulses that are carried to the brain by the auditory nerve and are interpreted into sounds.

The ear is also responsible for the balance of the body. Within the inner ear above the cochlea are three semicircular canals that communicate with each other; these contain a gelatinous fluid and thousands of tiny hairs connected to a cranial nerve that connects with the brain. When we move the head, the gelatinous liquid also moves, and the tiny hairs send information to the brain about the direction and speed of the movement. This allows the body to maintain its balance, which also becomes more stable with the help of sight. The sense of balance began to evolve in fish, then in amphibians and reptiles, without having much to do with hearing.

The sense of touch was the first to develop. From the first microorganisms that formed in the waters of the great ocean, the first organisms that came out of the water to settle on the surface, the sense of touch always existed. The first mammals introduced improvements in the sense of touch with the development of body hair that produced an improvement in motor coordination. Body hair, in addition to serving as thermal insulation, was used as receptors that provided information on how to move safely in enclosed spaces and avoid damage in the dark.

The sense of touch allows us as humans to detect temperatue, pressure, surface type, and vibrations of objects in our environment. us. The sense of touch even allows us to perceive sensation of internal pain. The information from these receptors is sent to the brain through nerve fibers. In addition to being the organ of the sense of touch, the skin also protects the body from physical, chemical, and bacterial agents. It also helps regulate temperature through sweat glands and blood capillaries.

Evolution has led us to the development of our wonderful nervous system, but it also resulted in a drastic change the location of the nervous system. After the first hominids descended from mammals about seven million years ago, they began to walk on two legs. When mammals walked on four legs, the nervous system was located in the front part of the body; when the animals began to walk on two legs, the nervous system moved to the top of the body. Located at the top of the human body, the nervous system is in a very privileged position next to the eyes, ears, nose, and mouth, where it receives sensory information before any other nucleus.

# Sharper Vision

The first insects evolved from the trilobites that lived in the great ocean about 400 million years ago. These insects were the first to emerge from the water to the surface, and they remain the most abundant animals on the surface of the Earth. They all have very complex, compound eyes. Insects developed their eyes independently but of the same genetic structure. In a microscopic lens array, they work together to form images. The more lenses, the finer the details of the image. The composed eyes of the insects were the most successful of the nature for its time.

The first fish that became shallow-water swimmers were the first vertebrates to use their eyes to see and explore the beauty of the Earth's surface. Those eyes continued in the creatures that conquered the surface and that became the dinosaurs after about 230 million years. For the next 160 million years, the dinosaurs dominated the animal kingdom.

One thing that made these animals so successful was their ability to focus on their prey.

The dinosaurs had the biggest eyes in history. Their eyes gave them a binocular vision to have better reach over their prey. In binocular vision, the vision of each eye intertwines with that of the other to result in a sweeping vision in three dimensions. The dinosaurs' vision then evolved to predatory vision, in which the eyes were closer together; vision in the prey evolved to protect it from predators, with the eyes farther apart. The rabbit, for example, has eyes that are extremely far apart, giving it a 360-degree view of its surroundings.

About 100 million years ago, when dinosaurs dominated the earth, mammals were no bigger than mice are today. They adapted to live at night to better protect themselves from the great predators and consequently developed the ability to see in the dark. Night vision is considered a success of the evolution of the eye and is essential for the survival of many mammals today. In some species that needed good night vision, the cornea of the eye became larger. Other mammals, such as felines, developed eyes that glow in the dark and function as a kind of reflecting mirror. With this type of eye, felines need only about 17 percent of the light that we need to see in the dark.

Even though we are mammals, humans do not have the ability to see in the dark like other mammals. This is because about thirty million years ago, our ancestors changed from nocturnal creatures to those who were awake during the day. When the primates came down from the trees, they had to develop eyes to see the world like never before, and that gave us the ability to see color. The human eye can see 2.3 million colors with greater speed and precision than a computer, making our color vision superior to that of many other mammals. Only a small number of species, including our primate cousins, can see a full range of yellows, blues, greens, and reds. This depth of vision did not exist in early primates. Its evolution has its roots because of the massive extinction of sixty-five million years ago, when the giant asteroid caused the extinction of the dinosaurs and allowed the mammals to emerge.

After the primates came down from the trees, they became a new species. One of those lineages became active during the day. These were the apes, the ancestors of today's monkeys and humans. They developed a new adaptation in their eyes not seen in past species. This included an expansion of vision to distinguish a standard range of colors consisting of blues and greens, one that now includes red.

Natural selection improved color vision so that primates could see food better. Red was developed to distinguish red from the leaves they ate. The redder the food, the more nutrients it contained. For that reason, these animals developed the ability to see leaves in the distance, which gave them greater opportunity to survive. This way they could save time and go straight to the red leaves.

Primates would also soon reap the fruit of another of their crucial adaptations: binocular vision. As mentioned, predators developed it first, but in primates it served a new function: depth perception, which is very important for an animal who has to jump from one tree to another. Over time primates developed a sixty-degree binocular vision alongside birds and prey animals. It served primates to capitalize on their coordination of hands and eyes.

The eyes are the greatest achievements of evolution. No two species look at the world in the same way, and sight evolved according to need. Among the most accurate eyes are those of the eagle. In most cases, the bigger the eye, the better the vision—but while the eyes of the eagle are almost the size and weight of ours, the eagle's vision is as much as three times sharper and better than ours.

The force that has driven this great innovation in vision has been evolution. The eagle has developed the most powerful eyes in nature, but the eagle's eyes are just one example of many that have evolved over time. The eyes on the animals have not evolved from the same ancestral eye. They have evolved several times in different animal lineages. However, evolution has used the same basic genes to form eyes in completely different animals like flies, squids, and even humans.

## Digestive System Adaptations

About 350 million years ago a species of fish discovered a new place of opportunity as it came out of the water to the surface, and a new way of feeding itself created new evolutionary opportunities. Some vertebrates on the surface developed digestive systems suitable for eating leaves. For example, birds, descendants of dinosaurs, use small stones called *gastroliths* to aid their digestion. These birds intentionally swallow the gastroliths with their food. These gastroliths lodge in the stomach or gizzard, the digestive organ of birds, where the gastroliths act as teeth to crush the food and extract the nutrients. This is the same system that dinosaurs used to aid their digestion.

When the first mammals emerged after the extinction of dinosaurs, a type of lizard also evolved to take advantage of the generous source of food. Snakes—slow-moving, cold-blooded animals without legs—invented a radical way to feed themselves. Because they don't have jaws or teeth enabling them to chew their food, they swallow their victims whole. They could swallow something larger in diameter than their head. Their entire body is a long digestive tube. After seven days the prey is digested, and most of it is stored as energy; as a result, snakes can go without eating for a long time, in some cases for years. Snakes are not the only animals that have developed extreme digestive tracts in order to survive. Other animals would make other special modifications as well.

Some twenty million years ago the australopithecus appeared; a small hominid in size, its brain was a little bigger than the brains of the other primates. With its jaws, teeth, and digestive system, the australopithecus developed improvements in its digestion. These hominids were our ancestors, but the new species developed a larger body, twice the size of its predecessor, while its teeth and stomachs were reduced. All these changes were due to radical changes in their diets. Each organ of the body needs its share of energy from food. The brain and the digestive tract are the ones that most require energy.

Australopithecus learned two things: to eat more food and to use tools to help get that food. They used tools to cut and crush the food, making digestion easier. But what most helped in the diet was the use of fire. They learned that cooked meat tasted better. Cooking food changed everything. It allowed us to get more energy from food with less effort, enabling us to get 40 percent more calories from food. All the energy that had been used to maintain large digestive tracts could now be used for the brain.

# Circulatory and Respiratory System Adaptations

Both the circulatory and respiratory systems of the vertebrates continued to evolve after the first fish became amphibian and left the water for the surface of the Earth.

Fish breathe through a system of gills where they pass oxygen from the water to their circulatory system, which is a closed system. Blood goes from the heart to the gills, then to the rest of the body, and finally back to the heart. Its circulation is simple, and its heart has two chambers: a ventricle and an atrium. Deoxygenated blood comes from the tissues of the body and passes to the ventricle, which sends it to the gills for oxygination. The oxygenated blood is then distributed throughout the body.

In amphibians, the circulation doubled through the appearance of the pulmonary circuit of circulation. In the pulmonary circuit, the venous blood is sent to the lungs for oxygenation and is then sent back to the heart. The systematic circuit of circulation then carries that oxygenated blood throughout the body, bringing back to the heart the deoxygenated blood collected from the tissues of the body. Amphibian lungs were small and underdeveloped, but they served the purpose of gas exchange with the external environment. In other words, they were able to breathe oxygen and expel carbon dioxide. Absorbed oxygen is diffused from these lungs into the blood of the circulatory system. Their heart is three-chambered consisting of one ventricle and two atria.

The circulation of reptiles doubles again because there are two circuits: one circuit takes blood to the lungs and after oxygenation returns it to the heart; the other circuit carries the oxygenated blood throughout the body, collects deoxygenated blood, and returns to the heart. The circulation of reptiles is also vascular because it leaves the heart through blood vessels. It is also closed because it never leaves these vessels; that is, there are no large spaces or gaps without blood. And it is also an incomplete circulation because deoxygenated and oxygenated blood are mixed in the ventricle, as in amphibians.

The heart of the reptile has three cavities: two atria and one ventricle, partially separated by a membrane that does not completely divide them. In the heart of amphibians and most reptiles, deoxygenated blood from the body reaches the right atrium and oxygenated blood from the lungs reaches the left atrium. Both auricles communicate with the ventricle. However, deoxygenated blood tends to remain in the right side of the ventricle to be pumped by the blood vessels into the lungs, while most of the oxygenated blood remains in the left ventricle to be pumped to the rest of the body. In reptiles, the separation of blood is more controlled because the right and left sides of the ventricle are separated by a membrane. All reptiles possess this three-cavity heart except for crocodiles, which have a heart divided into four chambers, as do mammals and birds.

In birds and mammals, as well as in crocodiles, the circulation is double, complete, and closed. The heart has four cavities: two atria, where blood enters, and two ventricles, where blood is pumped out of the heart. Into the right atrium comes the deoxygenated blood that comes from the tissues of the body; by contracting, the heart pumps blood to the lungs, which are highly developed in birds and mammals. In the lungs, blood collects oxygen through respiration, enters the left atrium, passes into the left ventricle, and is distributed throughout the body's tissues.

Hot-blooded birds and mammals have a high oxygen requirement, so their blood supply must be more efficient than that of cold-blooded animals. This demand resulted in the development of better lungs and a four-cavity heart. This new heart of birds and mammals is the same as the human heart. It has two left and two right ventricles, which separate the oxygenated blood from the deoxygenated blood, guaranteeing that the blood reaching the tissues of the body has the highest oxygen content possible. Coordinated contractions of the atria and ventricles form the cardiac cycle.

# Reproduction on the Earth's Surface

For hundreds of millions of years, animals remained confined to the Earth's oceans. But some 370 million years ago, a single lineage of fish began to move toward the shores of Earth. These animals were the amphibians, which developed legs from their fins as they lived for a long time in the marshy waters of the coast. Over time, those legs became strong enough to let them live out of the water and on the surface. But this new world represented unfamiliar problems in terms of reproduction.

In the great ocean, the ancestors of amphibians simply dropped their sperm into a stream of water to fertilize their eggs, a process known as *external fertilization*. But that would not work on dry land. So a group of these amphibians, the ancestors of reptiles and mammals, successfully changed their method of reproduction in a very different way. The reptiles developed internal fertilization and thus continued to evolve an extraordinary way to protect their creature: the amniotic egg. This marvel of evolution not only nourishes the creature in the egg, but its hard shell also protects the egg from drying out.

The amniotic egg gave reptiles the ability to conquer the Earth by reproducing, scattering, and growing on an unprecedented scale. But for dinosaurs this sexual activity could be a problem: mating was not always easy for these massaive creatures, whose very size could interfere with necessary sexual activity.

Dinosaurs evolved to be the largest animals that ever lived on Earth, but sex between big creatures could be complicated. Fossil records say that they did have sex and reproduced by internal fertilization like birds today. However, paleontologists don't yet know how the dinosaurs had sex. They obviously did, though, and did it well, as they lived and dominated the planet for more than 160 million years.

After the dinosaurs disappeared, the Earth became a site of waste where insects persisted. How they have survived is still a mystery. Maybe the impact of the asteroid caused a temperature change that may have caused the insects to hibernate; when they re-emerged they might have flourished, developing new forms of reproduction at high rates.

In the world of insects, sex is a sperm war. Females are looking for multiple sexual friends, hoping to have many males so that their offspring have a better chance of survival. In order to make this possible, insects have developed the largest variety of penis forms on the planet.!

The force that drives creatures to pass their genes on and ensure the survival of their race through sex is very strong and causes evolutionary changes. This process is called *sexual selection*. To be successful in terms of evolution, our genes must be contained in the next generation; to ensure the survival of the species, genes must be shared with beings who have better qualities. Animals don't mate with just anybody; they mate only with the best specimens that have the best chance of ensuring continuation of the species. Their mates must also share in the responsibility of protecting the young. Some males must even fight, dance, or do something else to attract a female.

Human beings emerged from their cousins the primates only a few million years ago. When our ancestors descended from the trees and began to walk on two legs instead of four, they had to make several changes regarding sex, since the female vagina, vaginal canal, and clitoris changed considerably. During the slow evolutionary process toward walking on two legs, the vagina changed its position of penetration. Before penetration was possible only from behind; in the new bipedal position, the vagina could also be penetrated from the front. The vaginal canal went from horizontal to vertical in the bipedal position, meaning the penis had to penetrate more deeply into the vaginal canal. That caused an enlargement of the penis. The clitoris also had to evolve and adapt to different shapes and sizes to provide more pleasure and the possibility of better orgasms. That was especially true for the woman's orgasm, because it stimulates the male ejaculation and thus ensures fertilization.

With the evolution of human beings, the cerebral cortex began to form a few million years ago. This caused the brain to get bigger. With the growth of the brain, sexuality also increased. However, the brain grew so much that it became a problem in sexual reproduction: the skull was too big for the baby to pass through the birth canal of its mother, which in turn had become narrower due to the weight and the additional pressure involved in upright walking. For this reason, babies can not be in the womb too long, or the skull would become so large that it would prevent passage through the vaginal canal.

The bonds between mother, child, and the whole family developed to guarantee survival of the species and thus deepen the love between human beings. Sex and the mind have interconnected, and humans have changed the mechanism of sex forever. Today people can reproduce without having sex; creatures can be cloned and fertilized without sex. With these developments, human beings are controlling their own evolution. In the future, parents will likely be able to choose the children they want to have—and may choose to have only those with the most desirable qualities in a type of artificial selection manipulated by the human being.

# 5

# THE HUMAN BEINGS

To become the human beings that we are today, we went through a long and lengthy evolution period from the Paleolitic and the Neolitic periods of Prehistory to the invention of writing that started our civilization. We descend from the hominids, from whom the homo genus (Homo Habilis, Homo Erectuus and Homo Sapiens) evolved. The people of today are commonly referred to as modern human and are the descendants of the Homo Sapiens. We inherited from them their intellect and the capability of language. It was the Homo Sapiens who brought us here in his great migrations from Africa. As modern humans, our behavior, thoughts, beliefs, and art have evolved to result in the culture and society we currently enjoy.

# 5.1 FIRST HOMINIDS: THE AUSTRALOPITHECUS

Primates evolved from mammals about seventy million years ago. From these monkeys or apes evolved a species known as the great apes, which included the bonobos, chimpanzees, gorillas, and orangutans. The members of this new species, separated from the great apes about seven million years ago, were forced to walk erect on their two hind legs to survive, thus giving rise to the so-called hominids. They constitute the family of the higher primates, from which later evolved the gender of the homos, and, in turn, man.

More than seven million years ago, the African continent underwent certain changes that would have great implications on that group of primates from which the first hominids formed and on the evolutionary process toward humans. Africa was becoming drier, which reduced the forests and jungles and made the continent more desert. This phenomenon happened after the formation of the Himalayas about four thousand kilometers east of the African continent.

Before the Himalayas, the climate in Africa was warm and humid all year round. But after the formation of the largest mountain range on the planet, the African climate began to change. When the Himalayan peaks rose to more than sixteen thousand feet, they impacted the global climate. In summer, the heat of the Sun generates a great ascending current of warm and dry air above the mountain range of the Himalayas, which descends toward Africa. Due to this current, an annual cycle occurred on this continent that includes a dry season. As a result, the Sahara Desert began to spread, and the area of moist forests dramatically reduced.

These new conditions forced the primates to have to walk on the surface in search of their food, since their trees had disappeared. The body structure of the primates had not been developed for this new way of moving from one side to the other. To look for food they had to raise their heads to see better, especially in areas of tall grasslands. In addition, having a raised head helped them see any threats, including predators. With primates being on two legs much of the day, they became accustomed to walking on their two hind legs and using their two front legs as hands. We call that position *bipedalism*, and we call species that walk on two legs *bipeds*.

This is how this group of primates evolved in the earliest hominids about five million years ago. These hominids were very similar to today's monkeys. From the hominids evoled the human beings. In fact, from a genetic point of view, the difference between the human and the monkey is very small: only 2 percent.

In addition to the ability to walk upright, these hominids developed a larger brain size, which allowed them to start the evolutionary race toward the human being. The first hominids could adapt to the life that they had to live in the African savannas and plains due to the climatic change.

One of the earliest hominids who walked upright on their two hind legs and with their hands free, as we do today, were Australopithecus, monkeys from the south who lived about five million years ago in what we know today as Ethiopia, Tanzania, Kenya, South Africa, and Chad, where their remains have been found. They had long limbs, powerful jaws, and strong molars. Like the chimpanzees, the Australopithecus fed mostly on fruits they picked from the trees. However, they also ate certain small animals like ants that served as an extra supply of protein in their diets, just as chimpanzees do.

The difference between these two species was the ecosystem in which each of them had to live. Chimpanzees lived in forests that did not undergo climate change, while the Australopithecus lived in the savannah, where they had to walk and travel long distances to collect their food. The Australopithecus lived most of their lives in savannah environments that probably included the presence of rivers.

The Australopithecus rarely exceeded a height of three feet and weighed about sixty-six pounds. They used their long, fine hands to press or to grab objects, fruits, and roots. They also had the ability to make some rudimentary tools of sticks and probably formed small communities in which each male lived with a group of females.

It is possible that the most glorious moment of those early hominids, of which we evolved, would have been when one of them grabbed a piece of wood and began to form mental images to revolutionize the world forever. By lifting that piece of wood, the early hominid invented a weapon to protect himself from his predators and even to kill other smaller animals and thus get his livelihood. Later, after a certain level of evolution, they made spears from their pieces of stick to defend themselves better from predators and more efficiently and safely turn larger animals into their prey. They also used pieces of wood to make primitive tools. Thus, began the flashes of intelligence in the small heads of those first beings from which we evolved. Their brains were not well developed, as their skulls had a volume of only about five hundred cubic centimeters.

The most famous Australopithecus was the so-called "Lucy," whose fossilized remains were found in Africa. Those remains were of a small female skeleton; approximately four feet tall, she was about twenty years old. She was a hominid because her position was erect.

It is believed that the Australopithecus disappeared due to the climate crisis that transformed the forested African savanna into deserts. These new conditions made it much more difficult to obtain their food, so they had to eat everything they found, including roots and even meat left in the bones by carnivorous animals. Before its disappearance, the australopithecus went through an enormous food shortage, which became a threat of death about two million years ago. Global cooling and a drought caused the tropical forests to decline and forced the australopithecus to retreat upward toward the equator. To survive this enormous food shortage, Australopithecus had to seek a new diet to replace the fruits as the basis of their daily diet.

According to the fossil record, two types of Australopithecus came into existence in southern Africa. One—referred to by paleontologists as *paranthropus*—incorporated roots into their diet and remained vegetarian. The roots eaten by the paranthropus apparently had great nutritional value and could be found all the time even though the weather was dry. These vegetarian Australopithecus were five feet tall and of robust corpulence. They managed to survive for something more than a million years or so eating their roots until they disappeared.

The other type of Australopithecus incorporated meat into their diets to become carnivorous about 2.5 million years ago. This new diet allowed the australopithecus to reach a height of 5.57 feet and gave it a very thin build, perhaps because of the long walks it had to do in search of food, which was mostly found in the leftovers of the prey that other animals discarded. In most cases, the leftovers were bones with little meat. However, the australopithecus scraped those bones to get the meat and the marrow inside the bones.

Unfortunately, the surviving Australopithecus then faced a crucial stage in their evolution: they had to cope with a number of adversities in the ecosystem of the Great African Rift in which they lived. The Great Rift Valley of Africa formed more than 30 million years ago. This valley is a great geological fracture about 62 miles wide that extends for about 3,700 miles from south to north. While most of it is along the African continent, one part extends to the Red Sea and the other to the Jordan Valley. This vast valley divided the African savannah into several ecosystems that led to the development of animals in different directions.

The wide development of animals in the various ecosystems of the Grand Rift brought new changes in the life of the carnivorous Australopithecus. In deciding to be carnivorous, it faced major challenges. To satisfy the demand to eat meat in its food, Australopithecus decided to have a safer source of food. That led to deciding to go after small animals to kill and eat them, which was the invention of the hunt. In that hunt, the Australopithecus had to compete with great carnivorous animals of the time. This would be a fierce competition to the point of putting their own lives at risk: lions and tigers were better developed and equipped and dominated the environment; in addition, the saber-tooth tiger liked to eat hominids.

The carnivorous Australopithecus was not yet ready to face this unequal fight, since it had neither the resources nor the intelligence by then. That would need to change later due precisely the new diet based on meat.

Eating meat had a significant impact on the growth of the brain, which is the part of the body that consumes more energy. The high caloric content of the meat could produce that energy. The more energy the brain received, the more it grew, and the more intelligence the Australopithecus gained. The disadvantages the Australopithecus had in the hunting of their prey was compensated for by their intelligence, through which it became a better hunter than the other animals. In addition, having more food for females resulted in many more offspring bringing, causing an increase in the population of the species. The Australopithecus showed new generations how to hunt and make tools, becoming better able to survive and making way for the evolutionary path of Homo Habilis and the rest of the Homos.

# 5.2 THE HOMOS

The homo genus evolved from the first hominids. The great characteristics very exclusive to the Homos include their intellect and language, which made them a unique species in the whole planet. The members of the genus homo are Homo Habilis, Homo Erectus, and Homo Sapiens. Homo Habilis were the first species that used and created tools of stone. They developed great abilities and became very skillfull. Homo Erectus managed to develop better tools. He also developed the ability to handle and control fire so successfully that he has been called the "Great Master of Fire." Homo Sapiens was the wise man that perfected tools, the control of fire, and oral language, which was very important in enabling him to transfer knowledge from one generation to the next.

## Homo Habilis

Habilis lived in Africa between 2.5 and 1.5 million years ago and is thought to have coexisted with the Australopithecus before they disappeared for good.

These hominids, descendants of the Australopithecus, also walked erect on two feet and had great abilities. This hominid had very strong and robust hands, which made them stand out as the first species that used and created tools of stone. He is represented by the illustration on the next page. In fact, their fossils were found with tools made of stone. In addition, they were the first to build a kind of hut with tree branches that were anchored to the ground with a pile of stones; the design of these huts simulated the crown of a tree, a place that was their home for a long time, when they were living on the trees.

Homo Habilis perhaps began using the stones available around them to throw them at their predators to protect themselves. After the Homo Habilis realized that he could even kill another animal with these stones, he then used them to hunt and obtain his food. Both in self-defense and hunting, the Homo Habilis became an expert stone shooter, apparently able to kill an animal with a single stone. Perhaps by accident he discovered that stones with sharp edges could cut his own hand; he then appears to have used sharp stones to cut the skin and meat of the animal. Taking advantage of the stone to improve living conditions ushered in what is known today as the Stone Age.

Homo Habilis had to adopt a more erect position than their Australopithecus ancestors because climatic variations made the grasslands grow, forcing them to stand straighter on their feet to better discern possible dangers. They had a brain of about 750 cubic centimeters, bigger than that of the Australopithecus. Their most important characteristic was the change in their way of feeding: they not only ate fruits and vegetables but also animals. The incorporation of meat in their daily diet was a very important factor in the development of the neocortex of the brain of the early Homos. Some evolved to become Homo Erectus.

The rest of the Habilis Homos became extinct about 1.5 million years ago.

## Homo Erectus

When the Homo Habilis realized that the more erect they walked the better they could see both opportunities and dangers, they ended up adopting the erect position completely when walking. That posture allowed them to better see the horizon above the herbaceous vegetation. As a result, Homo Habilis evolved into Homo Erectus.

The Erectus (or erect man) was tall-bodied, had great musculature, and had more pronounced facial features and thicker eyebrows than Homo Sapiens. Homo Erectus lived and prospered in the wooded savannas of Africa almost 2 million years ago and had a brain of about 1,100 cubic centimeters, much larger than the previous species and almost the size of the modern human brain. As seen at left, Homo Erectus managed to handle fire about 1.5 million years ago. He also managed to develop tools and appears to have had some sort of rudimentary language.

This ancestor of ours was a great innovator, developing techniques to work the stone and produce better tools. Among the tools of Homo Erectus were crushers and hand axes that could be worked on both sides and that were designed to cut and crush. There were also knives, as shown in the following illustration.

The Homo Erectus discovered how to remove slabs from a stone by hitting it near the edges with a stronger stone. The large piece of stone could become a heavy tool that could crush or grind. The slabs were turned into light tools like the scrapers used to prepare leather. These stones were usually of a type of sedimentary rock like flint, which is constituted of micro-crystalline silica. The flint is hard and tends to break into pieces.

To remove slabs from a flint stone, Homo Erectus held it firmly with one hand over the thigh of his leg or against another larger stone and then struck it with another stone. The stone was worked to remove slabs on the other side. With better tools, Homo Erectus became a better hunter.

Homo Erectus perfected the use of fire in such a way that he is known as the great master of fire. He managed to control it like no other species had ever done. To make fire, he held a stick at its top and turned it between his hands, transmitting a circular motion to the stic. The lower tip of the stick, in contact with a piece of dry wood, was heated by the friction until it began to burn. Blowing with his mouth, he managed to produce fire with the help of dry straw. Homo Erectus used fire to produce light during the nigh, protecting themselves from their predatorsThey also used fire for cooking.

Homo Erectus was the first hominid that traveled widely over the surface of the Earth, initiating the great journey to populate the planet. From Africa, Homo Erectus traveled to the southeast of what is now Asia, Europe, and even reached what is now China. As he faced the cold northern climate, he began to deveop clothing.

With the beginning of the glaciations about 120,000 years ago, seasonal weather became more rigorous and cold, and keeping warm was an indispensable requirement for survival. At first, Homo Erectus discovered that he could wear animal skins on his body. He then began to sew them using strips of the same leather and opening holes in the skin with his stone knife; later he turned his knife into a piercer and then into a needle.

During the glaciation, the Homo Erectus hunted animals to eat their meat and to shelter themselves with their skins. By that time, Homo Erectus already had control of fire and knew how to prepare the leather of the animal skins for clothing, which allowed him to live in zones near the glaciers during the glaciation.

Homo Erectus appears to have worn simple animal fur garments, judging from the tools and utensils that have been found, including drills and scrapers that were used to clean the skins with which they made the clothing. Perhaps the first treated skins were not used as clothing, but as material to cover the home. Skins were probably also used as a blanket or as camouflage while hunting. What is certain is that from this practice came the idea of covering themselves with furs to keep warm, especially while they were outside their abode and far from any of their fires.

In making clothes with the skins of the animals he hunted, Homo Erectusused his mouth as another tool. He held the skins with his teeth and used his hands to scrape the skins clean and prepare them for the making of the garments and for other uses. It is also possible to soften hard skins with blows.

Over time, perhaps thousands of years, the techniques were refined. The first improved scrapers, punches, and strips were used to join or sew the skins. What began as a kind of blanket used to cover the body became a sewn garment that was later perfected by Homo Sapiens.

## Homo Sapiens

Evolution did not stop with Homo Erectus, nor will it ever stop. Homo Erectus followed an evolutionary path that brought about significant changes. His physical features became less pronounced and he became smarter until he evolved into Homo Sapiens about 200,000 years ago. Homo Sapiens is the wise man who later evolved to become the humans as we know them; in fact, Homo Sapiens physically resembled the modern human.

Homo sapiens emerged on the African continent and developed a brain with a capacity of about 1,400 cubic centimeters. The brain of the early Homos continued to evolve over time until the neocortex of the Homo Sapiens was much larger than in any other species. The seat of thought, the neocortex contains the centers that compare and understand what the senses perceive. In addition, it governs what we think about and allows us to have feelings regarding ideas, art, symbols, and imagination. It is the neocortex that ultimately makes us human. In its evolution, the neocortex was creating mechanisms that would help the being to survive in the face of adversity. Thus, the neocortex came to design strategies and long-term planning that allowed the species to conquer the world.

The earliest fossils of Homo Sapiens found in Africa had a smaller jaw and a more prominent forehead, because a larger skull was needed to accommodate brain growth. The Homo Sapiens, therefore, had greater capacity of thought and was more intelligent. This allowed our immediate ancestors 170,000 years ago to invent the imagination. That transcendental event catapulted Homo Sapiens into a being that could solve a problem, had great technical capacity, and ushered in technology. Homo Sapiens first began to promote the manufacture of better tools and then perfected the control the fire.

The imagination allowed Homo Sapiens to make major changes in their behavior and way of life. The perfection of oral language was decisive in the progress achieved by Homos Sapiens, enabling them to transfer knowledge from one generation to the next. Language made them able to understand the world in a different way than anyone else had ever done before.

Before or during a hunting expedition, language enabled Homo Sapiens to exchange information on where the herds of animals might go, since those animals migrated to the rhythm of the climatic seasons. This allowed the Homo Sapiens to organize their hunting activity and predict its outcome. After a day of hunting, Homo Sapiens could gather to discuss and analyze what they did well or badly during the hunt, so they could learn from that experience and improve the next time.

About 35,000 years ago, Homo Sapiens had invented an instrument that allowed them to predict when animals would reach certain places, which greatly contributed to their planning of a hunt. In some cave paintings of the time, Homo Sapiens outlined their hunting plans on the walls of the caves where they still lived.

In addition to having better hunting techniques, Homo Sapiens also achieved complete control of fire, wore better garments, and used more and better stone and bone tools. For more than two million years, tools did not have any type of handle; it was not until about 200,000 years ago that wooden handles were used. The stones were fixed on these with strings of vegetable fibers or with resins; the latter were sometimes mixed with wax or bitumen. Small, pointed flakes were used to make arrows, spears, and harpoons and were used as knives or saws inserted in hand-carved wooden handles.

Clothing initially served a practical function but later assumed a more decorative one. Over the years, clothing evolved from simple and basic to very elaborate garments with some complexity. Some of these garments included shells and feathers as ornaments. It was Homo Sapiens who began to make distinctive designs. They differentiated suits of clothing for different purposes, for different sexes, and even over time for different classes.

We could say that fashion began during that part of human history when writing had not yet been invented. Later, in the Neolithic period or late part of the Stone Age, agriculture and livestock offered new materials for new garments. The complexity of societies increased, and clothing was a significant trait. The greater quantity of materials and its continuous supply that occurred with cattle raising and the agriculture in the Neolithic period allowed Homo Sapiens to practice and experiment with new fabrics and different types and styles of clothing.

All the advances made by Homos Sapiens resulted in an increase in the size of their populations, as well as their ritual and artistic manifestations. Homo Sapiens perfected the design and manufacture of tools, clothing, and language. He was the protagonist of the most significant changes in economic and social organization, as well as the first forms of agriculture, the domestication of animals, and life in towns and cities. With his great intellect, Homo Sapiens accomplished the great migrations from Africa to where we are today.

## Intellect: The Homo's Great Characteristic

The most remarkable and important characteristic of the genus Homo, from which the word *man* derives, is his intelligence. The members of this genus evolved from the Australopithecus and have been characterized by the large size of their brain. Most members of the genus Homo have brains of a distinct structure greater than 700 cubic centimeters, considerably larger than the early hominids and Australopithecus. The brain of early Homos was already more asymmetrical. The asymmetry between both hemispheres of the brain is related to the specialization of each of the brain regions in distinct functions. In the skulls of the early Homos, this cerebral asymmetry could already be observed.

In addition, they had a more developed frontal lobe, the front region of the cerebral neocortex. The frontal lobe is responsible for the exclusive complex thinking capacity of the Homos, in which the capacity for thought appears highly developed. Among the functions of the frontal lobe are to establish the sequence of movements of the speech apparatus to produce sounds, control of emotions, concentration, planning, anticipation, and control of memory.

Throughout human evolution, the cerebral neocortex, including the frontal lobe, has increased its development. The increase of the brain of the first Homos is related to more advantages for social development within the group. Also, the larger size of the brain is related to the development of linguistic abilities, which are necessary to greater social development. This brings us to the other characteristic of Homos: language.

## Language: The Other Great Characteristic

Language, the ability to orally transmit thoughts to others, is the other unique feature of Homos. To develop it, the earliest hominids likely continued to use vocal sounds in the form of a scream, growl, or moan in the face of fear, rage, and pain, which they had inherited from their ancestors, the great apes. These monkeys could, for example, when threatened by danger make a shout whose magnitude was reflected in the intensity of the cry.

Eventually different screams denoted distinct types of hazards. For example, the scream when an eagle approached could be stronger than when a tiger approached, since the eagle could catch them even in the treetop and represented greater danger. Most glorious is the fact that other monkeys managed to associate the cries with the perils and act to avoid the threat. It is at that moment that communication between them is born, because they managed to pass a thought from one being to another.

Over time, the hominids could use their free hands to indicate the direction of the danger in addition to emitting screams, which made communication more effective. They could make a sound and point to what they were referring to. They could also point to an object and try to communicate what they wanted through hand signals. Over time, communication progressed, especially with the arrival of members of the genus Homos. In addition to transmitting messages, the Homos could also exchange messages until they eventually formed a communication system using signs, gestures, and sounds.

Later the vocal sounds became words and the communication system became oral language, which was perfected with the arrival of Homo Sapiens about 200,000 years ago. Homo Sapiens already had developed the region of the brain called *broca,* where language is produced. In addition, his larynx was located below the face, which made the vocal cords resonate much better. Because the larynx is so high in other primates, they cannot articulate the precise sounds required to form words.

Homo Sapiens managed to articulate words and express them as they were generated in his mind. This breakthrough could have happened about 100,000 years ago. Language is born from the need to communicate ideas and thoughts with others. It is believed that this initial oral language was modified over time to include new experiences in the journey through life. It is probable that from that first language all the languages of the present world have been derived, since that language was taken with the Homo Sapiens in their great migrations throughout the planet. Such language has been key in the intellectual development of the human species.

# 5.3 GREAT HUMAN MIGRATIONS

Homo Erectus were the first hominids to migrate from Africa over the surface of the Earth. According to fossil records, they managed to reach China and Europe hundreds of thousands of years before the Homos Sapiens appeared. With the passage of the years, Homo Erectus developed bigger brains with more intelligence to form Homo Sapiens about 200,000 years ago. The Homos Sapiens spread throughout Africa and then migrated to what is today Asia,

India, Australia, Europe, and Northeast Asia until finally reaching the Americas.

After evolving from Homo Erectus, Homo Sapiens lived in Africa about 200,000 years ago. There they formed small social groups dedecated to hunting, fishing, and gathering the wild fruits to obtain their sustenance. They spread throughout the African continent from the east to the north and the south. They then spread out of Africa, undertaking several migrations. In one of the first, Homo Sapiens reached Egypt in northeastern Africa and then expand out of Africa to what is now Israel about 110,000 years ago. They settled in Egypt and Israel, remaining there until they were extinguished some 90,000 years ago. This first migration of Homo Sapiens is not considered of much impact since it did not have continuity.

The great migrations took place during the Quaternary period, when the glaciers advanced from the poles to give rise to the forth and last glacial period or ice age, which lasted about 100,000 years and that was followed by interglacial periods. As the poles froze, much of the water was held in the form of ice, which caused the sea level to fall and expose the land bridges between the continents that were previously under the sea. The bridge of the Bering Strait surfaced to connect Asia and North America. These bridges allowed animals and humans to migrate from one continent to another.

About 80,000 years ago, it is believed that in another migration out of Africa Homo Sapiens reached Asia in what is today the Arabian Peninsula through the Strait of Mandeb or Bab-el-Mandeb, which separates the Red Sea from Indian Ocean. It is very probable that Homo Sapiens had to build some sort of primitive boat to sail across the Straits of Mandeb, an act that would make them the first sailors. The crossing of the strait occurred at the time of glaciation, so the sea level was lower than at present and the width of the strait would have been about twelve miles. After crossing the Straits of Mandeb, the Homo Sapiens spread through the south of the Arabian Peninsula. They crossed what is today the Persian Gulf, probably by the Strait of Hormuz, until arriving at the India of today some 70,000 years ago. Then they crossed Indonesia to reach Australia about 60,000 years ago.

It is also believed that in another migration north from Africa north, Homo Sapiens crossed what is now known as the Suez Isthmus, a narrow strip of land between what is now the Red Sea and the Mediterranean Sea. This isthmus connects Africa and Asia. After crossing the Suez Isthmus about 50,000 years ago, Homo sapiens spread throughout the rest of the world: Europe, Asia, and the Americas. When Homo Sapiens arrived in Europe about 45,000 years ago, fossils show that some of them probably arrived and settled in the south of what is now France. Given that their remains were found in the French cave Cro-Magnon, this group of Homo Sapiens are sometimes referred to as the *man from Cro-Magnon*. These Homo Sapiens, with characteristics like those of today's humans, had a stature of 5.57 feet, a well-developed brain, better language, and improved social organization.

These Homo Sapiens had superior planning and technology. As for hunting, they had the ability to manufacture more efficient long-range tools, such as spears. As for food storage and preservation, their procedures were much more efficient. As for their relations with others, it seems that they managed with other groups of settlers of the region, which allowed them the trade and exchange of essential resources in time of scarcity.

Homo Sapiens could also cut down trees with axes to build their houses and canoes. They could make clothing and ornaments to wear, and cave paintings reveal that they had a distinct culture. In short, Homo Sapiens had better thinking skills.

During his walk-through Europe, Homo Sapiens encountered another group of humans somewhat different from him: the *Neanderthals*. This name means "Neander valley" in German and was used for this group of humans because its first remains were found in the Neander valley in Germany. Neanderthals, also belonging to the genus Homo, were specifically considered part of the Homo Erectus genus, which had been established and developed in that part of Europe much earlier, coming from Africa in earlier migrations.

The Neanderthals were short, strong, and broad-nosed, and they were also intelligent and skilled, having a skull of similar size and volume to that of Homo Sapiens. The Neanderthals had adapted very well to the extreme cold climate of glaciation, which turned their skin whiter. They dominated the handling of fire, were hunters, and made rustic tools with bones and stones. They also lived in social groups and practiced some cultural acts.

Fossil records indicate that Neanderthals buried their dead; remains have been found surrounded by weapons, food, and some utensils. They also practiced art; pigments of colors and remnants of red ocher dust have been found where they lived. They used caves to protect themselves, which would help strengthen family ties. It is believed that Neanderthals also had a type of language with certain limitations.

Better language and more advanced technology of Homo Sapiens allowed him to dominate the environment, leaving the Neanderthal at a disadvantage. It is thought that this disadvantage was a decisive factor in the extinction of the Neanderthals some 30,000 years ago. In the last fall of the temperature in Europe, the cold intensified and the glaciations covered the entire northern part of that continent.

To survive in such an inhospitable world, communication and the language were critical; because the Neanderthals did not have that resource, they disappeared.

After the interesting encounter between the Homo Sapiens and the Neanderthals, some of the Homos Sapiens continued their walk through Northeast Asia, where they arrived about 40,000 years ago. Then they managed to cross the Bering Strait, which was very accessible some 30,000 years ago. Then they continued to the American continent, arriving in North America about 15,000 years ago. Then continued to cross North and Central America and finally reached South America about 12,000 years ago.

Large human migrations virtually ended with the end of the last ice age about 12,000 years ago. As the glaciers receded, they sculpted the landscape of Earth. The continents were in the same position where they are today, with very few variations in the movement of tectonic plates. By then humans had already spread all over the world, gathering wild fruits and hunting and eating other animals, including the largest.

The Quaternary period is considered the human age, and with it, the period of the great prehistoric migrations had ended. The prehistoric migrations of yesterday had the same motivation as do migrations of today: people are looking for the sustenance to survive and better living conditions. While some human groups could be content to live in the new regions that had colonized, others were forced to go to explore new territories.

It is important to note here that as the Homo settled in areas other than Africa, he experienced significant biological changes to adapt to the conditions of his habitat. One of those substantial changes was the color of his skin, his eyes, and his hair. The pigment related to the color of the skin, eyes, and hair is *melanin*. Exposure of skin to solar radiation increases the production of melanin. The greater the melanin deposits in the body, the darker the color of the skin, eyes, and hair.

In hot climate zones where more ultraviolet radiation is received from sunlight, as in Africa, our ancestors tended to have darker skin with more melanin to protect themselves from that radiation. Their eyes and their hair were also black. In addition, black skin protects from the destruction of folic acid by ultraviolet radiation. Folic acid is an important nutrient in the reproductive years and prevents genetic defects. In cold climatic zones where less sunshine and less ultraviolet radiation is received, the skin tends to be lighter or white because less protection is required. The eyes and the hair also acquire different shades of a lighter color. In addition, white skin makes the production of vitamin D easier. Vitamin D is important for calcium metabolism and the formation of a strong skeleton in areas of insufficient sunlight. It may then be that the change in color of the skin from black to white has also arisen to achieve some advantages for the reproduction of those humans.

The change in color of the skin, the eyes, and the hair gave origin to a supposed classification of human race between blacks and whites. However, scientific evidence indicates that our species has not had significant biological modifications in the last 100,000 years. This classification of the race produced some social prejudices, but we must remember that there is only one human race. We all come from the black man and woman who came out of Africa and settled and colonized the rest of the planet.

# 5.4 HUMAN EVOLUTION

The human evolution or hominization is the process of transformation of the human species from its origin until our day. This encompasses all evolutionary changes, as well as all the progress that has taken place in the primates, and especially in the family of the hominids, until arriving at the present human species. Species of the genus Australopithecus and the genus Homo are members of the hominid family, including Homo Habilis, Homo Erectus, Homo Sapiens, and Modern Humans.

To reach what we are today from our Australopithecus ancestors, we have undergone many changes and innovations throughout the years that have made us human. Fossil records demonstrate that a large part of these changes were made on the African continent. One of the first characteristics that defined the human being was bipedalism.

## Bipedalism: Transcendental Changes

*Bipedalism* is the practice of walking upright on two hind legs; the two free front legs turn into hands. Achieving this new gait position imply a series of transcendental changes in human evolution. The bone structure would be greatly modified due to the upright posture and the bipedalism in the hominids. These modifications would have introduced adaptive advantages and would have helped the evolution of primates toward humans.

Among the advantages of bipedalism is being able to see food at great distances in mixed environments of jungle and savannah, as well as the manual transport of food collected in different places. Bipedalism also increases height and, therefore, the ability to see above the pastures and protect against potential predators. Bipedal males could carry food in their hands for their females and offspring, who could remain in their dwelling and establish a closer bond that favored survival of the family group. This bond is still in practice today: the father provides the sustenance, the mother cares for the offspring, and together they form a family.

The ancient species of hominids adapted to new environments to survive as their genes mutated, thus modifying their anatomy or body structure as well as their physiology, which includes the physical and chemical processes inherent in the functioning of the organism. The behavior of the first hominids was also modified. However, some of the behavior of the early hominids is still in us. For example, modern man and monkeys are very similar in many ways. The sexual practice of modern humans is very similar to that of chimpanzee monkeys. Throughout great periods of time, evolution deeply changed these beings and most of their ways of life. Facial changes toward our modern appearance came much later, about 100,000 years ago.

During the climatic changes through which Africa passed, hominids appeared about seven million years ago and walked in bipedal mode. The new bipedal form of walking introduced important modifications in the bodies of the hominids. These modifications also had an impact on the other species that evolved from hominids, such as members of the genus Homo. These changes include a rectilinear vertebral column in the apes, whereas in Homo Sapiens and its ancestors, the spine acquired curvatures that allow to better support the weight of walking on two legs.

This additional weight from the upright position caused the pelvis in the descendants of the hominids to become narrower, which causes the offspring to be born earlier so it can pass through the female's birth canal. If we add to this the fact that the members of the genus Homo had a larger skull, the difficulty of childbirth becomes greater.

Other bodily changes include those of the legs, joints, feet, and hands. The legs and joints changed to enable walking without the need to rotate the entire body. The foot was losing the ability to cling to the trees, having an important function in the support of the whole body. The upper limbs transformed into hands with which they could press and grab things. According to the Discovery Channel, the hominids turned their two front legs into hands out of love—doing so enabled them to make love to their partner much better.

Other very significant changes that have made us human are the expansion of the brain, the use of fire, and the development of our hands for the use and manufacture of tools. Another ultra-significant factor was the development of language.

## Stages of Human Evolution

After the first fish left the ocean to conquer the surface, terrestrial animals have experienced interesting periods of evolutionary changes in a relatively brief time of about 350 million years to become us. The evolutionary process can be summarized as follows:

---

**Bacteria ⇨ Fish ⇨ Amphibian ⇨
Reptiles ⇨ Mammals ⇨ Primates ⇨
Hominids ⇨ Homos ⇨ Humans**

---

After their evolution from the mammals, the primates continued their evolutionary process for about seven million years until becoming hominids and eventually becoming the men and women of today, as can be seen in the following.

---

**Australopithecus ⇨ Homo Habilis ⇨ Homo Erectus ⇨ Homo Sapiens ⇨ Modern Humans**

---

As we have already said, human evolution encompasses all the evolutionary changes that humans have undergone, as well as all the development and progress achieved from its inception with the earliest hominids to the present human species. To facilitate understanding, human evolution has been commonly divided into two major periods based on development and progress. A first period, called Prehistory, ranges from the emergence of the first hominids that preceded Homo Sapiens to the appearance of writing. The other period, called History, extends from the invention of writing to the present day.

# Prehistory

Prehistory began with the appearance of Homos in Africa some 2.5 million years ago and extends until the beginning of the invention of writing about 6,000 years ago in ancient Mesopotamia, the part of the Middle East where the human beings had come migrated from Africa. Prehistory comprises a period of about two million years; since there is no written record, everything we know about it comes from archeology. This science bases its study on the remains of materials found at the very site of events. These materials include vessels, carved stones, weapons, drawings, human remains, and graves. Prehistory isdivided into the Stone Age and the Metal Age.

## The Stone Age

The Stone Age is the period of human evolution when the first hominids began to use and develop tools, which were made primarily of sticks, bones, and stones. The Stone Ageincludes two different periods based on the sophistication of the tools manufactured by our ancestors. These periods are the Paleolithic, or ancient period of working the stone, and Neolithic, or new period of working the stone. Some consider Mesolithic to be another period, but this it is only a transition between the Paleolithic and the Neolithic.

The Paleolithic period began some 2.5 million of years ago and lasted until the beginning of Neolitic period 12,000 years ago. The Paleolitic is divided into the Lower and Upper Paleolithic.

During the Lower Paleolithic, the usual way to obtain food for the first hominids was the gathering of natural fruits and the ingestion of insects. Later the Australopithecus incorporated meat into its diet in an attempt to survive. To ensure the supply of this new component of his diet, he invented hunting, which led him to make tools of sticks, bones, and stones. The Lower Paleolithic saw the first creation of tools of carved stone by the successor of Australopithecus, Homo Habilis, about 2.5 million years ago.

Homo Erectus, the successor of Homo Habilis, developed group lifeand hunting technology, becoming a predator of herds of wild animals, such as mammoth and bison. He also developed fishing technology and began using nets to fish.

At that time the Homo Erectus, like their predecessors, were nomads—that is, they never stayed in the same place for long. When the food provided by the territory they occupied was scarce, they moved elsewhere. The social organization of Homo Erectus consisted of small groups living in camps on the banks of rivers, where water and food were easy to obtain for a time. Once the food became scarce, they migrated in search of food. At the time of the glaciations, life presented new challenges to survival because many of the animals that were hunted for food had disappeared. This led Homo Erectus to hone his hunting strategy. Another important aspect of this period was that fire was already well managed. That marked a very important advance in improving the lives of our ancestors.

Given the severity of the climate, prehistoric men lived in caves that protected them from the cold and from predators. There caves had definite areas for certain activities, such as the bonfire or the working of stone, bone, wood, and other materials. Some of these caves even had natural water troughs. Some other caves had areas for working and drying hides, areas for dismembering hunted animals, and areas for night protection fires.

The Homo Erectus also lived in huts constructed with diverse materials like sticks, bones, skins, and other materials. These human groups generally settled in certain places where food was abundant, such as fertile areas and those where large animals lived. Some of these settlements were occupied for several years.

Living in groups generates the ability to defend against external threats, as well as to achieve a better development of survival activities. This stage of human evolution began a differentiation of labor between men and women. Mothers cared for the young, since the young needed maternal care until well after birth. The task of obtaining food by hunting animals was a prolonged and arduous activity that females did not perform because they had to take care of the young.

The more advanced organization and planning came with the successor of Homo Erectus, the Homo Sapiens about 200,000 years ago. An important aspect of that development and progress was language, which allowed

Homo Sapiens to organize themselves to hunt or defend themselves from other animals, to communicate information on where to locate new sources of food, and to transmit knowledge from one generation to another.

About 40,000 years ago, Homo Sapiens had perfected the manufacture of utensils. That ushered in the Upper Paleolithic period of human evolution. In this sub-period, rock art was developed to promote prehistoric culture. Now the caves where our ancestors lived were a kind of sanctuary full of rock art in which magical beliefs were practiced. Other manifestations of this cultural transformation were rustic sculptures and small statues of bone or clay.

The Neolithic period began about 12,000 years ago and lasted until the invention of writing 6,000 year ago. It was characterized by the manufacture of polished stone tools and some pottery and pottery artifacts. During this period, the great Gobekli Tepe temple was built on the top of a mointain about six miles from the ancient settlement of Urfa in the southeast of what is now Turkey, near Syria.

This temple consisted of large T-shaped stone pillars decorated with a wide variety of animals and a kind of religious symbols carved in relief. See the above photograph.

In the photograph of Gobekli Tepe, you can still see the work in progress of a team led by German archaeologists to discover what is believed to be the oldest temple in the world. This team of archaeologists has been working on this project for more than a decade. The antiquity of Gobekli Tepe is about 11,000 years, before the discovery of agriculture, which also appeared during the Neolithic period, a year after the construction of the great temple.

After the last glaciation, the living conditions of our ancestors improved enormously: the abundant water from the melting of the glaciers produced more fertile soils, which caused the vegetation to flourish. Some areas were transformed into regions rich in edible fruits. With more edible vegetation, the animals also thrived, becoming more abundant. In this way, our ancestors gradually built more stable camps until they formed villages dedicated to gathering fruits and hunting animals. This is how our ancestors began to be sedentary.

Catal Huyuk in present-day Turkey is the best example of the first sedentary hunter-gatherer peoples. The abundance of fruits led Homo Sapiens to store the surplus of the harvest to eat when needed. At first, he made a hole in the ground for storage, and there he carried the fruits that he collected. He soon observed that some of the fruits of the hole and those that fell to the ground from the plants where he obtained them germinated and formed new plants. This great observation later led to the discovery of agriculture.

It is likely that agriculture started around these first food-storage villages and then spread out along what is known as the Middle East Crescent Fertile, which runs from the Nile Valley in Egypt to Mesopotamia in western Asia. Mesopotamia comprises the region between the Tigris and

Euphrates rivers. According to the registry, it was in this region of Mesopotamia where agriculture and the domestication of animals represented the most important development of that time, which turned these two activities into a true revolution that markedly changed the way of life of Homo Sapiens, marking a milestone in human evolution.

The breeding of animals began with their domestication. The first animal to be domesticated was the wild wolf, which was domesticated into a dog. According to a story from the Discovery Channel, the process of domestication started when the wolf saw the hunting practices and the way of life of the humans and decided to be part of that team. Perhaps the only thing missing from the humans was a keen sense of smell, which the wolf used in its hunting, and the wolf perhaps wanted to contribute that to the society that was about to be born.

How would the wolf get involved with humans? After all, these two species of animals competed with and could also eat each other. It is believed that the wolf realized the love that humans felt for their group, especially their offspring, and the wolf based his plan on that love. On one occasion the wolf saw that a human calf had been somewhat distant from the group. The wolf approached the baby, and when the humans realized that the wolf was near, they all went to where the baby and the wolf were. The humans thought that the wolf was going to eat the young, but as they approached they notice something they had never seen before: the wolf was playing with the baby, and the baby was laughing. The humans, who by then had deeply developed love and compassion, saw the wolf as loving, and from then until today the wolf went as a dog to be part of our family group. At least, that's how the story goes.

The domestication of animals by man continued. The breeding of other animals such as sheep, goats, cattle, and horses would initially begin in the extensive steppes of Asia, an area in which men became shepherds. Over time and thanks to agriculture, men also began providing food for the animals.

Some other activities that also evolved during the Neolitic were braiding and the looms. The fiber braiding technique evolved to make baskets for fruit picking, storage, and other functions. The looms were used to make fabrics out of which clothes were made. Along with agriculture and animal breeding, these new activities were important to the economy.

Homo Sapiens continued hunting, fishing, and gather fruits during this period and used more sophisticated tools made of bones and stones that were polished by rubbing. They also continued developing pottery and ceramics with which they made containers for liquids, thus facilitating the storage of water. As a result, they did not have to be permanently close to sources of water or to make so many trips to the source to obtain the precious liquid. Cooked clay vessels were also used to store grains, seeds, and other products.

In this period, Homo Sapiens became fully sedentary, and social life became more complex. The cultivation of the land and the domestication of animals forced them to settle permanently in the same place. In many places, villages or small towns were organized with huts and some rectangular dwellings that were divided into separate areas inside as their caves had been. Houses with rooms had arrived!

In this period the wheel was invented, facilitating transportation. Besides the Gobekli Tepe, other great monuments of stone called *dolmens* and *menhirs* were constructed, especially in Europa.

The Stone Age was coming to an end as Homos began using metals about 7,000 years ago. This was a process that occurred in several various places of the world at separate times.

## The Metal Age

The Metal Age of Prehistory begins at the end of the Neolithic period when humans began using copper to make some tools and utensils about 7,000 years ago. It is called the Metal Age because of the use of metals, and it is divided into three stages that are named after the metals man was using in each one. The oldest of these is the Copper Age, as copper was the first metal worked; later came the Bronze Age and finally the Iron Age.

As in the case of agriculture and animal husbandry, metals were not discovered simultaneously by all peoples. Those people who used copper imposed themselves on those who used only stone. Then those who discovered the use of bronze and later iron were imposed on those who had been left behind in technology.

Humans first began to use naturally occurring metals such as gold, silver, and copper. Gold was one of the first metals known to man; they were always very attracted to gold, perhaps because of its brightness, which reminded them of the Sun, to which they were also very attracted. Gold was found in the form of nuggets in the river sands or in veins containing gold. Silver is also found in nodules, completely in the natural state, on the surface of the Earth. But both gold and silver were very scarce, and their distribution on Earth was very irregular. Copper, like gold and silver, is also found in its natural state, but occurs with greater abundance and regularity. Copper was the first metal used in greater quantity.

The Copper Age began about 7,000 years ago when humans began working copper in a very simple way on the Anatolian Peninsula, an area northwest of the Fertile Crescent in present-day Turkey. The use of copper subsequently spread through Mesopotamia and Egypt.

At first, men struck with a stone hammer the copper in its natural or pure state at room temperature.

Subsequently, the copper was heated before it was hammered to avoid fractures and the loss of metal; with that was the advent of forging. Perhaps by accident, men discovdred that when copper overheated it became liquid; as the furnace fire was controlled, the casting process was discovered, a very important process in the next stage in the making of tools and metal utensils. By melting the copper in the oven, they could give it the desired shape by pouring it into molds.

When they could no longer obtain pure copper on the surface, it had to be obtained from mines. This is how mining was born. Extracting the materials from the mines, melting them, and alloying them with others led to ironwork or Siderurgy; when they are transformed in metallic objects, Metallurgy arises. Copper metallurgy seemed to occur in several places in the Middle East, in Asia, and in the Balkans in Europe.

Copper is a malleable, soft metal and is of little use for the manufacture of tools and utensils. As a result, only objects of adornment, such as necklaces, bracelets, rings, jewelry, and pins, were manufactured with copper. These were objects of luxury or social prestige for those who wore them. However, arrows, daggers, and axes made of copper have also been found. Given the low strength of copper, stone tools were still primarily used because they were more resistant. Humans continued to seek a solution to the problem of low copper resistance until they discovered bronze, a more resistant metal that ushered in another period, the Bronze Age.

By melting copper, humans saw that it was possible to mix the liquid copper with other metals. Thus, they discovered the alloys. In this way, bronze emerges as an alloy of copper and tin. Bronze is a metal much harder than its two components and is easier to melt and to work than copper.

The use of bronze began about five thousand years ago in what is now known as Armenia on the Asian continent; its use soon spreaded throughout Europe. The first bronze implements imitate the stone forms, so the first metal axes had the same triangular shape and lacked a handle, like those that had been made of stone.

With the progress in the use of the bronze, men could manufacture arms and luxurious utensils. Among the weapons was the sword, which characterized the warrior attitude that was developed in this period. Other weapons made of bronze were the daggers, the armors, the helmets, the spearheads, and the shields men used to protect themselves in combat. Luxurious objects such as pins, rings, jewelry, belt clips, necklaces, mirrors, and magical-religious statues were made of bronze. During most of the Bronze Age, agricultural implements were still made of stone and wood. Only at the end of the period were bronze sickles used to cut cereals.

Bronze had been used mainly for the manufacture of decorative objects and some weapons. However, man would continue his quest to make better tools, as he had done throughout his history (and continues to do to this day). As a result, man discovered iron, which was more abundant but that required higher temperatures to melt—and our ancestors were not yet ready to deal with those temperatures.

Meteorite iron, which fell as a meteorite on the surface of the Earth, had been known or a long time in certain places like Egypt and Mesopotamia. It had been used for about four thousand years to make small objects. However, the manufacturing of iron objects requires knowledge and technology completely different from that of bronze. But after a lengthy process of trial and error they succeeded in mastering iron metallurgy as well.

As implied by its name, the Iron Age began with the use of iron. With iron, men fashioned tools and arms that were much more resistant and powerful. A new craftsmanship and new tools arose: the tongs and the blacksmith's hammer.

The innovative technology of working iron demanded red-hot work and was a secret at first. The first to know this secret about 3,500 years ago were the Hittites, inhabitants of the Anatolian Peninsula in present-day Turkey. They guarded this secret very jealously for many years. After the fall of the Hittite supremacy, the innovative technology of iron began to spread to other places.

Iron had two advantages over bronze. The first is the abundance of iron: almost all geographic areas have iron ores. On the other hand, the componenets of bronze—copper and tin—had to be searched for, often in very distant places. The second advantage of iron over bronze is that iron weapons are more resistant, and while their flexibility allows them to deform, it is possible to repair them. Brass guns, on the other hand, were fragile and often broke with impact.

Iron was used to manufacture all kinds of tools for the countryside and to improve the work and living conditions of the people. However, during the Iron Age certain objects of bronze—such as bowls, cauldrons, and those of a religious or sumptuary character—continued to be manufactured.

The instruments made of iron were very diverse: axes, knives, pruners, forceps, hoes, sickles, plows, chisels, hammers, scissors, files, razors, and harnesses. These are instruments intended for agricultural activity or daily life. In the armament, iron was used for swords, the points of spears, daggers, shields, helmets, and horse bits. Manufacturing this wide variety of tools and instruments to make life easier gives us an idea of the development of the human intellect during prehistory.

# Development of Human Intellect during Prehistory

The intellectual development of the human species has determined their way of life. With development, the knowledge, skills, and customs necessary for survival are acquired, which includes the capacity to adapt to the environment to obtain the sustenance to live. Once humans learn the basic skills to survive, their talent will continue to evolve to invent tools and techniques that lead to a better life.

In the first humans, intellectual development arose with the evolution of practices to obtain its sustenance and to survive. One of those first practices used by the human species, which differentiates it from the other species, was the use and then the manufacture of tools as well as the use and control of fire. The use and manufacture of ropes, baskets, textiles, and ceramics as well as the discovery and development of agriculture, also show the intellectual development of the first humans. These new practices were developed and perfected as intelligence also developed in humans. Although these practices were implemented to meet basic needs such as nourishment and protection, they also contributed to the development of the intellect.

The first tool man used was instinctively a piece of stick from a tree branch, just as he would have done when he was still part of the great apes—in other words, before he evolved into a human. These monkeys always walked from stick to stick and even used a small stick to agitate and eat the ants in anthills. Using their instinct in an analogous way, the first hominids used a piece of wood to defend themselves against their predators. Then they saw that the same stick could be used to kill a small animal to eat. In this way, they had turned that piece of stick into a tool they used to protect themselves and get their food.

Over time, they also used their piece of stick as a club, their great companion for many years. They also discovered that a sharp point of their stick could puncture; over time, members of the genus Homos were able to sharpen a tip of the stick to turn it into a spear, which they could throw at an animal from a distance. If they succeeded in killing the animals with their spear, they could eat the animal. They could also fish with the spear, and they turned the spear into a harpoon. Thus, began the intellectual development of the first humans and their great inventions.

Probably in one of his wanderings trying to hunt some animal, the first humans realized they needed to throw something more. Looking around and not finding another piece of wood, he may have picked up a stone and thrown it at the animal. The idea of using the stone as a tool ushered in the Stone Age.

This period of the early life of the first humans includes one of the most important advances in the progress of human evolution, which happened when our ancestors acquired the ability to use and develop their own tools and, thanks to their intellect, to achieve survival. Like the stick, the stone served to obtain food and to defend against predators.

The oldest stone tools that have been found are about 2.5 million years old and were found in Africa. With them the first hominids and the first Homos hunted other animals to eat; they also used stone tools to protect themselves from predators. The use of these tools allowed our ancestors to survive in an environment full of challenges. The stone was also used to crush the bones of the animals to remove the marrow and eat it.

When early homos discovered that a stone with some edge could cut their hand, prehistoric man took edge to the stone and used it to cut the skin and meat of the hunted animal. The peeled bone was also used as a tool, and the part of the bone that was crushed to remove the marrow had a sharp edge and was used to make a tool with which they could open holes in leather to sew it.

By sharpening pieces of wood, stone, and bone, man used his intellect to make his own tools. One of the first humans to use stone tools was Homo Habilis, who used and made them with great skill during the Stone Age. However, it was with the advent of Homo Erectus that the Stone Age experienced its greatest development. Axes and knives of high quality were made, representing a huge leap in the manufacture of stone tools. This suggests that Homo Erectus was quite intelligent and able to plan actions in advance. Another example of the enormous intelligence of Homo Erectus was the way they came to dominate and control the use of fire.

Fire ignited the intellectual development of humans, which passed from one generation to another from the earliest Homos to Homo Sapiens. With his great wisdom, Homo Sapiens migrated from Africa to where we are today, living a life more comfortable than theirs thanks to the current technology—a technology that uses as base those great inventions of our ancestors during Prehistory. One of the most significant of those was fire.

The fire on the surface of the Earth arose after the first plants and forests appeared, about 400 million years ago. But that fire was started by lightning as it fell on the forest. At first all the animals feared the fire and fled from it. The members of the genus Homo were the first who did not flee from the fire. With their capacity of thought, they observed and analyzed fire until they managed to use it in their favor about 700,000 years ago. Initially they took a lighted branch very carefully to some convenient place, sheltered it, and added wood to it to maintain the fire. If it went out, they took a piece of firewood or burning branch from some other campfire or waited for another bolt of lightning.

It would take the Homos many thousands of years to learn how to light the fire, but they finally did it by rubbing a piece of stick with dry wood. The great master in the handling and controlling of fire was Homo Erectus. The fire became a great blessing; Homos could have light at night and heat in winter. Fire frightened other animals, even predators, so that humans could sleep peacefully inside a cave that had a bonfire at the entrance. Evidence has been found that the Homos also burned fresh bones full of marrow and fat to make torches to light in their caves and keep their dwellings warm when it was cold, thus displaying their great intellect.

In addition, fire could roast meat, giving it better flavor and softening the fibers so that it could be chewed more easily. Fire also killed germs and parasites in the meat, reducing diseases.

## Great Prehistoric Inventions

Despite the progress the first humans made, life was still difficult. During Prehistory, man lived on hunting, fishing, and gathering of wild fruits and was grouped into small nomadic communities that were mobilized as they followed migrating animals, which in turn were driven by changes in the climate. About 500,000 years ago, prehistoric man protected his body from the cold with animal skins and by living in caves or leather tents that provided protection and shelter. But life was still hard, especially during glaciations. It was extremely difficult to go out hunting in such freezing weather. In addition, the most abundant animals by then were very ferocious, such as the mammoth, bison, elephant, rhinoceros, bear, and lion. But necessity is the mother of invention, and man was forced to develop more efficient arms and forms of hunting in order to survive. He came to perfect the practice of using the spear from a great distance until he later invented the bow and arrow.

Another example of the development of the human intellect was the use and subsequent manufacture of strings and ropes. Throughout human evolution, strings have always been necessary for binding and tying or holding things during the daily chores. For example, strings can be used to join things, so they can be carried more efficiently. In addition, in hunting, the most important activity of that time, ropes were used to fashion traps to hunt some animals and to make nets for fishing. They also used ropes to tie tree trunks into rafts, another great invention.

Ropes were also used to climb to the top of some mountains caves as evidenced in Europe, where a braided rope of esparto was found in a cave and apparently used to access a high area in which was found a series of cave paintings. The rope was tied to the top of a wide stalagmite that was about twelve feet high. Although it dates to the Paleolithic more than 27,000 years ago, this rope is similar to the ones we use today.

Perhaps the first ropes used by humans during Prehistory were some stalks in the form of vexes that they naturally got from vines. They also used ropes drawn from the barks of the stems of some trees or the rachis or central axis of the palm leaves. Leather cords and animal ligaments or tendons were also used as ropes. Later they eventually developed techniques for making their own strings. Twisted and braided ropes were made from vegetable fibers obtained from plants such as spatters, reeds, and palms. Initially they made twisted, rather rustic but very efficient strings from these vegetable fibers. They simply took a bundle of those fibers, depending on the thickness of the rope they wanted to do, and twisted with their hands until they formed a part of the rope. To make the rope longer, they joined other fiber bundles to the first part. To complete it, they tied a knot at each end of the rope, so it did not come loose and unravel. Later, they improved this design by interweaving the fibers instead of twisting them to form a braided rope, which is stronger than the twisted rope. They also later learned how to make their ropes from animal fiber like wool.

Rope was also of significant importance building building the first dwellings, making the first clothes, and making sandals. Initial work with string led to basketry which in turn led to development of the weaving technique. With the technique of basketry, they invented baskets in which they could load and store food, especially after farming.

In making fabric, they invented cloth using instruments like the spindle, the loom, and other great inventions of the time. About 40,000 years ago, man managed to improve his clothes by making them more comfortable while cutting and sewing, thanks to the invention of the needle with an eye. Then he discovered the dyes obtained by macerating in water the bark of certain trees that contain tannins, such as the oak and the willow.

Thanks to the progressive development of their intelligence, humans manufactured arms and tools of stones through a technique they gradually perfected. They came to master the technique of carving the stone in the manufacture of their tools during the Paleolithic period of the Stone Age. Later, they also perfected the technique of polishing and drilling the stone for the manufacture of more precise tools during the Neolithic period. Along with fire management, these advances gave humans a better way of living by using and combing wood, stone, bone, and ropes in making composite tools more effective than the simple version tools like the spear and ax.

The composite lance was made using ropes to tie a stone knife to the tip of a stick. The simple lance, a piece of stick with a sharp point, was used by man for about 400,000 years and is perhaps one of the oldest weapons used by man.

The composite ax was used in Prehistory for about 250,000 years and was made of silica stones carved at one or both ends and fastened with ropes to a piece of wood at a right angle.

Similarly, combining sticks and strings enabled man to invent the bow about 30,000 years ago. A flexible rope like that of an animal tendon was tied to both ends of a piece of flexible pole and the rope was then tightened to create tension. The tensioned bow could effectively shoot an arrow over a distant range.

The arrow was a spear whose size was adapted to that of the bow and, of course, was within reach. The bow and arrow was a product of the evolution of man's thinking and enabled him to hunt in a more intelligent way than running at his prey or throwing a spear with his own arm. Undoubtedly the invention of the bow and arrow marked a point in Prehistory where things were no longer discovered by chance but were the result of much more advanced thinking.

These new inventions introduced great advances in Prehistoric technology. Prehistoric technology encompasses a set of knowledge, processes, and techniques that served to design and manufacture tools and objects to meet human needs during Prehistory. Early humans began to develop their technology by converting natural resources into simple tools.

Another aspect of significant importance in the intellectual development of the first humans was the emergence of their art. The initial expressions of art also give us an account of the degree of development of the human intellect during the Paleolithic period of the Stone Age. Various techniques—such as engraving, low and high relief, sculpture, and painting—were used by the prehistoric artist to perform his works on the deepest walls of caverns and is a definitive example of his extraordinary talent. One of the oldest known artistic manifestations are the rock paintings of about 45,000 years ago.

Thanks to his extraordinary talent, man had managed to increase the use and control over available natural resources. He learned to make finer and more effective tools with the stone that allowed him to cut trees and build his wooden huts. He also made rafts by joining tree trunks with ropes. He then made canoes with trunks hollowed out of trees; oars were added to enable him to guide and move the canoes from one side to the other. Eventually he managed to put sails on the canoe to create a ship that was used to sail the Nile about 30,000 years ago. Rafts, canoes, and sailboats were used for fishing and to start new migrations.

When man discovered that clay hardened in fire, he began to make a variety of clay objects such as figurines, vessels, pots, plates, containers, and other objects like the fusayolas used in spindles and the looms. He also invented the brick, which was used in the construction of houses. This brick consisted of a mixture of mud and straw.

Man started to make pottery with the potter's wheel, an invention that consisted of a manually operated turntable on which the vessel was shaped as it rotated. The great advantage of clay containers over baskets was that these containers could hold and transport liquids in addition to the other things normally carried in baskets. Later man developed the art of ceramic, in which an object made of clay was cooked in a kind of oven at a hot temperature. the result was an object made of clay that was exceptionally strong and resistant to leakage of liquid. Later man developed techniques to decorate the ceramics with figures and colors.

Thanks to his inventions and advances, man could take a decisive step in the production of his own food through the discovery of agriculture and animal husbandry in the Crescent Fertile of the Middle East. Man learned to sow the soil and to domesticate and raise animals. With the advent of agriculture, the invention of the wood plow, a tool used to prepare and remove the soil before planting seeds, followed about five thousand years later. At first the plow was pulled by people; later it was pulled by oxen, mules, and even horses.

After man developed cereal crops he invented beer from the fermentation of these cereals, perhaps by accident, about 3,500 years ago. The first beers were non-distilled spirits of bitter taste made from barley or rice. Later man developed grape crops and invented wine with the fermented grape juice. It is likely that prehistoric man first prepared fruit juice, which then fermented by natural action after some time.

Man also learned to spin to make thread from a mass of fiber that was pulled and twisted by hand to form the strand of thread. This thread was used to bind things. The fiber to make the thread could be of animal origin such as wool, as well as fibers of vegetable origin such as flax. Later man invented the spindle to obtain a finer and more uniform thread. The prehistoric spindle consisted of a cylindrical rod with a tip at the bottom end on which it could spin like a top when a rotary motion was applied at the top end. As the spindle was rotated, the part of the strand attached to the top end of the spindle twisted to form the thread, which was then rolled into the spindle. The spindle of the Neolithic period was usually of wood with a counterweight, fusayola, or malacate normally made of stone or clay in the bottom of the spindle. The fusayola maintained a rotational inertia to form the yarn from a mass of fibers.

Over time man discovered that interlacing the strands of thread could make a fabric, which he could use to make garments. He learned to weave and then invented the loom. There is very little archaeological evidence about the looms used in Prehistory, as most of the materials used to make the looms of that time were highly perishable. However, the stone or clay fusayolas or weights are the key evidence of looms used to make the clothing worn by our ancestors. According to the fusayolas found, the looms began to be realized during the Neolithic and have lasted until our days.

A simple primitive loom could have been constructed with about five sticks that formed the structure of the loom frame; the size of the frame depended on the garments to be made. The frame could consist of two pieces of long sticks placed vertically and another three pieces of shorter stick placed transversely. The joining and binding of the sticks were done with ropes. The configured frame could be supported on its top by a tree. In the first transverse pole of the upper part, the hanging threads were tied; at the lower end of the thread were attached the fusayolas or loom weights made of stone or clay. The fusayolas kept the threads tight. A roll of yarn was passed between each of the hanging strands of the upper crosspiece of the frame until a complete row of fabric was formed. Each time a row was finished, it was pressed up to make the fabric more compact. With the ability to spin and weave fibers, man could make his own fabrics, which had a significant impact on the making of the garment.

Like tools, clothing helped our ancestors survive, as the garments that covered their naked bodies also protected them. The intelligence of the first men allowed them to develop tools of stone, to dominate and control fire, and to make their clothes. However, his profound sense of improvement never ended, he was always looking for something else that would make his life easier. In that constant search, man discovered he could work metals to make better tools. With that, prehistoric man entered the Metal Age.

During the Metal Age, man obtained metals from the mines, thus inventing mining. When working the copper, the bronze, and the iron, he developed the foundry to manufacture tools and utensils. With this new technique he just had to pour the molten metal into a mold with the shape of the object he wanted to make. When alloying some metals with others, he discovered first  Siderurgy and then finished metallurgy. With iron, man made tools and weapons that were much more resistant and powerful.

     After discovering the bronze from an alloy of copper and tin during the Bronze Age, humans had to find tin, leading to an important trade route across the Mediterranean and the Atlantic. With the progress of metallurgy during the Bronze Age, the nail appeared, representing a revolutionary invention for that time. This allowed man to join the sticks or beams of wood and enabled him to build solid structures. Another invention of a great transcendence in the life man occurred at the same time, about seven thousand years ago. The wheel was a circular mechanical piece that rotated around an axis using the same principle already used in the rotating part of the potter's wheel. The wheel replaced the transport of some loads on trunks of sticks on flat surface. This great invention played a very important role in the development of transport in commercial as well as military activity. With the domestication of the horse, the first war chariots appeared.

     Luxury items such as mirrors and cosmetics were also invented. The first mirrors were used in Egypt about six thousand years ago. These were made of bronze, but the reflection of the image was blurry. At the same time, the first cosmetics were made to improve beauty, especially that of the face. The manufacture of toiletries continued to rise, which caused man to perfect the mirror by using other materials that improved definition of the image. Final perfection of the mirror was achieved with the discovery of glass, which involved melting at hot temperature silica sand, soda ash, and limestone; the resulting mirror reflected good light and a clear image.

# 5.5 MODERN HUMANS

The modern man who inhabits the Earth today comes from Homo Sapiens. This is a being that belongs to the class of mammals, to the order of the primates, to the family of the hominids, to the homo genus, and to the species Sapiens. Modern humans' behavior, thoughts, beliefs, and art have evolved with time to result in progress in their culture and society.

## Evolution of Human Behavior

All the social impulses of humans developed long before he developed the intellect. These impulses—such as mother's love, compassion, cooperation, curiosity, invention, and competitiveness—are intuitive, intrinsic, and shape behavior in the human being. All these social impulses were necessary in the survival of the first hominids and humans. As humans evolved, their social impulses could be modified with training to thus form a standard social behavior in the group.

Intellect and language, the qualities that separate humans from the rest of the other animals, slowly developed throughout the seven million years of human evolution. The more intellect developed in these beings, the better the communication between them and the more human they became. However, the intellect is not unique in humans, as it has also developed in some other animals. The intellect developed as a way of controlling the instincts to have a more adaptable behavior within the social group. This is extremely important to know, for today it seems to be ignored.

Throughout their evolution, humans could modify any normally intuitive behavior to obtain some benefits that would help them survive. This made them develop a great capacity for adaptation, which has been crucial in human survival and evolution. That process of controlling instincts is known as self-control or self-discipline and is the biggest difference between humans and animals, since animals use only their instincts in decisions about their behavior.

Self-control, then, can be a way of measuring the intellect. The more talent beings have, the more self-control they have, which makes them better humans. On the other hand, the less self-control they have, the more they will resemble the other animals, which lack intellect and act only by instinct. Instinct is the driving force in an organism's behavior and is directly determined by the genetic code of the organism. Millions of years ago, the first single-cell organismsdeveloped sensors to detect light and an instinct to swim into that light. Other organisms developed sensors to indicate when a prey was nearby. When their sensors told them that a prey was close, their instincts soared. With the development of sexual reproduction, the instinct of sexual desire provided the impetus for reproduction.

# Thought Evolution

Thought in the first humans arose from the perception and interpretation they began to have about their external world. Perceived sensations could be pleasant or unpleasant—and they were almost always more inclined toward pleasant sensations and awa from unpleasant ones. This interest is what triggers the mechanism of reason and thought. When you touch another body, you can perceive its shape, its texture, its temperature, and other properties. In this case, those sensations come from the body that is touched. All perceptions that beings receive from the outside world represent ideas, which can be either sensory or intellectual. Sensory ideas show the objects being perceived at the same moment. Intellectual ideas, on the other hand, are recorded in the memory and we can operate with them even when the objects are not in front of us. It is then believed that sensations are the source of all thoughts, with which we form value judgments about our surroundings. As a result, we can consider that everything that arises from our mind is a thought.

After our ancestors invented the imagination more than 170,000 years ago, the thought enters its best stage. The thought of Homo Sapiens was more logical than that of his predecessor because Homo Sapiens was wiser; he had a better understanding of his world, and his thinking was based more on reason. Logical thinking helped him analyze situations to find solutions to adverse events. As logical thinking evolved, thought entered a stage of advancement and generated creative thinking. Thus, Homo Sapiens was able to create in his mind an image of an object, visualize the actions he wanted to make of that imagined object, and then modify it to achieve its goal. In other words, Homo Sapiens could now transfer his future actions to images that were only in his mind. Transferring action to mental images means thinking. Indeed, thought is the faculty of having mental images and creating relationships with these images. Thus, the human being began to think and then used language to communicate his thinking to other people.

At first much of Homo Sapiens' thoughts were positive and based on reason, which helped them to survive. This could be a result of the fact that most of them had a similar reality. As their knowledge increased, they also expanded their ability to think, and they became creative. By that time the relationship of knowledge and thinking capacity was still in balance. However, with the passing of time a wide variety of new experiences occurred, especially with the arrival of shamanism, which was a type of beliefs practiced by some members of the genus Homo about 50,000 years ago to cure suffering with the help of the spirits. With shamanism, many thoughts arose that knowledge could not answer. During and after this period of spiritual beliefs and practices, our ancestors began to have contact with hallucinogenic substances and began to experience altered states of consciousness. Of course, this also altered our ancestors' thoughts and many of them began to distort what until then had been the common reality, which introduced dramatic changes in thought.

This difference of thought began in a certain way to divide humans. The new reality of that minority incorporated aspects somewhat distant from the real reality, and their thoughts moved away from the logical, creating some limitations in achieving the things necessary to lead a better life. However, the clear majority continued to use thought to find answers, solve problems, and invent in spite of the adversities of life itself, including the opposition of thinking based on those who had altered the common reality. The great thought of Homo Sapiens continued to evolve through the years until they perfected language. Thanks to these two fundamental tools—thinking and language—and thanks to the intelligence and adaptability of most of our ancestors, we have conquered the world.

Being able to pass his thoughts on to others introduced immense benefits into the life of Homo Sapiens. This improved their relationship with members of the social group also improved their safety, comfort, and the way they got their daily sustenance. Language has been a piece of transcendental importance in all the achievements of our ancestors. With it, the knowledge needed to guarantee the survival of humans is transmitted. Language has definitely made us conceive the world as never before.

# Origin and Evolution of Religious Beliefs

The goal of life has always been to survive. That is why every time our survival is threatened, fears are generated. From long before they evolved to humans, our ancestors went through many difficult situations in their quest to survive due to the changes that occurred in their habitat in Africa about seven million years ago.

After leading a comfortable life perched in the trees where they always had safe access to food, our ancestors had to make drastic changes as they began to lose their forests and had to walk erect on the ground in search of food. In this new stage, they traveled along paths full of much uncertainty, because by that time obtaining their food was not so easy. This produced more fears and concerns. One going in search of food could become food for another animal—so in addition to his fear of not finding what to eat, he also felt fear of death. He also feared the darkness, for anything could happen under the mantle of the night. That is why when they woke up each day and could see the light, they felt alive and happy. They began to feel a kind of adoration for the clarity of the day without understanding even what produced it. Perhaps to mitigate their fears a little, our ancestors began to develop some beliefs to help overcome their fears and thus continue to face the adversity of life. It's the same thing we do today: we remember our belief in God before we consider our fears and concerns.

As they developed their intellect, our ancestors became capable of formulating more complex thoughts on nature, natural phenomena, life, and death. But even after inventing the imagination; perfecting the skill of making better tools, utensils, and clothing; and perfecting language and greatly improving their life in social groups, Homo Sapiensstill could not explain many things that intrigued him.

Paradoxically, as is often the case, the more you know, the more you ignore.

When exposed to imposing natural phenomena that would endanger their survival—such as lightning, thunder, rain, volcanic eruptions, and fire—and seeing that he could do nothing to prevent them or defend himself against them, Homo Sapien's mind began to imagine everything possible for answers about how and why these events occurred.

Imagine what our ancestorthought as they saw a meteor streaking through the sky. His intrigue would have not only arise from seeing it coming, but after seeing the stone or meteor fall to the surface of the earth, he would have undoubtedly had more questions. In contemplating that stone of strange shape and texture, he may have thought it was the work of some supernatural power and that it had been sent to Earth as a message.

After many frustrations in trying to explain natural phenomena, he concluded that this type of event was due to a power much greater than his. Finding no answer on the cause of those events, came to think that such a thing could be related to his behavior, and he began to feel doubts about himself and fear toward that supreme power. He came to believe that natural phenomena were ruled by spirits. He also believed that spirits or hidden forces that could affect him in some way lived in him and in everything around him. In the face of so many destructive and threatening forces of nature, prehistoric man assigned to these events supernatural powers, something beyond his control. He began to fear the threat to his survival and even to feel respect for their great power. Eventually he considered them gods; he began to worship them, to have faith in them, and to offer tributes to appease their anger. Man, then went so far as to offer sacrifices of living beings to please their gods. He then felt the need to communicate with the spirits of all-powerful gods to influence them, and for this he used rites created by his beliefs, giving rise to the emergence of rituality, one of the important aspects of shamanism and of what would later be called religion.

Our ancestors did manage some natural phenomena by identifying patterns that allowed them to migrate to other places at certain times of the year. Along with these migrations came a kind of ritual to ask the alleged great creative power of events such as rain to start those events when they needed them. With the arrival of the rains came the creation of rivers and lakes, allowing plants and animals to thrive. They came to believe then that the water spirits were good—so good that without them plants and animals, including them, would perish. They acquired knowledge of life and death. They understood that some things, like plants and animals, lived a shorter time than other things, like stones. For this reason, they also developed the worship of the stones, which later led to their construction of great stone monuments.

Another event that had a major impact on the beliefs of human beings during Prehistory was the death of another being. Unable to find answers in his imagination about what might be happening to life after death, he began to weave a swarm of things and thus come to believe that something of being, like his spirit, separated from the body and would continue to be alive, and could even help the living. Perhaps this idea made our ancestors bury their dead with certain rituals during the Middle Paleolithic so that their spirits could help them survive. From the relationship of the living with the spirits is born spirituality, the other important aspect of shamanism and later of religion. By burying the dead with their household goods, food, and ornamental objects, we can infer that our ancestors believed in the existence of another life after death. Today there are those who still think the same.

Belief in a supreme being or god with the ability to produce events that no one else could make happen, as well as the belief in shamanism that the spirits of the dead would still be alive even after death, led the first believing men of shamanism to create an unreal or imaginary superior reality. Through such a reality they created a series of myths or fantastic stories to justify their beliefs. These myths could give a connotation of something real and sacred that they managed to sustain until today, passing it from generation to generation, first through oral language and then through written records.

The myths imposed a series of rituals on the most important activities of life, survival and procreation. Thus, for example, prehistoric men prepared for hunting by following rituals in the hope that their hunting would be productive and thus they would continue to survive. They disguised themselves as the animal they wanted to hunt because they believed that in this way they could seize the animal's spirit or that hidden forces would allow them to dominate the hunt of the animal. They also simulated hunting scenes and danced to the sound of primitive musical instruments in the light of torches in front of animal figures that had been painted or carved on the walls of the caverns or molded in clay or stone. Prehistoric men associated these objects or symbols with spirits and attributed to them derived powers in relation to natural phenomena.

Later, with the advent of agriculture and animal husbandry, prehistoric man also developed rituals to ask the gods for the fertility of the field to obtain good crops and good animals. The cult of fertility was developed during Neolithic time. The farmers of the time considered that the vital force resided in nature, that the woman was the symbol of human fecundity, and that the Earth was the source of the fecundity of all things about it. Mother Earth became the goddess or general deity. However, for the shepherds, fecundity resided in virility, which is why their gods were associated with the force of vigorous animals like the bull or the horse.

Rituals pretend to intervene favorably in the will of the supreme being with respect to natural phenomena such as the rains. For that reason, our ancestors observed and tried to give better explanation to the solar and lunar cycles, as well as seasonal changes and their relationship with the fertility of the field to try to determine the different energies that could affect their well-being and that of the group. With the development of belief, rituality, and spirituality, the first manifestations of shamanism arose, followed by primitive religiosity that was closely associated with magic, witchcraft, and superstition. Through these our ancestors tried to reproduce extraordinary phenomena contrary to natural laws using certain acts and rituals with the supposed intervention of the spirits. Thus, appears the religious cult as a way of showing reverence, devotion, and respect for something that is believed and considered powerful and divine.

In order to relate to the supreme being and obtain some benefit from it, humans used religious manifestations such as rituals or cults, which were to be conducted by people with experience and knowledge. What we know today as a religion is based on the primitive beliefs of primitive man and had its origin with the arrival of shamanism, which was a type of belief led by a Shaman, one of the first religious leaders dedicated to the knowledge of the occult. This was dedicated to healing the suffering of the human being with the help of spirits or souls, with whom he claimed they could maintain a certain relationship. Shamanism later led to the religions and shaman religious authorities we know today.

Prehistoric man believed that the spirits or hidden forces of nature would allow him to hunt, have children, and have fertile fields. There was so much faith in what he believed that he could see what he wanted, which further stimulated his beliefs. For this reason, he clung to those beliefs and tried to endorse the forces of nature such as the sun, moon, wind, water, and fire and represent those in the form of symbols to these gods to ask for help. He believed that if they could have representation in the form of painting, sculpture, or figures, they could also interfere with the spirits of that thing at their convenience. In trying to represent their gods in physical form, art emerged with their great paintings as found in Europe, with sculptures of animals such as the bison and the bull. They also painted and sculpted female human figures as a symbol of fertility as represented in the Venus of Prehistory. Finally, they constructed great monuments of stones like the menhirs and dolmens.

# Origin and Evolution of Art

At the beginning, the most important activity of Homo Sapiens was the hunt, because the sustenance and survival of the family and social group depended on it. They took hunting so seriously that before beginning a day of hunting, they initiated some type of ritual. The Homo Sapiens began to represent pictures of the hunt in paintings on the walls of the caves where they lived toward the end of the last glaciation. In this way arose prehistoric art that served a ritualistic and magic-religious function. The origins of prehistoric art, according to the findings made in Africa and Europe, date back to the end of the upper Paleolithic period some 30,000 years ago.

The manifestations of art that we know today as painting, sculpture, and engraving are artistic techniques that have a remote past in the religious manifestations of Homo Sapiens. Today we know with certainty that he painted the impressions or experiences of his daily life on the walls of the caverns or those of shallow caves. Homo Sapiens was a highly specialized hunter, so his artistic works naturally reflected it and wasrelated to it. That is why the motifs of this art in its beginnings are representations of animals or hunting scenes.

The prehistoric artist used various techniques to perform his works, from engraving and sculpture to painting. His work on the deepest walls of the caverns or on the shallow walls of the caves are called *rock art* and include *petroglyphs* and *pictographs*. Petroglyphs are drawings engraved on the rock, with incisions achieved by repeating a puncture, either intermittent or continuous. These incisions form a groove that clearly highlights the natural tone of the rock, also highlighting the drawing.

Pictographs or paintings are drawings made on the rock with the help of coloring matters. The simplest drawings were made with clay or pieces of charcoal. Later they were done with paint that was applied to the rock with the fingers or some sort of instrument such as bird feathers, twigs, bone chips, and bundles of animal hair in a primitive type of brush. The paints were obtained by mixing mineral pigments with some binder, which could be fat, oil, water, or some other vegetable, animal, or body fluid. Ores have excellent pigment properties, as they are stable and resistant to light and moisture. Pigments were also obtained from ocher soil, an earthy mineral consisting of hydrated iron oxide mixed with clay, quartz, gypsum, micas, or other elements. To convert the ocher to paint, it was washed, milled, and mixed with a binder such as oil, grease, or water.

The colors of the ocher are usually yellowish, orange, or reddish, depending on the mineral that is oxidized to give the pigmentation to the soil. The color of the ocher could be changed by heating it or toasting it; more variety of colors could be achieved by mixing the ocher with other ocher and then reheating it. For example, heating yellow ocher produced a purple-red color. The black colors of the paintings in the Paleolithic were obtained by mixing coal and dirt with manganese oxide. The white color was achieved from lime, while the blue was produced from a mixture of clay and the plant indigo blue. At first the most frequent colors used were red, white, and black.

In addition to petroglyphs and pictographs, prehistoric art also included combinations of engraving and painting. The groove or incision of the engraved drawing was filled with paint. Another special type of painting consisted of painting a flat object on the rock, producing a negative image of its outline. They also came to bathe the object in the painting and stamped it on the rock to obtain a silhouette or positive image. In this way the famous hands were made in negative and positive in several caves around the world.

The prehistoric artist managed to capture an elevated level of realism using colors in his paintings of animals or hunting scenes with human figures. But these manifestations of art are not the only ones that have been found; engraved art has also been found on objects such as tools, utensils, or adornments. Some prehistoric artistic manifestations have been found in the deepest walls of the caverns that seem to have been places of worship instead of housing.

Primitive man believed that it was possible to influence the spirits of the things or beings on which their survival depended by means of their representation in a drawing or painting. For that reason, made representations to guarantee an abundant hunt, which is why much of the rock art we have found was associated with the so-called "magic of hunting."

The caves in which sacred and worshipful prehistoric art has been found were almost inaccessible, and the paintings were made in the deepest and most difficult places of the caves. That made it necessary for the Paleolithic artist to use some artificial means of light, perhaps torches. In some shallow caves with prehistoric art, the caves were not the usual abode of primitive man, but places of worship where pilgrimages were made at certain times. The following illustration shows all the majesty of prehistoric art; it is a rock painting in the Cave of Altamira, Spain, that is preserved in the National Museum and Research Center of Altamira. (Used with with permission and license of Shutterstock.)

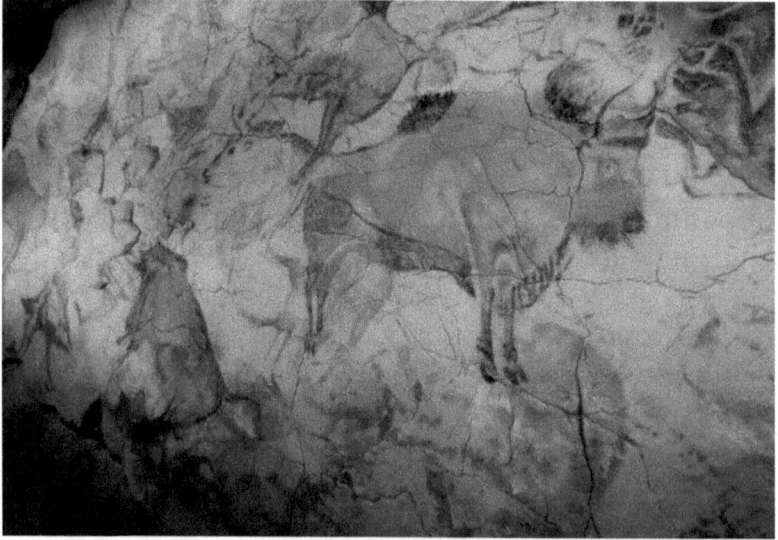

Many of the representations made by the man of the Stone Age were associated with hunting. The man from the Upper Paleolithic was a specialized hunter whose existence revolved mainly around hunting, the activity that allowed him to survive. That is why it came to art, to ensure its constant supply of food through its rituals. In this form the rock art was directly linked to the beliefs of these primitive groups.

In addition to rock paintings, prehistoric art also includes the art of figurines made of clay, stone, bone, or ivory and representing beings or things with influential in the activities on which their survival depended. An example of these figurines is the female figure as a symbol of fecundity called the Prehistoric Venus of about 22,000 years ago. These are statuettes of women with a faceless head and with a strong exaggeration in the size of the belly, the breasts, and the legs. This statuette is also known as the Venus of Willendorf, having been found near Willendorf, Austria. A good replica of the Prehistoric Venus is shown below.

During the Neolithic era also arose the megalithic art, with its immense monuments formed by large stones carved and erected for religious purposes. A good example of megalithic art is the temple of Gobekli Tepe about thirteen kilometers from the ancient Turkish city of Urfa, birthplace of the patriarch Abraham of the Bible. This temple is composed of megalithic structures with circles of *T*-shaped pillars built by hunters and gatherers 11,000 years ago. The large pillars carved out of *T*-shaped stone and decorated with animals and religious symbols carved in relief are buried in the earth. With a height of about sixteen feet and a weight of up to twenty tons, these pillars are interlaced with each other by low stone walls. Together they form a circular structure. The pillars are facing the center of the circle where there are two large columns of almost six meters and about forty tons.

Long after the construction of Gobekli Tepe, other monuments were built of large stones. These were roughly carved and erected alone or in combination to form structures erected either for research purposes, religious purposes, as burial sites for the dead, or as memorials of important events. The main megalithic monuments of these types include the *menhir, dolmen,* and the *cromlech.* The menhir, also called a monolith, is a large stone nailed vertically to the ground. The dolmen is a monument formed by several menhirs on which other large stones rest horizontally. Many of these dolmens served as burial chambers. The cromlech is a circle-shaped structure formed by several dolmens and menhirs. The best examples of these monuments are in Western Europe, the most famous being the Cromlech of Stonehenge built about five thousand years ago in Great Britain, shown on the following page.

Another important aspect of art is the art of music, which is also known today as the seventh art. Music has been part of life since its beginning. Making music is the art of combining sounds harmoniously so those sounds are logical, coherent, and pleasant to the ear. The organization of sounds requires harmony, melody, and rhythm.

The art of music arises perhaps from the attempt of the human being to imitate with his voice the sounds that existed in nature and sounds that came from the inner part of the human being, like the beating of his heart. It is believed that music appears with the language because a change of the tone of voice produces a song by prolonging and raising the sounds of the language. Later man would hit his chest with his hands or hit the palms of his hands like a clap to produce a sound to accompany his voice. As he sang and played, he also began to dance. During its beginnings, music had a magical purpose that was part of the rituals of hunting.

In time, prehistoric man invented musical instruments to further develop music and dance. It is believed that the first musical instruments were percussion instruments, perhaps because of their simplicity. Blows from stick to stick, stone against stone, or stone against stick existed for several centuries before the first more complex percussion instruments were created from percussion on dead animals and the resonance of the rib cage of these animals. In this way the stretched leather was used, first on the same bones of the animal remains; the duration of this instrument was very short due to the decomposition of the leather. When man discovered the drying and tanning of leather, he immediately used this art to construct percussion instruments of longer duration, which made possible a continuous improvement of these instruments. None of these remain, since the passage of time destroyed them. However, it is thought that the leather was tightened against the body of these instruments, which was made of wood.

Thus, primitive man was discovering some basic principles of acoustics: the bigger the body of the instrument or its box of resonance, the lower the sound. With this range of percussive sounds began to develop music as a means perhaps to dominate or control phenomena of nature and their spirits.

Prehistoric man was learning things associated with percussion and music over time by trial and error. Prehistoric man believed that if nature made a noise and water fell, then imitating that noise would also make water fall. Severe percussion instruments with their low frequency scared predators more than a lion roar. Similarly, acute percussive sounds produced a feeling of restlessness and nervousness, and percussion began to be used for producing feelings and moods much better than before. The different mix of frequencies produced different responses in the mood and therefore could be used for war, hunting, or ritual.

The musical instruments that followed percussion are the wind instruments, which appeared during the Upper Paleolithic. This great advance of prehistoric music is also seen as a great evolutionary advance of man. Perhaps this instrument was discovered by using blowguns or some other weapon or tool in which it was necessary to blow, thereby producing a sound. Three-hole flutes made more than 35,000 years ago have been found. After the wind instruments appear the ropes, which are born from the bow or weapon to shoot arrows. The bow as an instrument was apparently invented during the Paleolithic period more than 11,000 years ago. This instrument was used to create a sound different from the instruments of wind and percussion.

After discovering the three basic instruments for producing his music, which are still used today, prehistoric man continued to use the basic principle of percussion in everything else: the longer the tube of a wind instrument, the lower the sound it produces; the longer a string, the more severe the sound it produces. Thus, instruments could have a wide range of sounds: bass, medium, and treble. This principle was the basis of a whole musical culture that each community evolved in diverse ways. Contact between communities favored the propagation of discoveries and cultural exchange, for both worship and art.

## Evolution of Culture and Society

Since its appearance, the human being has been in a constant struggle to survive. As we have seen, prehistoric man had to use tools of stick, stone, and metal in his search for the daily sustenance. Human life evolved according to innovative ways of thinking that gave rise to innovative ideas about how to develop better ways of doing things to achieve a better life. The set of ideas and knowledge that people develop throughout their lives and that is passed from generation to generation through language is called *culture*. Among other things, culture includes the traditions, customs, beliefs, and art of the people.

Thanks to the culture and great capacity for learning and adaptation of our ancestors, they had colonized practically the entire planet almost by the end of the last glaciation, about 13,000 years ago. During this feat, our ancestors adapted to all the climates of the planet and managed to develop patterns of behavior so structured that they could successfully exploit the resources available in each of those territories. With development and progress during colonization, there was a significant and beneficial increase in cultural diversification at the end of the Paleolithic. Regarding livelihood activities, prehistoric man already dominated the manufacture of a wide variety of weapons and tools. With the diversification of culture emerged another important aspect, Paleolithic art. A variety of rites was represented by paintings, female statues such as the Paleolithic Venus, and burials both in caves and in the open air.

Another important aspect of colonization was the significant increase in the open-air settlements in some cases to form camps and communities. *Society* is a set of individuals who share a culture of behaviors and goals and interact with each other in full cooperation. Every society has its *culture*, and every culture is put into practice by people who are interrelated in society.

Culture has an individual and a social aspect. At the individual level, people with the learning of socialization are differentiating their way of life and their own identity. We transmit what we learn to other members of society, and in this way, we transform ourselves into people different from others. This is a fundamental aspect of culture.

Culture is the basis and foundation of who we are and will have a very influential role in the future life of societies and all their social organization, spirituality, art, philosophy, ethical and legal regulation, science and technology, economics and commerce, education, language, and literature. This set of disciplines and experiences form the cultural identity of the people and provides them with the necessary instruments for their development.

One of the ways in which people strengthen their culture and maintain their identity is through the knowledge and practice of their own values, something that seems to be forgotten today. It is important to emphasize that language is the fundamental pillar on which the culture is supported, being the vehicle of the acquisition and transmission of the knowledge and cultural values of the towns.

A key factor in having and maintaining a stable and solid culture will be the organization of society. The society of prehistoric man was organized in a hierarchical way, where the power was concentrated in a chief, perhaps the wisest or strongest of the group. Throughout Prehistory, the organizational form of societies underwent some variations. For this reason, both culture and society are constantly evolving, because over time they are influenced by new ways of thinking in human development.

About 12,000 years ago, the Neolithic Revolution occurred in the region of the Fertile Crescent of the Middle East; it is one of the most important processes generated by Homo Sapiens toward the transformation of human society. This revolution gave way to new forms of life that transformed the human being from nomadic to sedentary and from hunter-gatherer to producer of his own food as a result of the discovery of agriculture and then the domestication of animals. With agriculture arose the concept of property; humans who considered the land as their property were willing to protect it.

Agriculture and domestication of animals eventually produced more food than required to feed the entire population. This surplus introduced other changes in society, including the division of labor, since not all the population was required to work in agriculture and breeding. Those who were not farmers and breeders could engage in other activities, such as ceramics to make containers for storing seeds and crop products, the loom to make clothing for shelter, or housing construction. All this progress generated the necessary push for the people to develop the first cities, where people lived in an organized community governed by their own laws and central governments for the common good.

With the arrival of metals, the progress of society continued. The development of new customs and traditions, religious beliefs, and even new ways of life arose. With the metals they made weapons of great resistance, mostly out of iron. With these weapons they defended their lands and other property even with their own lives. This started the wars. To fight the injustices on the part of thieves and to maintain social order, they were obligated to make laws. Life in society requires establishing rules. At first, laws were based on the use and customs or traditional law that were transmitted orally, since writing had not yet been invented. Writing, one of the most fascinating inventions of the human intellect, introduced crucial changes in culture and society.

The advent of writing ended Prehistory, and the history of humanity began. The end of Prehistory also ends our story of trying to answer the big question of how we got here. In the pages of this book we traveled about 13.7 billion years to decipher our past and answer how we got here. We have seen how everything was formed—the universe, the solar system, the Earth, and life in it. We have seen how that life came out of the water to inhabit the surface and how it continued to evolve until we become human beings. We have seen how we got here.

With the arrival of writing, humanity has been able to write its own history. However, judging from the results of more than seven thousand years of civilization, another question comes up: Where is this civilization going? The possible answers to that compelling question will be the subject of our next book.

# ABOUT THE AUTHOR

Ivanni Delgado is a graduate engineer at the University of Tulsa, Oklahoma, with a master's degree in business from the NSU University of Talehquah, Oklahoma. He is a member of the Texas Authors Association and the author of *Life Under A New Perspective*, which he wrote to help people learn how to prosper and make their lives easy.

In this new book, *How We Got Here*, Ivanni tries to answer one of the most important questions about the existence of the human being, since, he thinks the answer will help us to have a better understanding of who we are and where we come from. Knowing the history of becoming human is fascinating and gives us a profound sense of accomplishment in finding out what we have done and endured in the struggle to become human. Knowing where we came from will help us choose better where we want to go. *How We Got Here* is an enlightened look at the past that will change your future.

# NOTES

## Chapter 1

*The Universe,* The History Channel, 2007

*The Planets,* NASA
https://solarsystem.nasa.gov/planets/

*The Universe,* NASA
http://starchild.gsfc.nasa.gov/docs/StarChild/universe_lev
el1/universe.html

## Chapter 2

*How the Earth Was Made,* History Channel, 2007

*The Planets,* NASA

https://solarsystem.nasa.gov/planets/earth/in-depth/

## Chapter 3

*The Violent Past, Miracle Planet,* The Science Channel, 2005

*Snowball Earth, Miracle Planet,* The Science Channel, 2005

*New Frontiers, Miracle Planet,* The Science Channel, 2005

*Extinction and Rebirth, Miracle Planet,* The Science Channel, 2005

*Survival of the Fittest, Miracle Planet,* The Science Channel, 2005

## Chapter 4

*Evolve*, The History Channel, 2008

*New Frontiers, Miracle Planet*, The Science Channel, 2005

## Chapter 5

Human Evolution, Smithsonian National Museum of Natural History, 2015

http://humanorigins.si.edu/evidence

## Ilustrations

Shutterstock under licence

NASA

Carmen & Son

www.ingramcontent.com/pod-product-compliance
Lightning Source LLC
Chambersburg PA
CBHW071410090426
42737CB00011B/1410